DAWNING *of the* RAJ

Warren Hastings, 1811. (Painting by Sir Thomas Lawrence)

DAWNING
of the RAJ

THE LIFE AND TRIALS
OF WARREN HASTINGS

Jeremy Bernstein

Ivan R. Dee

CHICAGO   2000

DAWNING OF THE RAJ. Copyright © 2000 by Jeremy Bernstein.
All rights reserved, including the right to reproduce this
book or portions thereof in any form. For information,
address: Ivan R. Dee, Publisher, 1332 North Halsted Street,
Chicago 60622. Manufactured in the United States of America
and printed on acid-free paper.

Illustration credits: Bodleian Library, University of Oxford, page 77 (272).
British Library, pages 37 (WD2460), 91 (P95), 93 (P47), 95 (P462), 223 (P376).
Corbis/Bettmann, page 221. National Portrait Gallery, London, pages ii, 27, 47,
55, 61, 115, 180, 233, 237, 255, 259, 283. The Royal Collection, © 1999, Her
Majesty Queen Elizabeth II, pages 19, 198.

Library of Congress Cataloging-in-Publication Data:
Bernstein, Jeremy, 1929–
    Dawning of the Raj : the life and trials of Warren Hastings / Jeremy
Bernstein.
        p. cm.
    Includes bibliographical references and index.
    ISBN 1-56663-281-1 (alk. paper)
        1. Hastings, Warren, 1732–1818.   2. Colonial administrators—India—
Biography.   3. Colonial administrators—Great Britain—Biography.   4.
India—History—British occupation, 1765–1947.
DS473.B45 2000
954.02'98'092—dc21
[B]   99-088030

The people of India, when we subdued them, were ten times as numerous as the Americans whom the Spanish vanquished, and were at the same time quite as highly civilized as the victorious Spaniards. They had reared cities larger and fairer than Sargossa or Toledo and buildings more beautiful and costly than the Cathedral of Seville.

—Thomas Babington Macaulay (1841)

The dominion excercised by the British Empire in India is fraught with many radical and incurable defects, besides those to which all human institutions are liable, arising from the distance of its scene of operations, the impossibility of furnishing it at all times, with those aids which it requires from home, and the difficulty of reconciling its primary exigencies with those which in all States ought to take place of every other concern, the interests of the people who are subjected to its authority. All that the wisest institutions can effect in such a system can only be to improve the advantages of a temporary possession, and to protract that decay, which sooner or later must end it.

—Warren Hastings (1777)

CONTENTS

PREFACE

Mankind are neither so good nor so bad as they are generally represented. Human life is a stream formed and impelled by a variety of passions, and its actions seldom flow from single and unmixed sources.

—George Bogle's Journal

The climax of this book will be a trial—the "trial of the century." It will involve the impeachment of a head of state, a zealous prosecutor, party politics and the media, as well as a dramatic setting worthy of a Shakespeare play. The century, however, was the eighteenth. To be exact, the trial began at high noon on February 13, 1788. The head of state was Warren Hastings. The state was British India, that part of India of which Hastings had been the first governor-general. The zealous prosecutor was Edmund Burke, for whom this impeachment had become a self-destructive obsession. The political parties involved were the Whigs and the Tories—Burke was a Whig, the majority party was the Tories. The trial, which took place in Westminster Hall in London, was a sensation, a spectacle. Even the queen was there on opening day. Hastings was charged with "high crimes and misdemeanors," which in this case could well have carried the death penalty.

In the body of this book I will not dwell on the parallels and differences between the British experience with impeachment and our own. But let me say a few words here. In Britain the origins of impeachment go back to the fourteenth century.[1] In 1376 the so-called Good Parliament impeached William, Lord Latimer. Latimer had been a minister to King Edward II, and this trial set the precedent for Parliament's being able to use the process of impeachment as a check on royal power. But it was little employed until the seventeenth century. The case closest to the one we will consider was that of Francis Bacon, the lord chancellor, who was accused of (and indeed pleaded guilty in 1621 to) accepting gifts from litigants.

When the framers of the United States Constitution drew up their clauses on impeachment they had the British example in front of them (though not the trial of Hastings, which occurred some months later). In both governments there were two bodies of legislatures: Commons and Lords in Britain, House and Senate in the United States. In both systems the "lower" house proposes the articles of impeachment, and the "upper" house disposes of them. But there the similarity pretty much ends. In the American system the only penalty is removal from office, while the British system provides for a full gamut of civil and criminal penalties. Bacon, for example, was fined forty thousand pounds, imprisoned by the king, and forbidden forever to hold governmental office. (He used the time, incidentally, to write some of his best-known philosophical works.) In Britain it was the rule that people undergoing impeachment were confined to the Tower of London. Hastings, exceptionally, was not. He was allowed a bail of forty thousand pounds. For whatever reason, as a practical matter, impeachment disappeared from Britain after the beginning of the nineteenth century. It could not in any case be used to impeach the king. It would, and did, take a civil war to do that.

Despite these differences, American readers will be continually struck by how remarkably similar some of the issues in the Hastings impeachment are to those they have encountered in their own history of impeachments. Let me give two examples. During the trial of Hastings the question was raised again and again: under what set of rules was he being tried? Were these rules that Parliament might set at its pleasure, or were these rules that held in a common court of law? For example, what evidence was admissible? This, as we shall see, played a decisive role in the outcome of the trial.

The second issue had to do with the dissolution of Parliament. This could be ordered by the king, and in 1790, in the midst of Hastings's trial, King George III did dissolve Parliament. When it was reconstituted, a debate arose as to whether the new Parliament needed to revoke Hastings's impeachment or whether the trial could simply continue. Finally, in May 1791, it was decided that it should continue, mainly on the grounds that, if it did not, the king could dissolve Parliament whenever he felt threatened by an impeachment of one of his ministers. One consequence was that any member of the House of Commons who in the interim had become a peer, and thus a member of the House of Lords, during the course of the trial functioned as both prosecutor and juror.

As unlikely as this trial was, even more unlikely was the creation of the British Empire in India. How did a tiny island, half a world away, come to dominate an entire subcontinent? To understand Hastings, and the trial, we must try to understand this situation of empire. This book, then, has a dual task: to recount the evolution of an empire and the biography of a man. The two are closely linked.

I WOULD LIKE to acknowledge Rishikesh Shaha, who inadvertently started me on this path in the spring of 1987, and Professor W. C. Dowling, whose mastery of all eighteenth-century things has guided me every step of the way. I am also grateful to my learned British e-mail "pal" Peter McInally for all sorts of wonderful lore, and to Professors Fred Whelan and Rosane Rocher, both authors of fine books on British India, for their careful reading of the manuscript; to Susan Rabiner for her help in forming this book; and finally to Ivan R. Dee for taking on this somewhat unconventional project with good humor and understanding.

J. B.

New York City
January 2000

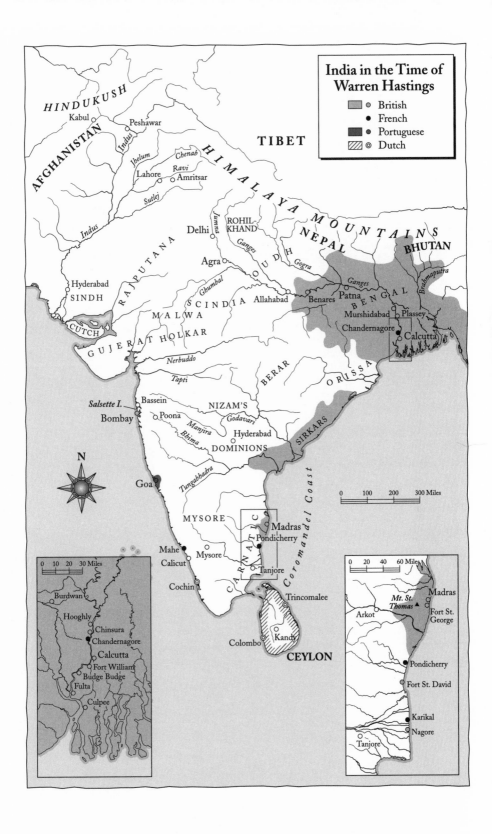

India in the Time of Warren Hastings

British
French
Portuguese
Dutch

HINDUKUSH
Kabul
Peshawar
AFGHANISTAN
Indus
Jhelum
Chenab
Lahore
Ravi
Amritsar
Sutlej
Indus
TIBET
HIMALAYA MOUNTAINS
Delhi
Jumna
ROHIL-KHAND
Ganges
NEPAL
BHUTAN
Agra
OUDH
Gogra
Ganges
Brahmaputra
Hyderabad
Ghumbal
SINDH
RAJPUTANA
SCINDIA
Allahabad
Benares
Patna
BENGAL
Murshidabad
Plassey
Chandernagore
Calcutta
MALWA
CUTCH
HOLKAR
GUJERAT
Nerbuddo
BERAR
ORISSA
Tapti
Salsette I.
Bassein
NIZAM'S
Bombay
Poona
Godavari
Manjira
Hyderabad
Bhima
DOMINIONS
SIRKARS
N
Goa
Tungabhadra
Coromandel Coast
0   100   200   300 Miles
MYSORE
CARNATIC
Madras
Pondicherry
Mahe
Mysore
Calicut
Tanjore
Cochin
Trincomalee

0 10 20 30 Miles
Burdwan
Hooghly
Chinsura
Chandernagore
Calcutta
Fort William
Budge Budge
Fulta
Culpee

Colombo   Kandy
CEYLON

0   20   40   60 Miles
Mt. St. Thomas
Madras
Arkot
Fort St. George
Pondicherry
Fort St. David
Karikal
Nagore
Tanjore

DAWNING *of the* RAJ

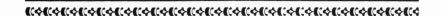

One

PROLOGUE:
GEORGE BOGLE

The first Governor-General of India conceived the plan of opening friendly commercial intercourse between the people over whom he ruled and the natives of the lofty table-land behind the snowy peaks to the north. On this grand object Warren Hastings bestowed much thought and he gradually developed a policy which was continuous while his influence lasted. He took a broad and enlightened view of the requirements of the case, and he appears to have seen from the first that the end could only be gained by persistent efforts extending over a long period.

It is owing to the absence of a continuous policy that this and many other great measures which were once full of promise have produced no permanent results.

—Clements R. Markham, *The Mission of George Bogle to Tibet and the Journey of Thomas Manning to Lhasa* (1876)

From early childhood I had the ambition—mainly from reading books—of going to the Himalayas. Growing up in Rochester, New York, and knowing no one else who thought this was reasonable, it seemed pretty far-fetched. Yet it came to pass not once but many times. In the fall of 1967, on assignment for the *New Yorker,* I spent several months in Nepal, both in Kathmandu and trekking to the base of Mount Everest and Annapurna. Then, in the fall of 1986, while trekking around the Annapurna range, I learned from people I

met, who had just come back from Tibet, that that country had now
opened itself up to more adventuresome tourism than simply flying
to Lhasa from central China on some sort of guided tour. Indeed, I
discovered that it was now possible to drive from Kathmandu to
Lhasa and then to make a loop to the Everest base camp in Tibet,
and even to climb above the camp on the glaciers leading to the
mountain itself. I decided that this was what I was going to do, and I
managed to get an assignment to do it from the *New Yorker.* Thus it
was in the spring of 1987 that I found myself once again in Kathmandu, but this time on my way to Tibet.

Since I was planning to write about my trip, and about Tibet in
general, I decided to spend the week or so I was in Kathmandu, before leaving, scouting bookstores and libraries to see if there were
books about Tibet that I had not discovered. Kathmandu has some
excellent bookstores that specialize in literature about the region,
and there are also some wonderful libraries—both public and private—that do the same. As it happened, in 1967 I had made a friendship with a Nepalese man named Rishikesh Shaha, who had a great
culture about both Nepal and the Indian subcontinent in general. He
often wrote about these matters. Over the years I saw him whenever
I came to Kathmandu. When I saw Rishikesh in the spring of 1987 I
told him what I was planning to do. He then gave me the run of his library. Many of the books were familiar to me, but one of them, *The
Mission of George Bogle to Tibet and the Journey of Thomas Manning to
Lhasa,*[1] was not at all. In truth, I had never heard of either of these
men. Indeed, when I first skimmed the book it did not seem especially relevant to my interests. It had been published in 1876 and had
been edited by a man named Clements R. Markham who identified
himself as with the Geographical Department, India Office. It turned
out that he was also the grandson of William Markham, who had been
one of Bogle's colleagues in India. Markham's book was a labor of
love.

Bogle's trip to Tibet, the one described in the book, began in the
late spring of 1774, and that of Manning's in 1811. The book also contains brief accounts of various other historical expeditions to Tibet. It
was not obvious to me, at first, how any of this material bore on what
I was about to do. But then I began reading it more carefully. While
the rest of the book is certainly interesting, it is Bogle's journey, and

his description of it, that stand out. Bogle's journal, which Markham publishes for the first time, was written fundamentally for an audience of one—Warren Hastings, the man who was responsible for Bogle's mission. By the time of his journey, Bogle knew Hastings well enough to know of his love of literature and language and of his interest in learning anything new about the people of India and their neighbors. One can imagine Bogle writing about Bhutanese women (the path to Tibet went through Bhutan) with Hastings in mind: "In all these different occupations of husbandry the heavy burden lies upon the fair sex; they have a hard lot of it. Besides all of this, the economy of the family falls to their share. They have to dress the victuals and feed the swine. They are not much troubled with washing or scrubbing: the fashion of the country renders this quite unnecessary. But not unfrequently one sees them with a child at the breast, staggering up a hill with a heavy load, or knocking corn, a labour scarcely less arduous. And with all this bitter draught they appear to have few of those sweetenings which might render it more palatable. They have none of the markets, fairs, churches, and weddings of England; they have none of the skipping and dancing of France; they have none of the devotion of the lower people in other Roman Catholic countries; they have none of the bathings, bracelets, &c., of the Bengali; and yeċ I know not how it comes to pass, but they seem to bear it all without murmuring; and having nothing else to deck themselves with, they plait their hair with garlands of leaves or twigs of trees. The resources of a light heart and a sound constitution are infinite."[2] And so they are.

George Bogle was the youngest of nine children—seven of whom survived—of George Bogle Sr. and Anne Sinclair. They were Scots, and Bogle was born on November 26, 1746, in Daldowie, the family seat near Bothwell on the right bank of the Clyde. Bogle's father was a successful Glasgow merchant who six times had been elected lord rector of Glasgow University. His mother, Anne, came from a distinguished Scottish family, the Sinclairs. Her father was a Scottish peer.

Bogle appears to have had a very happy childhood. One of the letters Markham quotes is an early one he wrote from Calcutta to his sister Anne, who was known affectionately as Chuffles. In it he describes scenes from his early life. "Throwing myself back in my great chair," he writes, "I am transported to the nursery in Daldowie. The

picture of Julius Caesar recalls to my mind the shows which you remember we used to make. . . . Do you remember how we broke open
the window at the bottom of one of the beds, to get at some shells?
Never shall I wish for anything so much as I did to get at those shells,
which we could always see, and never get at. All was one continued
scene of health and pleasure."[3]

Bogle studied briefly at Edinburgh University, but in 1764 he
went to France where he traveled for a year. His brothers Robert and
John were commercial people. John had established himself as a
merchant in Virginia, and some thought was given to Bogle's joining
him there. But it was decided that he should go instead to London
where Robert was a partner in the firm of Bogle and Scott. He became a clerk in the firm's "counting-house"—that is, a junior accoun-
tant. He remained there for four years, and in 1769, through the
influence of friends, he secured an appointment with the East India
Company.

The remarkable history of this company we will touch upon later,
but here are a few useful facts. On December 31, 1600, in the last
years of the reign of Queen Elizabeth I, 101 London merchants were
granted a royal charter for "The Company of Merchants of London
trading into the East Indies." This gave them exclusive rights to
trade in the Far East for the next fifteen years. Of particular importance was that the company was to operate free of royal constraints.
They were to be a law unto themselves. By Bogle's day the charter
had been renewed several times, and "Merchants of London" had
been replaced by "Merchants of England." It had become known as
the East India Company, or simply as the Honourable Company.
From very early in its history, the Company modeled itself in several
ways after the Dutch East India Company, which had preceded it
and with whom it had many military and nonmilitary confrontations.
The Dutch had created municipal corporations—communities—in
countries in the Far East where they did business. Following this
model, in 1639 an agent of the East India Company, Francis Day, negotiated with the local ruler the right to build, on what was essentially an unoccupied beach, the municipal corporation that over the
next decades became the city of Madras, one of the Company's
footholds in India. The other two were Bombay and Calcutta.

Bogle, like Hastings who had first arrived in India at the age of eighteen in 1750, entered the Company at the only rank possible, the lowest—that of "writer." This was a term of art which had been taken over from the Dutch "schryvers."[4] The writers were clerks. They toted up accounts. In the records of the East India Company there are many hundreds of thousands of pages of these accounts. The writers worked in so-called "factories"—places where the trading was actually done. In Bogle's day this would have been trading in spices, cotton, and silk, as well as opium, which, it is said, was introduced into the Indian subcontinent from the Middle East by Alexander the Great in the fourth century B.C. It became the Company's principal export to China, where it was exchanged for tea.

The writers were miserably paid—five pounds a year. A housemaid working in a manor house in England did not earn much less. The writers also had a monthly living allowance of twenty rupees (about two pounds), which allowed them just to get by. But if they survived the unhealthy climate for a few years (many didn't) and the other objective dangers, which included alcoholism, they stood to make themselves rich by trading on their own—encouraged by the Company—without paying taxes and duties to the local Indian rulers. They would then lend their rupee earnings to the Company in India and redeem the loans with interest in pounds when they returned to Britain. Often the sums involved came to hundreds of thousands of pounds, enough in some cases to buy a seat in Parliament. Thus it took some string-pulling to win an appointment as a writer, string-pulling that was done in London. Fortunately for Bogle, during the period in question a disproportionate amount of the string-pulling was done by and for Scots.[5]

The numbers are interesting. While one-tenth of the population of the British Isles were at this time Scots, about half of all the appointments of writers, cadets for the cadre of officers in the Company's army, and even assistant surgeons, were Scots. This was no accident. The Company always tried to curry favor with influential members of Parliament. In the mid-eighteenth century, Parliament succeeded in partially curbing the Company's independence. Without its influential Scottish supporters in Parliament, the Company's situation would have been much worse, as was later the case. That aside, it was in 1707 that Scotland had been incorporated into Britain, which made it possible for Scots to be employed by this chartered

English company, and since many in the Scottish gentry were not well off, seeking one's fortune abroad was fairly common.

Bogle's brother Robert no doubt had suitable connections. He presumably also had the wherewithal to underwrite Bogle's expenses in taking up his new position. These expenses included the cost of the passage by sail, which was typically more than a hundred pounds. There were also various items of clothing and even soap. One list I saw[6] included a pound and a half for two wigs. I have never seen an eighteenth-century portrait of anyone from the Company in India wearing a wig. The tropical climate must have discouraged extraneous headgear, though wigs were worn by the imported British judges when they were hearing a case. In any event, Bogle embarked on January 25, 1770, on one of the Company's great sailing ships— "Indiamen" they were called, usually four or five hundred tons—the *Vansittart*.

To better understand some of the rest of our story, it is important to realize what this sort of passage to India involved. It was the end of February before Bogle's ship cleared the English Channel. It did not arrive in Calcutta until August 19—seven months later. This was fairly typical. An extremely fast passage might be four months. Some passages landed—unwillingly when they were blown off course— first in Brazil before they turned east across the South Atlantic Ocean and around the Cape of Good Hope at the southern tip of Africa. Many vessels were lost in storms, and some were captured by hostile forces, such as the French. Markham does not tell us if Bogle went via Brazil, but he does tell us that after rounding the Cape the ship touched one of the Comoro Islands in the Indian Ocean. Then it went northeast across the Indian Ocean until it reached the coast of India. It made a stop at Madras and then sailed up the coast until it arrived at the mouth of the Hooghly River. Then it had to travel some eighty miles upstream to reach Calcutta. It is clear from this description that directing the activities of the Company from London in anything like real time was impossible. Decisions had to be made on the spot in India; the directors of the Company in London could react to them only months later—and, of course, vice versa. A year might go by before a response to a query, or an order, was received.

The location of Calcutta upstream on the Hooghly was partly accident and partly design. The Hooghly is the westernmost channel in the delta by which the Ganges reaches the sea. It was, at the time, the main outlet for the river. It was more or less navigable by ocean-going ships up to about where Calcutta stands. But there is no obvious reason why this particular mud ridge was selected by the city's founder, Job Charnock, in 1690. Three nearby villages, Kalikata, Sutanuti, and Govindapur, all became parts of the city, which took its name from the first. As anyone who has visited Calcutta knows, the climate during the monsoon season, when the city becomes a kind of malignant Venice, borders on the insufferable. One can imagine British traders trying to flog their stout wool cloth—which at first they did—to the locals. What happened was the reverse. The British soon found themselves paying in silver, much of which came from Mexico, for the cottons and silks of India. "Calico" takes its name from Calicut, now officially Kozikode, an Indian city on the southwest coast.

One of Hastings's biographers[7] has given us a vivid description of Calcutta's appearance in the mid-eighteenth century. I offer this in some detail because most all Englishmen, including those who later were to judge Hastings in Parliament, had never been to India. They had no firsthand knowledge of what living there meant.

"One edifice [Fort William], confronting the river, dominated the low-lying horizon, the citadel built by Charnock's successors to defend the infant settlement. There the Union Flag proudly waved from a lofty flagstaff, proclaiming the rule of English law. The long outer wall of Fort William was comparatively low, but inside, rising well above the houses that clustered about it on the flat bank, were the main buildings of the seat of government of the settlement, the Governor's House and the Factory offices, well designed buildings and worthy of their dignified function. Landing at the steps below the Fort, one passed by the watergate through the main entrance into the Factory, and thence into the heart of the settlement."

The description goes on: "Behind the Fort was a wide promenade and to the southeast a large square open space known as the Park, in the middle of which a reservoir, known as the Tank, provided the settlement with its main water supply. The Park was the center of the little community. [Known as Tank Square, it is still there and is still widely used.] To the north, facing the Park, was the community church, and next to it the Writers' Building. . . ." [This building now houses the departments of the government of West Bengal.] "Eastwards lay the Court-house . . . southwards the Hospital and the Cemetery,* whilst on all sides scattered about within easy reach of the Fort were the dwelling-houses of the principal members of the settlement, most of them three-storied buildings, and built in the typical English Georgian style of the period. The whole area was less than one square mile. Immediately beyond, principally to the north, lay the native town, already grown to a considerable size and increasing rapidly."

All of this sounds almost Arcadian, but the description goes on: "Few places in the world could have held less attraction than eighteenth-century Calcutta for the refined and cultured Englishman fresh from home. Though Bengal has sometimes been called a Garden of Eden—for reason of its rich fertility—Calcutta was emphatically no paradise. As late as 1780 . . . it was described by a visiting traveler as 'that scattered and confused chaos of houses, huts, sheds, streets, lanes, alleys, windings, gutters, sinks and tanks, which, jumbled into an undistinguished mass of filth and corruption, equally offensive to human sense and health. . . .'

"The surrounding swamp was poorly drained, the jungle was malarious [sic], the innumerable ditches were cesspools, putrefying bodies of men and animals lay on the banks of the river and in the streets and watercourses, the only drains were open canals, the scavenging was done by jackals at night and by vultures, kites and crows by day, sanitation of even the most primitive kind was nonexistent, and even in the great tank, which provided the settlement with drinking-water, pariah dogs with mange were known at times to bathe and drink."

How anyone survived this for very long is difficult to imagine. You couldn't even get away to the mountains during the hot season. The idyllic hill stations one associates with British India were a cen-

---

*I am not sure which cemetery is being referred to here. In 1767 the British opened the South Park Street Cemetery. In 1988, when I visited Calcutta, I very much wanted to see it, but I could not convey to the taxi driver what a cemetery was. In Calcutta, as in most places in the subcontinent, the dead are cremated and their ashes deposited. In Calcutta they are put into the Hooghly River. I finally managed to explain that this cemetery was a place where the English visited their ancestors. That worked.

tury in the future. It was commonly said that very few of the English arrivals survived more than three monsoons. What's more, when Bogle arrived in Calcutta in 1770 he was greeted by a desperate famine. He describes it vividly in a letter to his father written not long after he arrived in the city:

"Last year the crops failed to an extent never known before in the memory of man, which has reduced the inhabitants to utmost distress. [According to different estimates, between a third and a half died.] The town was better provided for than most others, and yet it has suffered amazingly. The Governor [John Cartier] and Council had a magazine of grain with which they fed fifteen thousand every day for some months, and yet this could not prevent many thousands from dying of want, and the streets from being crowded with the most miserable objects. There were sometimes 150 dead bodies picked up in a day, and thrown into the river. In the country the distress was greater, as it was further removed from the sea and not so easily supplied from distant countries. Whole families perished of hunger, or fed upon leaves of trees, or, contrary to their religion, ate animal food; some even subsisted on the dead carcasses. Their distress is unparalleled, and it shocks one to think of it. A million and a half people are said to have famished in the provinces that belong to the English. There is one thing that must amaze everyone that has been used to a free country. There is an indolence and indifference about them that is astonishing, and despair rather increases it. They have died without a single effort to obtain grain either by force or even by toil and labour. What mobs and commotions there would be with us were grain to increase to three times its price! and in many places it was a hundred times what it usually is."[8] By the following December the worst of the famine was over.

Bogle, now approaching his mid-twenties, was a little older than the typical writer recruit. Perhaps it was because of this, or perhaps it was because his superiors realized his special abilities, that he was placed as an assistant with the so-called Select Committee, which transacted the political business of the Company. This gave him the opportunity to study how it operated. Like Hastings, but unlike most of his colleagues, Bogle began learning the languages of the subcontinent. At the time, Persian was the language of diplomacy in this part of the world—no doubt reflecting the fact that Bengal was part of the

Moghul Empire. Urdu, now the national language of Pakistan, has an Arabic script and a plethora of Persian words. Both Bogle and Hastings learned Persian and Urdu. They certainly knew Bengali. This gave both of them an ease in dealing with the local people that most of their British contemporaries did not enjoy.

After Bogle had been in Calcutta for eighteen months, Hastings arrived there from Madras where he had been stationed. He was about to take up his duties as the newly appointed governor of Bengal. From here on the careers of the two men became intertwined. In an attempt to rejuvenate a dormant bureaucracy, Hastings made a number of new appointments. Bogle became assistant secretary to the Board of Revenue. In this capacity he accompanied Hastings on a four-month visit to the interior of Bengal. It was at this time that Bogle's brother Robert suffered severe business losses, and it looked as if his father might have to sell their home at Daldowie. Bogle dedicated himself to earning enough money to pay off his family's debts. Over the next several years he managed to transmit 4,500 pounds—a very large sum—to his family. He was also steadily gaining the confidence of Hastings and moving up the Company ladder. One can see why Hastings might have chosen Bogle to lead the first British diplomatic mission to Tibet.

To understand the events that led to this mission, we need to say a little about the geography and history of India's northern neighbor, Bhutan. If you fly north from Calcutta to Paro in Bhutan—the country's only airfield—you first fly over what appears to be the absolutely flat seabed of an ancient sea, which indeed it is. During the monsoon season this area is largely under water. But then one abruptly runs into the "coastline." This is a line of steeply rising Himalayan foothills which are densely covered by forests so thick that you cannot see the ground. The hills rise to about seven thousand feet and level off on a plateau, the first step to the Tibetan plateau which is over twelve thousand feet in altitude. At eighteen places river valleys cut through these foothills. These valleys are known as "duars"—related to the Hindi world *dwar*, for "gate," and to our own word "door." The duars provide the only viable passages from the plateau down to the plains of India.

In the late eighteenth century Bhutan was not a unified country; it was split into various fiefdoms ruled by local warlords. The warlord who ruled from what is now the capital of Bhutan, Thimpu, became known to the British as the Deb "Raja." The northernmost border state of India, on the Bhutanese border, had the colorful name of Cooch Behar. It had its own raja. From time to time Bhutanese raiders came down the nearest duar and invaded Cooch Behar. In 1772 they abducted both the raja and his brother. The regent—the deputy ruler—of Cooch Behar, appealed to the British—in particular to Hastings, who was now the governor of Bengal—for help. He proposed to pay half the state revenues if the British could rid Cooch Behar of the invading Bhutanese. Hastings accepted—a pattern that would be repeated with other frontier states.

In December 1772 a force of *sepoys*—mercenary Indian troops—under the command of Captain John Jones was sent into Cooch Behar to deal with the Bhutanese. They learned, as the British would continue to learn in the Duar Wars of the next century, that the Bhutanese were tough customers. With heavy losses on both sides, these skirmishes lasted into the spring of 1774 when the British finally administered a sound drubbing to the Bhutanese. The Deb Raja was forced to resign, and his successor began suing for peace. In the interim Hastings had been corresponding with the directors of the Company in London, partly to get permission for what he had already done during the interval between letters, and partly to promote the idea of trading with the Bhutanese and the Tibetans, something he had had in mind from the time he became governor of Bengal. Here, at last, might be a place to dispose of the heavy British woolen cloth.

The Bhutanese, as Buddhists, had a spiritual allegiance to the Buddhists of Tibet. Nominally, the spiritual and temporal ruler of Tibet was the Dalai Lama in Lhasa. But at this time, as often happened, the Dalai Lama was a child, and a regent was the de facto ruler of the country. Next in line was a second lama, the Panchen Lama, whom the British usually referred to as the Teshu Lama (their own variant on the "tashi" or fortunate lama). The Panchen presided over the Tashilhunpo monastery near Shigatse, the second largest city in Tibet, some two hundred miles from Lhasa and that much closer to Bhutan. The Bhutanese were now intensely concerned about the intentions of the British, so they appealed to the Panchen whom they regarded as their protector. The Panchen had somehow heard of Hastings, and so it was, on March 29, 1774, that Hastings received a remarkable letter in Persian from Tibet. The letter has been variously translated, but I much prefer the savorous version in Markham's book.[9]

It begins, "The affairs of this quarter in every respect flourish. I am night and day employed in prayers for the increase of your happiness and prosperity. Having been informed by travellers from your quarter of your exhalted fame and reputation, my heart, like the blossom of spring, abounds with gaiety, gladness, and joy; praise that the star of your fortune is in its ascension; praise that happiness and ease are the surrounding attendants of myself and family. Neither to molest nor persecute is my aim; it is even the characteristic of my sect to deprive ourselves of the necessary refreshment of sleep, should an injury be done to a single individual. But in justice and humanity I am informed that you far surpass us. May you ever adorn the seat of justice and power that mankind may, under the shadow of your bosom, enjoy the blessings of happiness and ease."

This out of the way, the Panchen now gets down to business. "By your favour, I am the Rajah and Lama of this country, and rule over numbers of subjects, a particular with which you have no doubt been made acquainted by travellers from these parts. I have been repeatedly informed that you have been engaged in hostilities against the Deb Judhur [the previous Deb Raja], to which it is said, the Deb's own criminal conduct, in committing ravages and other outrages on your frontiers, has given rise. As he is of a rude and ignorant race (past times are not destitute of instances of the like misconduct, which his own avarice has tempted him to commit), it is not unlikely that he has now renewed these instances; and the ravages and plunder which he may have committed on the skirts of the Bengal and Bahar [sic] provinces have given you provocation to send your vindictive army against him. However, his party has been defeated, many of his people have been killed, three forts have been taken from him, and he has met with the punishment he deserved; and it is as evident as the sun your army has been victorious, and that, if you had been desirous of it, you might, in the space of two days, have entirely extirpated him, for he had not power to resist your efforts."

Now the admonition. "But I now take upon me to be his mediator, and to represent to you that, as the said Deb Rajah is dependent on the Dalai Lama, who rules in this country with unlimited sway (but on account of his being in his minority, the charge of the government and administration is committed to me), should you persist in offering further molestation to the Deb's country, it will irritate both the Lama and all his subjects against you. Therefore from a regard to our religion and customs, I request you will cease all hostilities against him, and in doing this you will confer the greatest favour and friendship upon me. I have reprimanded the Deb for his past conduct, and I have admonished him to desist from his evil practices in future, and to be submissive to you in all matters. I am persuaded that he will conform to the advice which I have given him, and it will be necessary that you treat him with compassion and clemency. As to my part, I am but a Fakir, and it is the custom of my sect, with rosary in our hands, to pray for the welfare of mankind, and for the peace and happiness of the inhabitants of this country; and I do now, with my head uncovered, entreat that you may cease all hostilities against the Deb in future. . . ."

This extraordinary document inspired Hastings to conclude a ten-article peace treaty with the Bhutanese in a matter of weeks. It restored some land that the British had taken from the Bhutanese in exchange for five Tangun ponies. These charming animals (Bogle was soon to make use of them) are one of the delights of anyone traveling in the backcountry of Bhutan, where they trot along with bells jingling. The Bhutanese were also allowed to send an annual trade delegation to the northern India border town of Rangpur. Peace was restored, and the scene was set for Bogle's mission. In Hastings's mind, Bhutan was now a sideshow. The real object was to open diplomatic relations with Tibet, which might in turn bring improved trade relations with China, an Eldorado promising untold riches to the Company.

By mid-May 1774 Hastings had officially appointed Bogle as his "deputy to the Teshu Lama, the sovereign of Bhutan."[10] In a footnote Markham suggests (and I agree) that by "Bhutan" he meant here *bhot*, a reference to Tibet and a transliteration of the Tibetan word for "Tibet"—*pö*, the origin of the name "Bhutan," land of the Bhots. Hastings uses "Bhutan" in this sense elsewhere. But he does not seem to realize that the Panchen is not in Lhasa where he proposes to send Bogle. He charges Bogle with investigating the prospects for trade in such items as "gold, silver, precious stones, musk," and "rhubarb." Bogle is also charged with studying the geography of the country—terra incognita to the British. Bogle is to report back "from time to time" on his progress. Hastings had the idea that Bogle might establish a "residence" in Lhasa—something that did not happen until the twentieth century and then only by force of arms.[11] Hastings also asked Bogle to draw on him for all charges. It seems as if Hastings paid for this expedition out of his own funds. Finally, he appointed an assistant surgeon named Alexander Hamilton to go along on the mission. The two men would be without a military escort.

This was the formal public letter of appointment. Three days later, however, Hastings sent Bogle a private commission which, in my view, illustrates Hastings at his best. This is what he asked Bogle to do:[12]

1. To send one or more pair of animals called tús [goats] which produce the shawl wool. If by a dooley, chairs, or any other contrivance they can be secured from the fatigues and hazards of the way, the expense is to be no objection.

2. To send one or more pair of the cattle which bear what are called cowtails [yaks].

3. To send me carefully packed some fresh ripe walnuts for seed, or an entire plant, if it can be transported; and any other curious or valuable seeds or plants, the rhubarb and ginseng especially.

4. Any curiosities, whether natural productions, manufactures, paintings, or what else may be acceptable to persons of taste in England. Animals only that may be useful, unless any that may be remarkably curious.

5. In your inquiries concerning the people, the form of their government, and the mode of collecting their revenue, are points principally meriting your attention.

6. To keep a diary, inserting whatever passes before your observation which shall be characteristic of the people, the country, the climate, the road, their manners, customs, buildings, cookery, &c., or interesting to the trade of this country, carrying with you a pencil and a pocket-book for the purpose of minuting short notes

of every fact or remark as it occurs, and putting them in order at your leisure while they are fresh in your memory.

7. To inquire what countries lie between Lhasa and Siberia, and what communication there is between them. The same with regard to China and Kashmir.

8. To ascertain the value of their trade with Bengal by their gold and silver coins, and to send me samples of both.

9. Every nation excels others in some particular art or science. To find out the excellence of the Bhutanese [Tibetans].

Warren Hastings

10. To inform yourself of the course and navigation of the Brahmaputra, and of the state of the countries through which it runs. [This would have been quite a task, for the Brahmaputra has it source in far western Tibet, near Mount Kailas, and ends up draining in India not far from the border with Burma.]

W. H.

Not mentioned in the commission was Hastings's charge to Bogle to plant potatoes at every rest stop, which he faithfully did, noting the exact number in his journal.* In addition, Hastings provided Bogle with an historical memorandum about Tibet which he wrote himself. He must have read quite widely in the sources available to him. But this only whetted his curiosity. He writes in one paragraph, "It is said that in Tibet it is very common for one lady to have several husbands. I should wish to know if this practice obtains in all ranks of society, and whether those husbands who all have intercourse with one woman have not likewise other women that are their wives, with whom likewise they hold an intercourse in common. We have instances in other countries where, though each man in a family had a wife that was properly his own, all the men in the family had likewise an intercourse with all the women in it. Perhaps this may also be the

---

*The potato comes from South America. It was brought to Europe in the sixteenth century and thence to Asia where, at least in the Indian subcontinent, it is now an essential component of the diet. I have always thought that the two most important legacies of the British in India were the English language and the potato.

case in Tibet; and if we knew anything of the laws of succession in Tibet, or to whom the children of a wife with several husbands were understood to belong, one might be able to discover how the fact stood, though we had no direct information with regard to it."[13]

Armed with these instructions, Bogle and Hamilton left Calcutta in mid-May 1774 with a cadre of Bengali assistants, none of whom had ever seen snow, to follow a route that no Englishman had ever traveled. Their first destination was the Tashichodzong in what is now the present capital of Bhutan, Thimpu. In Tibetan, or Dzongkha, the national language of Bhutan, *dzong* refers to a fortress-monastery. The Tashichodzong, which the British called the Tassisudon, was the seat of the government of the Deb Raja. Its buildings, which are still on the same site but have been reconstructed several times, house the present Bhutanese government. One can drive in a day from the Indian frontier to Thimpu following a route up the Buxa Duar which, as far as I can tell, is the same one Bogle took. On foot and pony it took him ten days. His encounter with the Deb Raja was most cordial and led to the peace treaty mentioned above.

The next step was to travel into Tibet to meet the Panchen. Here a snag developed. Communications arrived from Tibet saying that Bogle was not welcome and should return to India. Different excuses were offered: that an epidemic of smallpox made traveling into Tibet unsafe; that the Chinese, who were at this time enjoying a period of influence in Tibet, objected. Later Bogle discovered the real reason: the Panchen had been informed that two "Fringies"—foreigners— had arrived in Bhutan with a large retinue, the Bengalis. Having no experience with the British, the Panchen thought, reasonably, that this might be some sort of military expedition. In time it was reported to him that the group seemed to have only peaceful intentions, so they received permission to enter Tibet. By the time they left the country, it was October.

To enter Tibet they crossed a high pass from which two of the most magnificent mountains in the world are visible. Chomolhari, at 24,000 feet, is on the Bhutan-Tibet frontier. It is a sacred mountain to the Bhutanese, and Bogle was warned not to try to hunt animals within view of it. But he also glimpsed what he describes as a "snowy hill."[14] This, from its location on the frontier between Sikkim and

George Bogle in formal Bhutanese clothing presented
to him by the Deb Raja. (Detail from a painting by
Tilly Kettle)

Nepal, was surely Kanchenjunga (28,208 feet), the third-highest
mountain in the world.

The Panchen was not in Shigatse; the city was suffering a smallpox epidemic. So the two met in a small palace a day's march away
from the city. They got along well at once. It turned out that the
Panchen's mother was from Ladakh, close to India, so that he had
learned Hindustani from her, a language that Bogle knew. From
Bogle's journal it is clear that, by the time he left Tibet, he had made
himself fluent in Tibetan.

Bogle spent more than five months in Shigatse with the Panchen and his family. His description of his stay is one of the high points of the journal. When he was not having long talks with the Panchen, he passed the time playing chess or fortune-telling or in like activities. "... The Tibetans have a great faith in fortune-telling," Bogle writes, "which indeed seems to be common to all mankind except our European philosophers, who are too wise to believe in anything."[15] On one occasion the Panchen asked Bogle to describe Europe to him. He was particularly interested in Russia. The Russians and Chinese were then engaged in border skirmishes. (In the next century this would become the Great Game, with the British drawn in as well. It would become the excuse for the 1904 British invasion of Tibet.) The Panchen also wanted to know about the Christian religion. Jesuits had entered Tibet earlier in the century but had been expelled from the country. The Panchen asked Bogle to explain the Trinity. Religion was not Bogle's strong suit, and he did not feel up to the task. But when the Panchen asked Bogle to say something in English so that he could hear what the language sounded like, Bogle recited some verses of Gray's "Elegy in a Country Churchyard."

Meanwhile he was reporting continually to Hastings about what he was learning. On the polyandry he noted, "Montesquieu and other political writers insist that it is destructive of the population; and the women cry out that it is unjust and unreasonable that so many of their sex should be subjected to the pleasure of one man. But in this country they have their revenge. The elder brother marries a woman, and she becomes the wife of the whole family. They club together in matrimony as merchants do in trade. Nor is this joint concern often productive of jealousy among the partners. They are little addicted to jealousy. Disputes, indeed, sometimes arise about the children of the marriage; but they are settled either by a comparison of the features of the child with those of its several fathers, or left to the determination of the mother."[16]

The Panchen made a request which Bogle passed on to Hastings. There had been a Buddhist temple in Calcutta that had been destroyed when the Muslims had taken Calcutta for a time from the English. Could the governor have a new one built? As soon as he learned of the Panchen's request, Hastings ordered a Buddhist temple and center for Buddhists built on the banks of the Hooghly. But if Bogle hoped for a visit to Lhasa, it could not be arranged. The politics were simply too complicated, and while the Panchen was agreeable, the people in Lhasa were not.

In early April 1775 Bogle began his return trip, covering essentially the same route he had traveled a year before. By June he was in India. Markham quotes an excerpt from a letter that Bogle received from Hastings upon his arrival: "I am perfectly satisfied and pleased with every circumstance of your conduct, and equally so with the issue of your commission. . . . I have many thanks to make for your journal, which the world must have. Its merits shall not be lost where I can make it known. . . ."[17] True to his word, on August 7, 1775, a scant few weeks after Bogle's return, Hastings wrote to Samuel Johnson, whom he had gotten to know in London, enclosing a copy of Bogle's journal. "When I read the account of your visit to the Hebrides," he wrote, "I could not help wishing that a portion of that spirit which could draw so much entertainment and instruction from a region so little befriended by nature, or improved by the arts of society, could have animated Mr. Bogle, the author of this journal, but I flatter myself that you will find it not unworthy of perusal. I confess I received great pleasure from it, and I assure myself, that whatever originality you may discover in the description of the countries and inhabitants of which it treats, you will at least be pleased with the amiable character of the Lama, which has been confirmed to me by the testimonies of other travellers, who have visited his capital. . . ."

Hastings goes on: "I am afraid it may look like an ill compliment to tell you that I have endeavoured to prevail on the writer to put it into a more connected form, and to send it, with some additional materials, to England for publication. If it would not be assuming too great a liberty, I should request to be favoured with your opinion upon the propriety of this intention. The first copies of these sheets were taken, and intended for your perusal, long before I had any thoughts of making them public, and I cannot now deny myself the satisfaction of accomplishing that design whatever may be their future lot. . . ."[18]

Nothing came of this request, and the journal was not published until a century later.

↘

TO EXPLORE the details of the next six years of Bogle's career, when his destiny became interwoven with that of Hastings, would get us ahead of our story. Here let me note that in or around 1775, Bogle's portrait was painted by the English artist Tilly Kettle, who was then living in India. It is the only portrait of Bogle I have seen. But Kettle's portraits of Hastings are so much like the other paintings of him that I would assume that this is a good likeness of Bogle as well. He is shown in what appears to be a Bhutanese outfit. He has bare feet and is wearing a hat that resembles a flower pot. Two Tibetans seated next to him are smoking pipes. Through the open window one can see a monastery. The setting does not look much like Shigatse, but Kettle would not have had much visual documentation to work with.

In 1779 Hastings appointed Bogle collector of revenue in Rangpur, a town on the Bengal-Bhutan frontier. Then, in 1781, Hastings promoted Bogle to be a member of the Committee of Revenue in Calcutta. He immediately took up the position, but shortly after he arrived in Calcutta he contracted a fatal illness and died on April 3, 1781. He was thirty-four. He is buried in the South Park Street Cemetery in Calcutta, where there is a massive monument in the form of a sarcophagus with a simple dedication to the "Late Ambassador to Tibet." Had Bogle lived, Hastings planned to send him back to Tibet on a second mission, this time all the way to Lhasa.

When I first read Markham's account of Bogle's death, I was puzzled by this passage: "George Bogle left two daughters, named Martha and Mary, who were sent to Scotland. . . ."[19] Why no mention of the girls' mother? Who was she? This was a complete mystery to me until I came across a memoir entitled "George Bogle and his Children" written by H. E. Richardson, who was the last British Resident in Lhasa before the Chinese takeover of Tibet in the 1990s. In his book *Tibet and Its History*,[20] Richardson had described a startling discovery about Bogle's children, and this memoir brought the story up to date. Richardson had come across evidence that the girls' mother was a Tibetan who may well have been related to the Panchen. It was even suggested that she was the Panchen's sister, something that Richardson thinks was impossible. It may have been one of the nieces whom Bogle writes about affectionately. She must have come back with him from Tibet. That the girls had a Tibetan ancestry was, it turned out, part of the Bogle family legend. Markham must have known this, because in reconstructing Bogle's journal he spoke with members of the family. But to the Victorians this sort of liaison was not something to be discussed. Indeed, as Richardson notes, there is evidence that Bogle had had other children with native women before his relationship with his Tibetan wife. This too was not to be discussed, though in Bogle's day it was commonplace.

When I first encountered Bogle's journal in Rishikesh Shaha's library, all those years ago, I read it with the eye of a traveler, on my way to Tibet. Warren Hastings for me was, at the time, a secondary figure. What I knew about him I had learned from Bogle's journal. But over the years I found myself haunted by him. I kept asking myself, why was this man brought into disgrace? Was Bogle completely wrong in his assessment of him? Who was Hastings? How did he come to cast such a giant shadow over a country like India? That is the mystery we now begin to unravel. It has taken me a decade.

Two
A BIBLIO-BIOGRAPHICAL
INTERLUDE

When he [Hastings] landed in his native country, he had
attained his fifty-second year. . . . In his person he was thin, but
not tall; of spare habit, very bald, with a countenance placid and
thoughtful, but when animated full of intelligence. Never perhaps
did any man who passed the Cape of Good Hope display a mind
more elevated above mercenary considerations. Placed in a
situation where he might have amassed immense wealth without
exciting censure, he revisited England with only a modest
competence. . . . In private life he was playful and gay to a degree
hardly conceivable, never carrying his political vexations into the
bosom of his family. Of a temper so buoyant and elastic that the
instant he quitted the Council board, where he had been assailed
by every species of opposition, often heightened by personal
acrimony, he mixed in society like a youth upon whom care had
never intruded.
—Sir Nathaniel W. Wraxall, M.P., *Posthumous Memoirs* (1836)

As one might imagine, in the last two centuries many biographies
and biographical sketches of Hastings have appeared, beginning
with contemporary reminiscences. Hastings himself never wrote an
autobiography, though in old age he set down some autobiographical
notes. But he left an incredible paper trail—some *three hundred* volumes. In that era people wrote *letters*, by the thousands! Further-

more Hastings was not only obliged to minute all his actions as a government official in India, he also carried on a vast correspondence with the authorities in London as well as with innumerable friends, family members, and associates. The first individual who seems to have come to grips with this nachlass was the Reverend George R. Gleig, rector of Ivychurch in Kent, who in 1841 published a three-volume work—an "official" biography—entitled *Memoirs of the Life of the Right Hon. Warren Hastings, First Governor-General of Bengal.*[1] Gleig's successors have happily quoted from the original documents found in his book while declaring that, as a biography, it borders on the worthless. (To cite a minor but characteristic example, Gleig has decided that Bogle's first name is William!) For Gleig, Hastings was a giant without flaw. Hastings's widow was still alive when Gleig was working on the book. She died in 1837 at the age of eighty-nine, three months before the ascension of Queen Victoria. The presence of Hastings's widow and members of her family, whom Gleig acknowledges, certainly influenced what he wrote, a task which he says took him four years. Indeed, Gleig notes that "It was not my good fortune to become acquainted with Mrs. Hastings till the last shadows of old age had fallen upon her; and we are seldom able to determine with accuracy, if we see them for the first time in so dim a light, how either men or women may have comported themselves when they were young. Yet I can testify that even then she was no ordinary woman; while they that knew her better and had other and more extensive opportunities of judging, assure me, that long after she had passed the period of middle life, she was altogether fascinating."[2] In his acknowledgments Gleig thanks Hastings's stepson and daughter-in-law for their help in collecting materials for his book. They too surely had an influence.

The first person to lower the boom on Gleig was his contemporary, the English historian Thomas Babington Macaulay. In October 1841 Macaulay published what was an ostensible review of Gleig's book in the *Edinburgh Review*. It is "ostensible" because in a "review" of more than 125 pages, Gleig's book is barely mentioned and then only to ridicule it.[3] Nonetheless this essay has stood like a colossus over subsequent Hastings biographers. There are several reasons for this, not least of which was that Macaulay had actually served for five years—1834–1838—in the government of India. He did much to try to bring equality of Europeans and Indians under the law—which Hastings would surely have approved of—and to inaugurate a system of national education that was more British than Indian—which Hastings would surely have disapproved of. He understood firsthand what Hastings had accomplished, and his essay reflects that. After his service in India, Macaulay returned to England and reentered Parliament, where he remained until 1847 when he was defeated for reelection. Meanwhile he was at work on his monumental four-volume *History of England*, whose first two volumes were published in 1848. Essays like the one on Hastings were apparently "busy work."

For anyone with an ear for the English language, Macaulay's writing is like champagne. Very few historians (Hastings's public schoolmate Edward Gibbon being an exception), indeed very few writers, have ever used the language with such power. The writing is so marvelous that one is often lulled into forgetting what Macaulay is saying. In the case of Hastings, he makes clear his point of view in the first paragraph of his essay. He writes, "He [Hastings] had great qualities, and he rendered great services to the state. But to represent him as a man of stainless virtue is to make him ridiculous; and from a regard for his memory, if from no other feeling, his friends would have done well to lend no countenance to such adulation. We believe that, if he were now living, he would have sufficient judgment and sufficient greatness of mind to wish to be shown as he was. He must have known that there were dark spots in his fame. He might also have felt with pride that the splendor of his fame would bear many spots. He would have wished posterity to have a likeness of him, though an unfavorable likeness, rather than a daub at once insipid and unnatural, resembling neither him nor anybody else. 'Paint me as I am' said Oliver Cromwell, while sitting to young Lely. 'If you leave out the scars and wrinkles, I will not pay you a shilling.'"[4]

It is by no means clear that Hastings would have agreed that there were "dark spots in his fame." (Incidentally, in the thirty-odd portraits and busts of Hastings I have seen, I find none with "scars and wrinkles.") He certainly would not have agreed that the dark spots were the ones that Macaulay singles out. Indeed, to each of Macaulay's "spots" one can associate quotations from Hastings in which he denies their "darkness." Nonetheless, all subsequent biographers of Hastings keep finding Macaulay peering at them. They too find

Thomas Babington Macaulay, 1853. (Painting by John Partridge)

flaws with Hastings but, they insist, not the ones that Macaulay emphasizes.

By the end of the nineteenth century the British Empire was well established. The Sepoy Mutiny, which led to a major Anglo-Indian war, had occurred in 1857. In 1858 Parliament passed the Government of India Act, which effectively put the East India Company out of the business of governing India. Governors-general became viceroys, and Queen Victoria became Empress of India—the jewel in the crown. Biographies of Hastings written at the end of the century reflect this change. The most interesting to me is the one written by Sir Alfred Lyall.[5] Lyall was in the Indian service, both in India and Britain, from 1855 to 1902. While in India he helped to govern some of the provinces which in Hastings's day were at the outer fringes of the Company's territory. He had a much better understanding of

these provinces than Macaulay did and, in my view, convincingly re-
futes some of Macaulay's contentions. He too finds flaws in Hastings.
But they are precisely what Macaulay says they are not. In particular
he finds in Hastings an "inability to see or admit that a view may
have been wrong or an action blameworthy."[6] But Lyall and
Macaulay do agree that, faults and all, Hastings was a very great man.
Indeed, when Macaulay proposed his review to the editor of the *Edinburgh Review*, he wrote, "I hardly know a story so interesting and of
such various interest. And the central figure is in the highest degree
striking and majestic. I think Hastings, though far from faultless, one
of the greatest men England ever produced. He had pre-eminent talents for government, and great literary talents too; fine taste, a
princely spirit, and heroic equanimity in the midst of adversity and
danger. . . ."[7]

By the 1930s it had become clear, at least to some people, that the
British in India might be living on borrowed time. This was, after all,
the age of Gandhi. It was also a time when democracy, at least as an
experiment, was being introduced to India. The turmoil this created
was reflected in A. Mervyn Davies's biography of Hastings, *Strange
Destiny*, published in 1935. He writes, "English liberal thought came
in the twentieth century to govern policy [in India]. In pursuit of the
democratic ideal, a vast constitutional experiment was initiated with
the object of giving to India popular representative institutions on a
western model, a form of government radically different from any
hitherto known in the country, unfitted to the character and needs of
the people, and ill-adapted to the peculiar conglomerate racial and
political circumstances of the country. Whatever may be said about
the future benefits that democracy will bring to India, it can hardly
be denied that its hasty introduction, without adequate preparation,
has helped in bringing about the present situation, the chief features
of which are new and growing racial antagonism, a militant national-
ism, widespread political, social, and agrarian discontent, revolution-
ary movements, outbreaks of crime, bitter discord between rival
religious communities, and a general feeling of uncertainty about the
future; all of which threaten to destroy not only the Empire but the
political unity of India, to plunge the country into anarchy and start it
on the same road that China has taken. An increasing alienation of
the people of India from their English rulers has succeeded the har-

mony of interests, aims and methods that was the central feature of Hastings's policy."[8]

Davies, who was a literary agent, had been interested in Hastings since his undergraduate days at Oxford. He apparently spent five years writing this book. I do not know how much time he spent in India. The result is a delightful, anecdotal account, which is not always accurate. For example, Davies has Bogle being received in *Lhasa* by the Panchen Lama, which indicates to me that he never studied the sources with much care. If one reads his book more as an historical novel than as serious history, one will be better off. If it is history one wants, the book to read is Keith Feiling's 1954 biography, *Warren Hastings*.[9] While the book is gracefully written, the reader must be prepared to parse innumerable sentences of the form "There were jealousies between the brilliant Nana Phadnavis, and his rivals, who suspected his intimacy with the infant Peishwa's mother, and rival ambitions of the military chiefs, Scindia and Holkar." The mind begins to reel. By the time Feiling wrote his book, India had been independent for some seven years. Democracy was no longer an experiment but an established fact. Hastings was becoming a part of history like the buildings the British constructed[10] and the language they left. Very few monuments were ever erected in Britain to Hastings—none by the government. His real monument is this history. Our story now begins.

Three

HASTINGS, 1732–1769

I happened to sup with him not long ago, when the conversation turned upon *Robinson Crusoe*. Everybody present gave their opinion of the book, of course without reflection. While the rest of the company were talking, Mr. Hastings seemed lost in a reverie, in which I little suspected that *Robinson Crusoe* could be concerned. At last he gravely declared, that he had often read the book with singular satisfaction; but that no passage in it had ever struck him so much, as where the hero is said to have built a monstrous boat at a distance from the sea, without knowing by what means he was to convey it to the water. "And by Jove," says Hastings, "the same thing has happened to myself an hundred times in my life. I have built a boat without any further consideration, and when difficulties and consequences have been urged against it, have been too ready to answer them by saying to myself 'Let me finish the boat first, and then I'll warrant, I shall find some method to launch it.'" This is the man's own political picture drawn by himself.

—Philip Francis (circa 1778)[1]

I: HASTINGS WHEN YOUNG

Sometime during the long course of his impeachment trial, one of his counsel, Robert Dallas, handed Hastings a poem of his own composition. Hastings liked it so much that he copied it in his own hand. As he wrote a good deal of poetry, and as it was found among his papers, it was sometimes attributed to him. He certainly shared the sentiments. The poem reads,

> Oft have I wondered that on Irish Ground
> No poisonous reptiles yet were found;
> Reveal'd the secret strands of nature's work,
> She sav'd her venom to create a Burke.[2]

Edmund Burke, who was Irish and was the principal spokesman for the prosecution in the trial, loosed a stream of venom upon Hastings during the course of it which bordered on the obscene. He was often admonished by the Lords who sat in judgment, but this had little effect. Burke was playing to a wider audience. Here is a sampler:[3]

"This swindling Maecenas—swindling of glory, and obtaining honour under false pretences—a bad scribbler of absurd papers, who could never put two sentences of sense together."

"A common-place dog-trot of the meanest of mankind."

"He is a captain general of iniquity—thief—tyrant—robber—cheat—sharper—swindler. We call him these names, and are sorry that the English language does not afford terms adequate to the enormity of his offences."

"Sir WALTER RALEIGH was called a spider of hell. This was foolish of Lord Coke [who presided over the impeachment of Raleigh which led to his execution]. Had he been a Manager in this trial, he would have been guilty of neglect of duty, had he not called the prisoner a spider of hell."

"A sink not only of filth and excrement to shock the natural senses, but of filth and excrement to shock the moral sense of every visitor."

As flagrant as these insults were, there is one that must have cut

Hastings very close to the bone. Burke described him as "A man whose origin was low, obscure, and vulgar, and bred in vulgar and ignoble habits—more proud than persons born under canopies of state, and swaddled in purple." If Burke had chosen to look back a number of generations, he would have found Hastingses who *were* "swaddled in purple." In the fourteenth century the family had more than its share of barons and earls. By the seventeenth century, however, the family estate at Daylesford in Worcester could barely support Simon Hastings and his eleven children from two marriages. One of his sons, John, was forced to sell part of the estate, and *his* son John chose the losing Royalist side in the Civil War. It ended with the victory of Oliver Cromwell and the beheading of King Charles I. John fled the country for a time. When he returned, he married Elizabeth Penyston of Cornwell in Oxfordshire. This marriage produced three generations of sons and grandsons all named Penyston, or Penniston, Hastings. Warren Hastings's grandfather Penyston was an Oxford graduate who became rector of Daylesford. His oldest son, Penyston III, was Hastings's father.

By 1715 the estate in Daylesford had been sold to a Bristol merchant named Jacob Knight. When the rector, Hastings's grandfather, died in 1752 he was bankrupt. Penyston III, Hastings's father, was a disaster from the beginning. He failed to graduate from Oxford but took holy orders and in 1730 married Hastings's mother, Hester Warren. Gleig makes the romantic claim that Penyston when he married was a youth of not more than fifteen. Feiling, who has looked into the matter with more care, finds that he was about twenty-five. The following year Hastings's older sister Anne was born, and on December 6, 1732, Warren was born. Within a few days his mother died, and within seven months Penyston had remarried—the daughter of an Oxford tradesman. What happened to her is not clear, but it is recorded that Penyston was using the small trust funds of his two children to pay his own debts. He then decamped to Barbados as the rector of Christ Church. He remarried again, and by 1744 he was dead. Whatever there was left of the children's legacy went to Penyston's Barbardos widow. It is not surprising that, when late in life, Hastings was asked about his father, he replied, "There was not much in my father's history that would be worth repeating except that when he became old enough he entered into holy orders, and went to one of the West India Islands where he died."[4]

I have not been able to discover what happened to Hastings's sister Anne in the immediate years after the death and disappearance of her parents. At least in the beginning, her fate probably resembled that of her younger brother. He was first put in the care of a woman in the village, whom the parish paid a pittance to take care of orphaned children. Then, until the age of eight, he lived with his grandfather Penyston, the rector, who was certainly helped in the raising of the children by his sister Elizabeth. (Throughout his life Hastings retained a fond relationship with his Aunt Elizabeth. He provided her with a stipend even when he had to borrow the money to pay it.) When Hastings was two, his grandfather was forced to leave Daylesford, locating in an equally modest clerical position in the nearby community of Churchill. Hastings was sent to a charity school along with the most impoverished children of the village.

Even then, however, he had an awareness that somehow he was different. Very late in life he remembered a stream, the Kingham brook near Churchill. He recalled, "To lie beside the margin of that stream, and muse, was one of my favourite recreations; and there, one bright summer's day, when I was scarcely seven years old, I well remember that I first formed the determination to purchase back Daylesford. I was then literally dependent upon those whose condition scarcely raised them above the pressure of absolute want; yet somehow or another, the child's dream, as it did not appear unreasonable at the moment, so in after years it never faded away. God knows there were periods in my career, when to accomplish that, or any object of honourable mention seemed to be impossible, but I have lived to accomplish it. . . ."[5]

In 1740, when he was eight, Hastings was taken into custody by his father's brother Howard. This was an extraordinary bit of good fortune since Howard had a decent position in the Customs House and could afford to send him to a boarding school at Newington Butts, near London. The education was good, the food less so. Hastings blamed it for the fact that he never grew taller than about five feet six inches. He appeared frail, but as many of his enemies were later to find, he had more stamina and will power than any of them.

In 1743 his uncle sent him to Westminster, one of the best public schools in England. Among his schoolmates were two future prime ministers, the poet William Cowper, and the historian Edward Gibbon. His best friend was a boy named Elijah Impey, whose destiny would interlock with his in India. Macaulay, who periodically breaks into flights of imaginative fancy, writes, "We know little about their school days. But, we think, we may safely venture to guess that whenever Hastings wished to play a trick more than usually naughty, he hired Impey with a tart or a ball to act as fag in the worst part of the prank."[6] Of course, when he wrote this, Macaulay knew that during Hastings's tenure as governor-general of Bengal, Sir Elijah Impey would be the chief justice of its Supreme Court.

At Westminster, Hastings was an outstanding student, one year at the top of his school of 350 students. For this his name was engraved in gold letters on the wall of his dormitory. He learned to love Latin poetry and in later life wrote odes in imitation of Horace. He must also have learned French since he spoke it and often used French phrases in his letters. (As far as I know, he never visited France.) He appears to have tried to fly. He designed a pair of wings and managed to break his nose. But all this came to an end in February 1749 when his uncle died.

Physicists like myself are highly sensitive to initial conditions. The flapping of a butterfly's wing on a Pacific island can lead weeks later to a typhoon halfway around the world. If Hastings's uncle had not died in 1749, would there have been a British Empire in India? Would Hastings ever have gone there? Could there have been an empire without him? One wonders. He was apparently headed for a brilliant university career. With his scholarly bent, evident all his life, he might have become an Oxford don or gone into British politics. Instead he became the ward of one Joseph Creswicke, who was a member of the family his father had first married into. Meanwhile his sister Anne had married an attorney named John Woodman. For reasons unclear, Creswicke insisted that Hastings leave school. It wasn't the money, it seems. Gleig reports that when Dr. Nichols, headmaster of the school, was informed, he said, "What, lose Warren Hastings—lose the best scholar of his year! That will never do at all. If the want of means to keep you here—aye, and at college too—be the only hindrance, we can easily remove that. You shall go on with your education at my charges. I cannot afford to lose the reputation which I am sure to obtain through you."[7]

In later life Hastings remembered that it was his own idea to go out to India when he was forced to leave school. He had been left no inheritance and, apart from whatever Mr. Creswicke was willing to give him, he was destitute. Creswicke did have the contacts to get Hastings an appointment as a writer. He must also have paid for the course in accounting that Hastings took in London. But there was no course offered in what to expect in India. Not until the next century did the Company provide its own training courses for people going to India. Mr. Creswicke must also have put the money up for Hastings's passage and for his kit. In any event, he sailed from Gravesend on January 27, 1750, on the East Indiaman *London*. He was seventeen. As he wrote in the notes he left for his autobiography, "On the 8th of October 1750 I arrived in Bengal the last of eight young men who composed the same list of that establishment."[8]

SOME DECADES BEFORE Hastings's arrival in India, the so-called Old Company, whose charter went back to Queen Elizabeth, and the New Company, composed of independent operators who had simply set themselves up as a rival enterprise, had joined to become the United Company of Merchants of England trading into the East Indies. By 1750 the United Company had three enclaves in India in various states of relative precariousness. The settlements in Madras and Calcutta had been built from more or less nothing. As mentioned earlier, what became Madras was founded in 1639, an inspiration of a Company agent named Francis Day. It was an unlikely choice for a location. The nearest significant habitation was a fort at San Thomé, which at the time belonged to the Portuguese, who were none too friendly. It is said that Day had a lady friend in San Thomé, which is why he negotiated with the local Indian ruler to build a fort—St. George—a few miles up the beach.

The founding of Calcutta in 1690 on the Hooghly River was, as we have noted, the inspiration of Job Charnock, who also dealt with the local ruler for the use of the territory. Calcutta too was built of whole cloth.

With Bombay the situation was quite different. In 1661 the off-shore islands on which Bombay was built were given to Charles II, the son of the ill-fated Charles I, who became the first king after the monarchy was restored, as a wedding present. The islands had been in the possession of the Portuguese. Charles II had married the Portuguese Princess Catherine of Braganza, and Bombay was part of her dowry. Like many wedding gifts, the recipient was eager to exchange it. It consisted of twenty square miles, mainly of water, and came with an obligation to help the Portuguese fight their battles. Thus when the Company offered to take it off of Charles's hands in 1668, he was delighted. This was the one place in India where the Company had taken over a terrain that was already in some sense British.

From 1658 until his death in 1707, the Moghul emperor Aurangzeb ruled most of India.[9] He was an austere man and a devout Muslim whose capital was Delhi. Dissenters and revolutionaries were dealt with summarily. A particular concern were the Marathas, a warrior caste of Hindus who came from the hills near Bombay. They put up a fierce resistance to the Muslim domination of Aurangzeb and would later play an important role in the struggle of the British to maintain their presence in India throughout the entire period of Hastings's involvement. If the Marathas had ever been able to consolidate under a single strong leader for a substantial period of time, they might well have come to rule all of India and force out the British. Aurangzeb spent much blood and treasure trying to control them. After his death the Moghul Empire imploded and the Marathas became a powerful force. But while Aurangzeb ruled, it was with him or his local *nawabs* (nabobs)—Muslim governors—and the other Indian princes that the British dealt. It was with Aurangzeb that the British signed an agreement in 1690 allowing them to trade in Bengal. After his death the British had to deal with the local nawabs who claimed pieces of the Moghul Empire. They also had to deal with the French.

The French East India Company (Compagnie des Indes Orientales) had been founded in 1664. It had two important enclaves, one at Pondicherry, some eighty-five miles down the coast from Madras, and the other upriver on the Hooghly from Calcutta at Chandernagore. In both places the French competed with the British for trade and influence. The French evolved an idea of how colonies

Headquarters of the East India Company on Leadenhall Street in London, late eighteenth century. (Watercolor by James Malton)

should operate in India, which as the eighteenth century progressed became the British model as well. Before mid-century the British in India resembled tenants trying to renew real estate leases with erratic and often grasping landlords, the nawabs. According to one estimate, in 1740 the Company had about 2,000 troops—native sepoys and Europeans—in all of India. (By 1782 there were an estimated 115,000.) At first these soldiers acted as policemen who kept civil order and prevented theft from the warehouses. The first full regiment of regular British troops in India arrived in Madras in 1754, and the sepoys were not given uniforms until 1757. Above all, these troops were not used for territorial expansion, something that the Company explicitly forbade. They were, as it turned out, not much use in defending the territory they already had. Events came to a head not long before Hastings arrived in India.

In the early 1740s the French and English were engaged in a war on the European continent over the claim of Maria Theresa to the succession in Austria. By the time news of this conflict reached India in 1744 the matter had been decided, but in the outpost on the sub-

continent this did not become known until later. Hence the French
and the English began their own war in India. The French governor
of Pondicherry was Joseph François Dupleix, a man of substantial
abilities and a vivid nationalist bent. He was abetted by a strong
French fleet under the command of Admiral Mahé de la Bourdonnais. Bourdonnais, and the ground troops he commanded, captured
Madras in September 1746. Very few shots were fired in anger in defense of the city, and most of the population eventually found their
way to Fort St. David, a small British settlement nearby. Among the
escapees was Robert Clive—later Lord Clive, more precisely Baron
Clive of Plassey, a title he received in 1762—who had come to
Madras as a writer in 1744 at the age of nineteen. Clive reappears in
our story shortly.

Having captured Madras, the question for the French was what to
do with it. As far as Bourdonnais was concerned, it was simply a matter of looting the city and leaving. But Dupleix had other ideas.
Madras, he felt, should become a French city, a triumph over the English. Meanwhile the local nawab, Anwar-ud-Din, whose territory
this was after all, decided that he had had enough of these foreigners
and would push them all into the sea. This decision, as reasonable as
it seems, led unexpectedly to a decisive transformation in the balance of power on the Indian subcontinent. Bourdonnais had with him
a contingent of French troops, now at Dupleix's disposal, who were
equipped with the latest armaments of modern warfare. Most significant was the rate of fire of the French guns.[10] The Indian guns could
fire about once every three minutes while the French guns could fire
several times a minute. This meant that while the nawab's troops
might vastly outnumber the French, they could be mowed down like
so many game birds. And this is precisely what happened. This revolution in warfare led to an entirely new idea of how French, and then
British, colonies in India should operate. Instead of being timorous
outsiders begging to be tolerated, they could now attempt to control
the situation. The idea was to install by force their own puppet
nawabs, who would then do as they were told, at least until they re-
volted.

For the English, this tactic was still in the future. Meanwhile they
were in danger of losing any remaining hold they had in southern
India. While they were forced to give up Madras in 1746, they were

able, just, to hang on to Fort St. David until 1749. When the English and French signed the treaty of Aix-la-Chapelle, it momentarily ended the fighting in India and restored what was left of Madras, after its sacking, to the English. Thus when in 1750 Hastings made his voyage to Bengal, he was able to touch down at both Fort St. David and Madras before arriving in Calcutta.

There seems to be no record of what Hastings did during his first two years in Calcutta. Very likely his first employment was in keeping a written account of some part of the Company's transactions. It is reasonable to suppose that he began to learn the languages of the subcontinent. The Company offered cash bonuses—ten pounds, twice the annual salary of a beginning writer—to employees who learned Hindustani and somewhat less to those who learned Persian. Hastings learned both and certainly enough Bengali to deal with the local people.

In 1752 he was sent upriver to the important trading post at Kasimbazar, which was next to the nawab of Bengal's capital at Murshidabad, a substantial city known for its Moorish palaces and rich bazaars. During the next four years Hastings mastered the details of inland trade, especially silk. He never forgot them. Indeed, Gleig quotes a letter that Hastings wrote some twenty years later when he had become governor-general, with all the cares of that office on his shoulders, to a young colleague about silk. A little bit of it gives a sense of why these young men thought so highly of him. He writes, "I will frankly confess to you that I do not see the same advantages in the expensive works which you have annexed to your reels. I mean the bassines, the furnaces, and bars of iron for the tender threads of silk to pass through. These will prove a heavy article in the Company's dead stock. They will for ever require repairs, and by being made the necessary appendages to your improvements, which, otherwise, I think are admirable, they will preclude the inhabitants from adopting the same method of winding the silk from the cacoons. Why will not your reel, with the earthen pots, the occasional moving stoves, and other simple implements to which the natives are accustomed, which are all within their reach, and cost nothing, answer all the purposes of a more complex or a more showy mechanism? I propose these as doubts, or queries, not as assertions. A better information from you may possibly show that I am mistaken. . . ."[11]

Until the events of 1757, Hastings moved steadily, if not spectacularly, up the Company ranks. He was promoted to storekeeper and in 1756 represented the Company in trade disputes in Murshidabad. He also began, on a small scale, the sort of inland private trading that the Company expected its ill-paid factors to carry on. But to appreciate the events of 1757 we must return to Robert Clive, whom we left in 1746, fleeing, disguised as a Muslim, from Madras.

II: THE BLACK HOLE

Clive was born on September 29, 1725, in Shropshire, England.[12] His father was a lawyer and a small landowner. To employ anachronistic terminology, Clive was a juvenile delinquent. He had a fierce temper, which was one reason he was forced to leave several schools. At one point he led a gang of like-minded youths who charged protection money—protection from themselves—to local merchants. By the time he reached seventeen, his father had had enough. He used his influence to obtain for Clive an appointment as a writer for the Company, so that he would be sent off to India. It is not clear that Clive senior ever wanted to see his son again. More than half the people whom the Company sent to India at this time died there. Clive, at least in his early years in India, absolutely hated the place. He wrote, "I have not enjoyed one happy day since I left my native country."[13] And he meant it. Twice he tried to blow his brains out with a pistol. It misfired both times, and he decided that Providence must be preserving him for something. He also fought a duel. On the positive side, he began a program of self-study using books from the governor's library. He didn't, by the way, master any of the local languages; throughout his career he had to use interpreters. What would become of him no one could predict.

While the English and French had signed a formal truce, nothing prevented them from backing rival nawabs—with force if necessary. Here Clive found his true vocation. A British-backed nawab was being besieged by a French-backed nawab in the coastal town of Trichinopoly, not far from Arcot, the capital of the Carnatic region that contained Madras and Pondicherry. This was not a trivial matter. Dupleix and his puppet nawabs were in the process of taking over all of southern India. Dupleix had set himself up as a sort of oriental potentate. Trichinopoly stood in the way of a French hegemony. Clive, who was in Fort St. David, secured a commission as a "captain" in the Company's private army, and in the summer of 1751 he led some two hundred British soldiers and three hundred sepoys in a daring move to lift the siege. The force had only eight officers, four of them civilians like Clive, and six of them had never seen combat.

The first thing this unlikely contingent did was to capture Arcot itself, which was possible only because the nawab had taken his troops to Trichinopoly. The nawab then withdrew four thousand of his troops from Trichonopoly, effectively lifting the siege there, and laid siege to his own capital. Clive had anticipated this; he and his men held out for nearly two months until they were rescued by Maratha troops. (During this period the British and French formed temporary alliances with the Marathas whenever it suited their purposes.) A British puppet nawab was installed in Arcot, and the Clive legend was created.

What characterized Clive in this and his future engagements was his seemingly total indifference to his own mortality. He entered all forms of warfare in a state of euphoria. By the end of his life Clive was addicted to opium, and one wonders if this played a role in his state of mind when he went into battle. Opium, as noted earlier, was an important product in the Company's trade. It was manufactured in India and exchanged in China for tea.*

For the next two years Clive engaged in various military opera-

---

*The Chinese government tried unsuccessfully to block the importation of opium, but then, as now, it got through anyway. It is perhaps not generally realized that the tea that the American revolutionaries dumped into the Boston Harbor in 1773 had come to Boston from China on boats belonging to the East India Company. It had presumably been exchanged for opium.

tions, all successful, against the French and their native allies. His health suffered, and in 1753 he retired from the Company and returned to England with his new bride Margaret Maskelyne, sister of an eminent mathematician, Nevil, who had been the Astronomer Royal. Clive was now twenty-seven. Along with various trophies of war, he had amassed a sizable amount of money, and it appeared as if he would settle down in England. He was hailed as a war hero and even got himself elected to Parliament, an election that was overturned by a vote of Parliament itself. After two years in England, during which he spent most of his money on lavish living (and some to settle his father's debts, which must have come as a surprise to the old man), he applied once again to the Company for a position and was appointed governor of Fort St. David with the rank of lieutenant colonel in the regular army. His path and that of Hastings were about to cross.

In 1756 the nawab of Bengal, Ali Vardi Khan, with whom the British has been dealing on a satisfactory basis, died. As he had no sons, he had designated the son of his youngest daughter, one Siraj-ud-Daula, as his successor. Siraj was then twenty. In all the literature about him, one cannot find a single favorable comment. In describing him Macaulay surpasses himself. He writes, "Oriental despots are perhaps the worst class of human beings; and this unhappy boy was one of the worst specimens of his class. His understanding was naturally feeble, and his temper naturally unamiable. His education had been such as would have enervated even a vigorous intellect and perverted even a generous disposition. He was unreasonable, because nobody ever dared to reason with him, and selfish, because he had never been made to feel himself dependent on the good will of others. Early debauchery had unnerved his body and his mind. He indulged immoderately in the use of ardent spirits, which inflamed his weak brain almost to madness. His chosen companions were flatterers, sprung from the dregs of the people, and recommended by nothing but buffoonery and servility. It is said that he had arrived at that last stage of human depravity, when cruelty becomes pleasing for its own sake, when the sight of pain, as pain, where no advantage is to be gained, no offence punished, no danger averted, is an agreeable excitement. It had early been his amusement to torture beasts and birds; and, when he grew up, he enjoyed with still keener relish the misery of his fellow creatures."[14]

Almost as soon as he had been installed as nawab, Siraj decided to rid Bengal of the British. As a first step he took as prisoners all the Company personnel, including Hastings, who were stationed in Kasimbazar, the trading post adjacent to his capital at Murshidabad. They were treated vilely. One commentator[15] maintains that Hastings was forcibly circumcised, something that frequently happened when non-Muslim men were taken prisoner. His life was saved by some Indian friends and above all by the head of the Dutch factory, who paid a bail to have him released. Hastings never forgot it. When this man died, Hastings paid out of his own pocket an annual pension of three hundred pounds to his widow until her death in 1793. This was long after Hastings had left India and, indeed, after the impeachment had ruined him financially.

As badly as Hastings and his colleagues were treated in Murshidabad, it paled by comparison to what happened in Calcutta. In 1756, the same year of Siraj's installation, the Company had decided to make modest improvements in the defensive capacity of Fort William. For example, a ditch had been started in 1742 which was supposed to help repulse a hypothetical invasion by the Marathas. It was never completed and had filled up with rubbish. Now it was cleared and a new battery of guns installed. When Siraj got wind of this he was outraged, seeing it as an affront to his authority. It became one of his stated reasons for seizing Calcutta. He was also under the false impression that the British must have a vast treasure stored there. In any event, immediately after he had taken Kasimbazar he marched on Calcutta with an army of several thousand men. To defend the city, the British were able to mobilize 515 poorly armed volunteers. At the sight of the nawab's army, every English man, woman, and child who could find a place in a boat, including the governor and the commanding officer of the British troops, fled the city. They went down river to a village called Fulta, where boats bound for Calcutta often stopped to take on pilots. It was such a miserable hamlet that most of the refugees chose to sleep on the boats in which they had escaped.

Not everyone got away. How many remained is still open to question. John Zephania Holwell, the chief magistrate, who was designated commander-in-chief as the boats were pulling out, and whose account of the events that followed is most often cited, said that 146 were left in Calcutta. Recent Indian studies give a figure of 64.[16] In any event, Holwell raised a white flag, and the remaining English were taken prisoner by Siraj's soldiers. Holwell was certain that at least one woman and several wounded soldiers were among them. The Indian soldiers had been instructed to secure the prisoners, so they had to find a place to hold them. Fort William had a punishment cell on its first floor which was next to a large barrack room. The cell was about eighteen feet long and fourteen feet wide, with two small barred windows that were the only source of ventilation. It was an extremely unpleasant dark and dank place, even for one or two unruly soldiers to be confined in, so they had named it the Black Hole. As evening came on June 20, just before the monsoon, when the climate in Calcutta is almost unbearable, the prisoners were force-marched into the fort.

At first they assumed they would be spending the night in the barrack, which would have been uncomfortable but not intolerable. Instead they were shoved into the Black Hole by guards bearing clubs and scimitars. Holwell, whose description of the events of that evening is known to every British schoolchild, writes, "This stroke was so sudden, so unexpected, and the throng and the pressure so great upon us next to the door of the Black Hole prison, there was no resisting it, but, like one agitated wave impelling another, we were obliged to give way and enter; the rest followed like a torrent, few amongst us, the soldiers excepted, having the least idea of the dimensions or nature of a place we had never seen; for if we had, we should at all events rushed upon the guard, and been, as the lesser evil, by our own choice cut to pieces."[17]

Once they were incarcerated, Holwell tried to keep everyone calm so that they wouldn't panic and trample each other to death. They were so tightly wedged in that they could not stand or sit at will. It was so humid that most of them took off their clothes. Many began going mad from lack of water and air. The only thing that saved the survivors was that many of their fellow prisoners died quickly, leaving more air for the rest. Holwell lost consciousness at about 2 a.m. and, as he was doing so, hoped that he would die soon.

In the morning he was taken to the window so that he might revive enough to talk to the guards, as he was the senior officer of the group. At 6 a.m. an officer of the nawab's army was found, and the twenty-one survivors were let out.[18]

The nawab sent for Holwell. He was so physically traumatized by the ordeal that until he was given water he could not speak. When he could, the nawab asked where the treasure—which did not exist—could be found. Then the survivors were ordered to leave Calcutta (whose name the nawab had changed to Alinagor) before sunset or their ears and noses would be cut off. They made their way to Fulta.

Hastings was still in Murshidabad, where he was now more or less free. He began an attempt to negotiate with Siraj to ease the plight of the English who were still there. Siraj was willing to return only the French and Dutch concessions, not the English, for the payment of a large fine. At one point he made a public display of his personal wealth, which he said came to some 85 million pounds. With the nawab's erratic moods, it became too dangerous for Hastings to remain, so he too made his way to Fulta.

News of the fall of Calcutta finally reached Madras, about a thousand miles away. As it happened, a small body of British troops had already been sent from Madras when rumors reached the city of Siraj's first moves against the British factory in Kasimbazar. They arrived in Fulta in July but, at only two hundred strong, they were in no position to move against Calcutta. If anything, they were a burden on the meager resources—especially safe drinking water—that the town could provide. Along with the rest of the refugees, they began dying of disease. The real effort to free Calcutta did not begin until a strong naval and army force under the command of Admiral Charles Watson and Clive was dispatched by the authorities in Madras. It took them until mid-December to reach Fulta, some six months after Calcutta had been taken. Clive and Watson first tried to resolve the matter diplomatically by demanding restitution and compensation from Siraj. The Company's main concern was to restart its commerce. There seemed to be no great moral outrage over the Black Hole incident; that came later. When Clive and Watson got no response from Siraj, they began moving upriver with both warships and troops. In addition to those from Madras, they recruited able-bodied men from Fulta. Hastings, armed with a flintlock musket, was among them.

The first obstacle was a fort with the picturesque name Budge-Budge. The plan was to soften it up with a naval bombardment and then storm it. A drunken sailor from the fleet wobbled ashore and let himself into the fort through one of the holes created by the shelling. He announced to the startled guards, while waving his cutlass, that he was capturing the fort. Several of his comrades in like condition came through the breach and completed the operation. The sailor was later court-martialed but was given leniency when he promised not to capture any more forts. Then the British turned their attention to Calcutta.

Calcutta was taken easily, but the city was in ruins. Siraj's occupation had resulted in an estimated two million pounds' worth of damage. Meanwhile Siraj had regrouped his army and was marching once again on the city. Clive mounted a small operation which produced a large number of British casualties and resulted in a sort of stalemate. The question then arose as to whether Clive should attack at full bore. Here he was reluctant. The reason is interesting: Clive had decided that he wanted to be governor-general of Bengal. In practice, since all the British controlled were a few enclaves on the river, and since the policy of the Company was not to engage in territorial expansion, this meant being the governor of Calcutta. Clive understood full well that the Company had much less interest in punishing Siraj than in getting back to business. So the British tried to negotiate with him, which was a little like shooting bullets through fog. In particular, Siraj had already given the French, who had an enclave upriver in Chandernagor, all the concessions he had confiscated from the British. The French were not about to relinquish these without a fight, and the rumor was that they were sending troops into Bengal. In fact, the Seven Years War between the British and French had already begun in Europe. Thus this phase of British territorial expansion in India, like others, became a reflection of conflicts elsewhere in the world. The real battle for Bengal was now joined, and, when it was over, the British had the beginnings of an empire despite themselves.

The name of Clive will forever be associated with the battle of Plassey, which took place on June 23, 1757, a year and ten days after Calcutta had fallen. But the capture of the French fort at Chandernagor earlier that spring was at least as important. It was certainly a

Lord Clive receiving the homage of the nawab, c. 1761–1762. (Painting by Francis Hayman)

much harder struggle and cost the British incomparably more casualties. And it produced two significant consequences: it essentially eliminated the French influence in Bengal, and it put Siraj into a state of panic which encouraged an opposing faction in Murshidabad to take more decisive action. The great Jagat Seth banking family, originally from Rajasthan, who had come to Bengal early in the eighteenth century, had been badly mistreated by Siraj, and they had informally hired the British to get rid of him. In the event, the Jagat Seths awarded more than 1.25 million pounds to individuals from the Company for this activity.[19] The British had already begun negotiations with Siraj's potential successor, a man named Mir Jafar. And they were still trying to negotiate with Siraj, which, as usual, turned out to be impossible. Hence they began moving upriver towards Murshidabad.

The armies met at Plassey. Nominally Siraj's army consisted of some fifty thousand men and the British of some three thousand. But Siraj's troops had by this time such conflicting loyalties that only about twelve thousand were willing to fight—a ratio of four to one in favor of the Indians. This was a match the British could easily handle, and the battle was won with fewer than thirty British casualties. They next entered Murshidabad and installed Mir Jafar. Two weeks later one of Mir Jafar's sons assassinated Siraj, and Bengal now belonged in large part to the British.

Hastings, meanwhile, had married. His wife, Mary Allot Buchanan, was the widow of John Buchanan, one of the British officers who had been trampled to death in the Black Hole. She had two infant daughters with whom she had escaped to Fulta. The daughters were apparently sent back to Ireland where their grandmother lived; they vanish from our story. Hastings married Mary Buchanan just before he marched off with Clive to liberate Calcutta. In December 1757 their first child, a boy they named George, was born. A daughter whom they called Elizabeth was born the following autumn, but she died a few weeks later.

Not a great deal is known about Mary Hastings. In a letter to his old guardian Mr. Creswicke, Hastings said he "experienced every good quality in my wife which I always wished for in a woman."[20] There seems to be no portrait of her. She moved upriver to Kasimbazar when Hastings resumed his post there. By 1758 he was essentially in charge of the Company's operations in Kasimbazar and Murshidabad. His relationship with Clive became more complicated when it became clear that under the umbrella of war reparations, Clive and the Company were sucking Bengal dry.

As noted, Siraj had made a great show of counting his wealth publicly, professing a figure of 85 million pounds. When the British made a recount, they found it to be closer to 1.5 million. Of this, Clive took about 234,000 off the top for services rendered; eventually he became one of the wealthiest men in England. His officers and ordinary soldiers and sailors pretty well cleaned out what remained. Mir Jafar began giving land grants to the Company and to individuals like Clive since he no longer had any other capital with which to pay his debts. Hastings soon realized that this policy would kill the golden goose, and when he objected he began getting letters from Company officials in Calcutta, including Clive, complaining that he was becoming too pro-Indian.[21] But Clive had begun to get letters too. These were from the directors of the Company in London. Their complaint was that profits in Bengal had not risen commensurate with the military expenditures that Clive now wished to make. It was becoming clearer and clearer that Clive had in mind taking over as much of India as he could and really creating an empire. This aim had begun to attract the attention of Parliament. The last thing in the world that the Company wanted was parliamentary oversight, and sharp exchanges of letters with Clive ensued. In 1760, in progressively failing health, he returned to England.

On July 11, 1759, Mary Hastings, who had now become seriously ill, died. Hastings was devastated. In the course of a year he had buried a wife and a daughter. He kept his son George with him in India until the following year, but then, concerned about his young son's state of health, he sent him to England. Where he sent him, and why, is one of the most fascinating incidents in Hastings's private life, not reported in full detail in any of the Hastings biographies.*

When Hastings discovered the need for a surgeon in Kasimbazar, he wished to appoint the doctor who attended his wife in her last illness. But Clive preferred to appoint his surgeon from Madras, Tysoe Saul Hancock. Clive won out, and in 1759, not long before Mary Hastings died, Hancock arrived in Kasimbazar. He was close to fifty. He brought with him his wife of seven years, who was some twenty years younger. She turned out to be Jane Austen's aunt Philadelphia, the sister of her father George. The three Austen children—George, Philadelphia, and Lenora—had a history not unlike that of Hastings. Their parents had died when they were young, and they were then shunted among relatives who were not eager to support them. Philadelphia was dispatched to cousins, the Freemans. She was, as Hastings had been, a destitute dependent relative, but, as a woman, she was expected to marry as soon as possible. She was an attractive and witty young woman, but she had no dowry, and without a dowry

*One wonders whether this reflects some sort of reticence on the part of these biographers or whether they simply didn't know. I suspect the former. I stumbled on it by searching the World Wide Web under the rubric "Hastings." Much to my astonishment, two biographies of Jane Austen surfaced: *Jane Austen: A Life* by Claire Tomalin (New York, 1997), hereafter *Claire*; and *Jane Austen* by David Nokes (London, 1997), hereafter *Nokes*. Of the two, Nokes's account is somewhat more complete. Nokes belongs, alas, to the "As Jane Austen sat by the window she could only have been thinking . . ." school of biographers. But his quoted source material is invaluable.

none of the eligible local men would consider her for marriage. Her uncle, Frank Austen, handled Hancock's financial affairs in England. The common practice was for Company functionaries to buy precious jewels in India, such as diamonds, and send them back to Britain to be resold. This is what Frank Austen did for Hancock. Hancock must have told him that he was looking for an English wife—dowry or no—and Philadelphia seemed to be a reasonable candidate. Hence in 1751, after applying to the Company for permission, she was allowed to sail to Fort St. David on the East Indiaman *Bombay Castle*. She was one of eleven single women, including Clive's future wife Margaret Maskelyne, who made the long voyage on the *Bombay Castle* for essentially the same purpose. Philadelphia was not quite twenty-two when she landed in Fort St. David. What she thought of Hancock when she met him is unrecorded, but six months later they were married. And now she was in Kasimbazar.

Hancock and Hastings—and of course Philadelphia—became quite close. The two men began the sort of private trading enterprise that Clive, and the other senior members of the Company, approved of. Everyone was doing it. This much appears in the standard biographies of Hastings. What does not concerns the relationship that seems to have developed between Hastings and Philadelphia.

In December 1761 the previously childless Hancock marriage was blessed with a daughter who was named Elizabeth, in memory of Hastings's dead child. He became her godfather and conferred on her a very large gift of five thousand pounds. A few years later, when Philadelphia and her daughter had moved back to England, he gave them an even larger gift of ten thousand pounds. Elizabeth, who was fourteen years older than Jane Austen, recreated herself in London as "Eliza." She was a central figure in Jane Austen's life and, unlike anyone else in the family, a bird of exotic plumage. She traveled the Continent with her mother and eventually married a self-styled French nobleman named Jean Capot de Feuillide, said to have been the handsomest man in his regiment. She later described herself as Countess de Feuillide. He, on the other hand, thought she was a rich heiress who was somehow related to "Lord Hastings." The one child they had, a son, was named Hastings.

The "Count" de Feuillide was in fact the son of a lawyer, untitled. At the time he needed money to drain swampland in his native

Landes in the hope of turning it into agricultural terrain. He had the permission of the king to do this but lacked the funds. Enter Eliza. Hastings was tipped off to Eliza's role in this scheme by his lawyer brother-in-law, who wrote in 1781 that "They [the de Feuillide family] seem already desirous of draining [her] of every shilling she has. . . ."[22] Since these "shillings" came from Hastings's gift to Philadelphia, he had good reason to be interested. The money was still in trust. But there was more to it than the money, as we shall see. In any event, after the marriage in 1781, Eliza began helping finance her husband's project. Whatever might have come of it ended with the French Revolution. In 1791, when the revolution made life dangerous for her as the wife of someone associated with the king, Eliza returned to London. Her husband remained in France, but in February 1793 he was arrested and guillotined—the death of the aristocrat he had always wanted to be. Eliza remained in England and, much to the surprise of the Austen family, in 1797 she married Jane's older brother Henry. He was twenty-six and she ten years his senior. She informed Hastings of this and managed to withdraw whatever money remained in the trust, which was soon used up. The couple, who remained childless, had a tendency to live beyond their means.

Philadelphia died in 1792, having long outlived her husband, who had died in 1775 in India. Eliza's child, Hastings, died in 1801 at the age of fifteen. He had never been very healthy. Henry, Eliza's husband, appealed to Warren Hastings for money to support himself and Eliza, but Hastings refused. That seems to have ended any connection he had with Eliza. She died in 1813. Before her death, Henry, probably with the hope of reinforcing the connection, sent Hastings the just-published *Pride and Prejudice*. Hastings wrote Jane Austen a letter telling her how much he liked it.

These are the bare bones. But we have skirted the real question: what relation did Elizabeth Hancock—Eliza—have to Hastings? Every indication is that she was his daughter. Although this was never acknowledged by Hastings, it seems to have been an accepted fact in the Austen family. After Jane received Hastings's letter, she wrote to her sister Cassandra that despite her brother Henry's attempts to find out, "Mr. Hastings never *hinted* at Eliza to the smallest degree."[23] But the suspicion of such an affair must have been rather widespread in India. At one point Clive wrote to his wife, who it may be recalled had come out to India in the first place with Philadelphia, "In no circumstances keep company with Mrs. Hancock for it is beyond a doubt that she abandoned herself to Mr. Hastings."[24]

Somehow the Hancocks and Hastings must have reached an understanding which allowed them to retain their friendship. When Hastings left India for the first time in the spring of 1765, it was on the same ship with the Hancocks. And when, after his wife's death, he sent his son George back to England, it was to Philadelphia's brother George, Jane's father, who had just become the vicar of Steventon in Hampshire and was teaching boys in order to supplement his income. George Hastings died of what seems to have been diphtheria six months after he arrived at the Austens. Hastings never saw him again. Hancock himself returned to India in 1768, and he never saw his wife and daughter again. But his letters to Philadelphia hint at something that was never really resolved. In one of them, after Philadelphia suggested that Eliza might come out to visit Bengal, Hancock advised that it would not be a good idea. The place had become "lewd." And, he added, "You yourself know how impossible it is for a young girl to avoid being attracted to a young handsome man whose address is agreeable to her."[25]

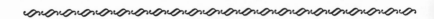

III: A PASSAGE FROM INDIA

In the hundreds of letters that Hastings wrote throughout his career in India, there is no suggestion of racism. Certainly there were Indians he disliked. Indeed, one of them he thoroughly hated. He was a Hindu Brahmin named Nand Kumar or Nandakumar—the British often spelled his name Nuncumar. Nandakumar is a contraction that means "son of Nand," one of the names for Krishna (the Hindu deity worshiped as an incarnation of the preserver god Vishnu). Why Hastings hated him we shall learn. But even of him, Hastings regarded the individual and not a symbol of the race. On the other hand, one has barely to scratch the surface of, say, Clive's correspondence with Hastings, to find instructions such as, "I would leave all the trickery to the Hindoos and Mussalmen to whom it is natural, being convinced that the reputation we have in this country is owing . . . to the ingenuity and plain dealing for which we are distinguished."[26] This at a time when the Company was descending on Bengal like a flock of vultures.

Hastings, unlike most of the servants of the Company, including Clive, spoke the Indian languages, which meant he could deal face to face with his Indian counterparts as individuals. But he had learned these languages because of his genuine interest in and respect for the country. When most young Englishmen arrived in India to take up junior posts, one of the first things that struck them was not the exotic fascination of the place but the standard of living of their seniors. These people had fine, often very large homes and were attended by a veritable army of servants. Even Hastings, who showed relatively little interest in such matters, soon began to buy houses. For these young men the immediate question was how they could begin dipping into the till.

The key turned out to be acquiring what was known as a *banyan*. This was a sort of personal middleman, or agent, who would trade in the name of the person in the Company whom he represented. It was not difficult to find a banyan. Indeed, they would try to find you. Their eagerness had to do with how inland trade worked. As noted, the Company enforced a monopoly on export trade. Anyone who tried to infringe on it was considered a pirate whose ship could be sunk or, better, confiscated. Inland trading took place among cities and towns in India, and, in the course of it, export items such as silk, opium, or salt, to take a few examples, found their way to the factories in places like Calcutta where they could be shipped abroad. Local Indian governments financed their operations by taxing this inland trading. In so far as the Company controlled or influenced these governments, they could arrange for their own employees to be exempted from these taxes and tariffs. The exemptions were granted in the form of a laissez-passer known as a *dastak*. If a banyan could use the dastak belonging to a junior clerk in the Company, all sorts of wonderful possibilities presented themselves. The banyan could begin trading as if he represented the authority of the Company and impose conditions on, say, the silk weavers in a village that they were helpless to resist—especially if the banyans were backed up by the Company's sepoys, who might very well be in on the take. This wretchedly corrupt system was, in Clive's time, bankrupting Bengal.

Clive knew this and made gestures toward controlling the system, but then he left India. He was replaced by a man named Henry Vansittart, who was in spirit rather similar to Hastings but who lacked Hastings's incredible toughness. When Vansittart arrived in Calcutta, Hastings was still in Murshidabad, where he was, as chief of the Company's factory in nearby Kasimbazar, the Company's ambassador to the court of Mir Jafar. But in 1761 he was appointed to the Council Board in Calcutta, the entity which, in collaboration with the governor, ran the Company's affairs in Bengal. Among the local population there was a growing dissatisfaction with Mir Jafar, who was losing control of his territory. He had been put in an almost impossible position. If he allowed the system of dastaks to run amok, he would lose the revenue he needed to pay for services he could offer to his increasingly mutinous population; if he cracked down, he would come into conflict with the British. As he was in no position to crack down, his financial situation was spiraling out of control. The British decided to step in by replacing him with his son-in-law, Mir Kasim, from whom they thought they might be able to extract further concessions.

Hastings favored this move, for he regarded Mir Kasim as an able and energetic man who seemed to have a favorable disposition toward the British. In this he misjudged, and this misjudgment led to his first resignation from the Company. It might well have finished his career altogether. It was true that Mir Kasim was able and energetic, but these very qualities led him to oppose vigorously the whole British-imposed system of freelance trading which was depriving his government of the revenues it needed. Hastings himself made a trip of inspection and concluded that Mir Kasim had a good case. The British flag was flying illegally from every improvised trading post one could imagine. Next he made a joint fact-finding visit with Vansittart. The two of them, upon returning, proposed a compromise arrangement which would have given Mir Kasim more of the revenue

Warren Hastings, c. 1766–1768. (Painting by Sir Joshua Reynolds)

he was entitled to. This compromise was turned down by the rest of the Council in Calcutta. By 1763 the situation had become explosive. The Council, with Hastings in strong dissent, decided to try to reinstate Mir Jafar. This led to bloodshed, which Hastings had predicted. Several Company employees were massacred and Mir Jafar was restored by force, only to repeat the same cycle of events that had led to his displacement in the first place. Hastings and Vansittart resigned, and Clive was recalled to India to try to restore order. Thus in 1764 Hastings and the Hancocks found themselves on the same boat to England.

Hastings had made enough money in India so that he thought he might live comfortably in England. He had about thirty thousand pounds saved, most of which he left in India, where the returns were higher, to be invested. It is not clear what he planned to do with himself. He was only thirty-two. He rented different homes in London—one near his sister and her family, another near the Hancocks. We know he visited Samuel Johnson because, when Boswell was foraging for material for his biography, he wrote to Hastings to see if he still had any letters from Johnson. He had three, it turned out, which he gave Boswell the use of. Indeed, they are in the biography.[27] The first one, dated, March 30, 1774, begins, "Sir, Though I have had but little personal knowledge of you, I have had enough to make me wish for more; and though it be a long time since I was honoured by your visit, I had too much pleasure from it to forget it. . . ." He goes on to remind Hastings of their idea to introduce the instruction of the Persian language in Britain. Perhaps it was through Johnson that Hastings met Joshua Reynolds and commissioned him to do his portrait. It is, as far as I know, the first one done of Hastings. It must have cost him a small fortune. Reynolds charged twenty guineas for a head, fifty for a half length, and over a hundred pounds for a full length. The Hastings painting is somewhere between a half and a full. In it he is unwigged, and his hair is beginning to recede. He is wearing a suit of clothes that look extremely expensive. His hand rests on some sort of scroll. He looks for all the world like a young lord—some have even said like a young fop.

He spent like a young lord as well. He spent money he did not have. He bought paintings and a carriage, which he had decorated with his arms. He spent like someone who had known poverty and hated it. And, inevitably, the money ran out. His investments in India failed. He sought reemployment with the only employers he had ever known, the British East India Company. After some reluctance, they hired him to be "second" to the newly elected governor of Madras, Josias Du Pré. Before leaving England, Hastings arranged to have three chests of claret and one of hock sent to him annually. He brought books such as Hume's *History and Essays* for the six-month voyage. On March 26, 1769, he sailed for India on the 499-ton East Indiaman *Duke of Grafton*. On board, as it happened, was a fellow passenger who would transform his life.

Four
HASTINGS, 1769–1772: MADRAS

Mr. Hastings is a man who is every way fitted for the station which he holds. He possesses a steadiness, and at the same time a moderation of character; he is quick and assiduous in business, and has a fine style of language, a knowledge of the customs and dispositions of the natives, whose tongue he understands, and, although not affable, yet of the most ready access to all the world. During his administration many abuses have been reformed, and many useful regulations have been established in every department of government. The natives are possessed of a code of laws far more ancient than Justinian, which have been handed down through a succession of ages, are interwoven with the system of their religion, and are framed to suit the manners of the people for whom they are intended. To revive these laws is at present a principal object with Mr. Hastings, and some progress has been made in translating them into English. This work, when done, will do great credit to Mr. Hastings, and will furnish an excellent guide to the decisions of the Courts, while it pleases the people, who are attached to their own laws and usage's.

—George Bogle (1773)[1]

One does not usually think of the historian Thomas Babington Macaulay as a figure of romance. He lived much of his adult life, and very happily, with his sister. Nonetheless his writing periodically breaks into romantic passages that one almost wishes could be accompanied by music. Here is one that occurs in his essay on Hastings:

"The situation was indeed perilous. No place is so propitious to the formation either of close friendships or of deadly enemies as an Indiaman. There are very few people who do not find a voyage which lasts several months insupportably dull. Anything is welcome which may break that long monotony, a sail, a shark, an albatross, a man overboard. Most passengers find some resource in eating twice as many meals as on land. But the great devices for killing time are quarrelling and flirting. The facilities for both these exciting pursuits are great. The inmates of the ship are thrown together far more than in any country-seat or boarding-house. None can escape from the rest except by imprisoning himself in a cell in which he can hardly turn. All food, all exercise, is taken in company. Ceremony is to a great extent banished. It is every day in the power of a mischievous person to inflict innumerable annoyances; it is every day in the power of an amiable person to confer little services. It not seldom happens that serious distress and danger call forth in genuine beauty and deformity heroic virtues and abject vices which, in the ordinary intercourse of good society, might remain during many years unknown even to intimate associates."

What inspired Macaulay to indulge in this rhetorical outburst was the presence on the *Duke of Grafton,* in addition to Hastings, of the Baron Carl von Imhoff, his wife, and their young son Charles. The Baroness von Imhoff's full maiden name had been Anna Maria Appolonia Chapusettin. She was born in 1747—making her twenty-one when she sailed from England—of a French Huguenot family that had settled in Stuttgart. The baron, who seems to have been considerably older, had been in the Württemberg army when he married his wife. They had left a six-month-old infant named Julius in England. Besides soldiering, the baron had a second profession. He did miniature portraits.

Despite his title, the baron had no financial resources. He had first come to England to try to ply his trade, but then had used a social connection with Queen Charlotte, the German-born wife of King George III, to become a cadet in the Company's army—something that was not easy to come by, though it was easier than being appointed a writer. His go-between was one Frau Schwellenberg, the queen's mistress of the robes. Macaulay, with characteristic reticence, refers to her as the "old hag from Germany." Frau Schwellenberg was able to pull enough strings so that the von Imhoffs were now traveling on one of the Company's ships to India. This one carried, in addition to its relatively small passenger complement, troops and ten guns for the artillery in Madras.

Hastings, as the Company's most senior official on board, had booked what was called the roundhouse—the most luxurious accommodation on the ship. The von Imhoffs occupied a state cabin on the deck below. It is not clear how much English they spoke. The baroness, whom Hastings for some reason thereafter called Marian, never lost her German accent, and her letters, of which dozens have been preserved, often display a most ingenious personal form of English. It seems that during the passage she and Hastings spoke mainly in French. Gleig, who must have learned this either from the baroness in old age or, more likely, from her sons, is the only source of what supposedly happened next. When they rounded Cape Horn, he informs us, Hastings took seriously ill. This might well have happened, but one should keep in mind that in the thirty-odd years he spent in India—except for the very last year or so when he was under the most extreme pressure—he never seems to have been sick at all: something of a miracle. The family lore, reported by Gleig, was that the baroness nursed him back to sound health. By the time they reached Madras, it had been decided that they would all live together in Hastings's house. Tysoe Hancock, Philadelphia's husband, now back in India and communicating with his wife in England at intervals of six months (the time it took the packet of letters to get there) wrote the following in April 1772, by which time there had been developments.

"There is a lady, by name of Mrs. Imhoff, who is his [Hastings's] principal favourite among the ladies. She came to India on board the same ship with Mr. Hastings, is the wife of a gentleman who has been an officer in the German service, and came out a cadet to Madras. Finding it impossible to maintain his family by the sword [the salaries were very low], and having a turn to miniature painting, he quitted the sword and betook himself to the latter profession. After having painted all who chose to be painted at Madras, he came to Bengal the latter end of the year 1770. She remained at Madras, and lived in Mr. Hasting's [sic] house on the Mount [a reference to St. Thomas Mount, then a fashionable location some eight miles west of Madras] chiefly, I believe. She is about twenty-six years old, has a good person and has been very pretty, is sensible, lively, and wants only to be a greater mistress of the English language to prove she has a great share of wit. She came to Calcutta last October. They do not make a part of Mr. Hasting's family, but are often of his private parties. The husband is truly a German. I should not have mentioned Mrs. Imhoff, but I know everything relating to Mr. Hastings is greatly interesting to you. . . ."[2]

The last sentence tells us something about Hancock's lingering feelings about the triangle. Curiously, this letter was found among *Hastings's* papers. One wonders how and why it got there.

By early 1772 Hastings was back in Calcutta for the first time in seven years. But now he was governor-general, a tale I shall recount shortly. Two years earlier, the baron had been given permission by the Company to ply his trade in Calcutta. He left Madras without wife and child. They remained there for a year, when they too went to Calcutta, leaving Hastings temporarily in Madras. But a few months later he joined them in Calcutta, and in 1773 the baron returned to Europe alone. The domestic relations of Hastings and the baroness during this period are a little murky, but some indication is given by the following snippet from a letter to Hastings by a former colleague in Madras. The worry was that there might be an attempt to poison the newly appointed governor-general. The warning was, "Do not employ any black cook; let your fair female friend [the baroness] oversee everything you eat."[3] Hastings remained intact, and in July 1777, after receiving a sizable sum from Hastings, the baron obtained a German divorce and the baroness and Hastings arranged their wedding.

A view of how all of this appeared to at least one observer is found in a letter written in 1777 by Philip Francis to a friend in England. Francis (who is responsible for the Robinson Crusoe anecdote at the beginning of the preceding chapter), was brilliant, incredibly nasty, and hated Hastings. He writes, "To complete the character, as it will probably conclude the history of this extraordinary man, I must inform you that he is to be married shortly to the supposed wife of a German painter with whom he has lived for several years. The lady is

Marian Hastings (Engraving by Ozias Humphry)

turned of forty, has children grown up by her pretended husband, from whom she has obtained a divorce under the hand of some German prince. I have always been on good terms with the lady, and do not despair of being invited to the wedding. She is an agreeable woman, and has been very pretty. My Lord Chief Justice Impey [Hastings's old school friend], the most upright of all possible lawyers [meant cynically since Francis hated Impey as well], is to act the part of father to the second Helen, though his wife has not spoken to her this twelve month."

The "lady," incidentally, was thirty, and Hastings was fifteen years older.

The baroness, in her unmarried situation, had been snubbed by some of the tonier ladies in Calcutta. Rest assured, once the marriage had taken place on August 8, the baroness got hers back, something that Francis referred to as "toad eating." Hastings presented a lakh of rupees (a hundred thousand) to his wife as a wedding settlement. This compares favorably to the twenty rupees a month he had received for his living expenses when, seventeen years earlier, he had begun as a writer, but it was somewhat less than the sum he had given to Philadelphia Hancock and her daughter.

A BIT MORE of the history of the British East India Company is necessary in order to make what follows comprehensible. As noted earlier, on December 31, 1600, Queen Elizabeth I granted a charter to a group of 101 men[4] for the exclusive right in Britain to send boats to the East Indies. The first twelve voyages were financed by separate subscriptions. They were a relatively high-risk gamble since a boat might return with, say, a cargo of peppers, a very valuable commodity, or might be wrecked or captured by pirates or a foreign navy. Starting in 1613, the Company began financing itself by selling stock in joint ventures, which could involve several voyages with correspondingly less risk. A year later it had twenty-four sailing ships. These ships weighed a few hundred tons apiece and, considering where they were going, looked almost like toys.

The Company survived the vagaries of the descendants of James I, Elizabeth's successor, and even the revolution and Cromwell, still more or less intact. What threatened to put it out of business once and for all was the presence of rivals in Britain, especially after the Glorious Revolution of 1688 which brought William of Orange to the throne. These new societies and the old Company were merged into the United Company in 1709. The United Company had well over three million pounds in shares owned by some three thousand stockholders, and it sent more than thirty ships each year to Asia with annual sales of as much as two million pounds.

What interests us is how this very substantial enterprise was managed. There were two levels, a Court of Directors and a Court of Proprietors. The twenty four directors were required each to own 2,000 pounds' worth of stock, while the considerably larger group of proprietors each needed to own a minimum of 1,000 pounds. The proprietors (by the end of the eighteenth century there were some 2,000) could vote to overturn decisions of the directors. They also elected the directors. This was a system that lent itself to all sorts of permutations and combinations. In particular, the more stock you owned, the more votes you had, so that a director who had a great deal of stock could keep himself or his friends in power almost indefinitely. And there was Parliament, which in this period was threatening to step in and govern the Company. In 1767, two years before Hastings set sail again for India, Parliament had temporarily been bought off with an agreement by which the Company was bound to send to the government 400,000 pounds each year from India—money which in many years it did not actually have. In Britain there was a great illusion about the wealth of Bengal, the richest province in which the Company had a presence. This was fostered by the nabobs—men like Clive—who returned to Britain with fortunes and proceeded to flaunt them. Among other things, they bought seats in Parliament. Hence it was assumed that Bengal must be a land of streets lined with gold. But for various reasons, such as droughts and crop failures, in many years the Company could scarcely meet its expenses in India, let alone send 400,000 pounds back to the motherland. One must bear this in mind in attempting to understand the problems that Hastings had to deal with.

During much of this period the chairman of the Court of Directors was a man named Laurence Sulivan. Unlike many of his colleagues, Sulivan had actually served in India. Feiling characterizes him as follows: ". . . down to his death in 1789 the politics of the India House [the name of the building on Leadenhall Street in London where the Company had its headquarters] largely turned on his sincere zeal for peace and reform, his inextinguishable love of power, and his financial misfortunes."[5] He was chairman during much of Hastings's tenure as governor-general.

Until Plassey and its aftermath, Sulivan and Clive had been allies. But then Clive began suggesting that the British government take over Indian territory. In his famous letter of 1759 to William Pitt, the Elder, Clive wrote: "Now I leave you to judge, whether an income of two millions sterling [a delusional figure as it turned out], with the possession of three provinces [Bengal, Bihar, and Orissa] abounding in the most valuable products of nature and of art, be an object deserving the public attention, which would prove a source of immense wealth to the kingdom."[6]

Sulivan too received a letter from Clive, a classic which read:

"Experience, not conjecture, or the report of others, had made me well acquainted with the genius of the people and nature of the country, and I can assert with some degree of confidence that this rich and flourishing kingdom may be totally subdued by so small a force as two thousand Europeans. . . . [The Indians] are indolent, luxurious, ignorant and cowardly beyond all conception. . . . I am persuaded you will believe I do not want to aggrandize the Company at the expense of all equity and justice; long may the present [nawab] enjoy the advantages gained him by our arms, if he abides strictly to his treaties. But you Sir, who have resided so long in India, are well acquainted with the nature and dispositions of these Muslims, gratitude they have none, bare men of very narrow conceptions, and have adopted a system of politicks more peculiar to this country than any other, viz. to attempt everything by treachery rather than force. . . . What is it, then, can enable us to secure our present acquisitions or improve upon them but such a force as leaves nothing to the power of treachery or ingratitude?"[7]

This sort of thing inspired Sulivan to write to Clive and his followers that "you seem to have acted like men divested of your understanding."[8]

This riposte signaled the end of whatever civilized discourse Clive and Sulivan had with each other and might well have been the end of any relationship between Clive and the Company except for two related facts. On the one hand, by Company rule no chairman could serve for longer than four successive years, though after a hiatus he could be reelected; and, on the other hand, the massacre of the Company's employees at the hands of Mir Kasim in July 1763, the event that helped force the resignations of Hastings and Vansittart, had not been forgotten. With the situation in Bengal one of chaos, in desperation the Company turned to Clive in 1764 to save it on any terms he chose. In addition to insisting that Sulivan and his people have no say in his affairs in India, Clive demanded absolute power as governor of Bengal. He stipulated that he would be subject to no restraints by the Council in Calcutta, and that he would also be commander-in-chief of the army. A further condition reflected Clive's concern about feathering his own financial nest. It may be recalled that after Clive had dispatched Mir Jafar he had pocketed 234,000 pounds from the mir's treasury for services rendered. But there was more. He was also granted an estate—a *jagir*, as it was called—which paid to Clive, as opposed to the Company, an annual rent of some 30,000 pounds. This arrangement, to which Sulivan vigorously objected, remained valid only as long as the Company approved of it. As part of his arrangement for returning to India, Clive had it extended for the next ten years. As he shot himself to death on November 22, 1774, ten years later when back in England, the question of a further extension turned out to be moot.[9]

Studying this history, one constantly asks, is it possible to pinpoint a time, or an event, when the Company began the transformation that led to the British Empire? It is tempting to say it was the Battle of Plassey, and indeed this is often said. I do not find this choice convincing. The issue at Plassey, and the campaign that led to it, was really the restoration of the status quo ante. Whatever Clive might have thought, the Company had no interest in anything but trade, that is, the exchange of goods, or silver and gold, against native products which could then, hopefully, be sold at a profit. If Siraj-ud-daula had negotiated on an equitable basis with the British, or vice versa, Plassey never would have happened. Even so, there was no empire before Plassey and there was none immediately afterward. But during Clive's second tour in India, the one now in question, something did happen, something that changed everything.

Just before Clive left for England in 1759, he had been offered by the nawab, on behalf of the Company, the *diwani* of Bengal—the power to collect taxes directly from the province. This was quite different from trade, though the two got mixed up as tax revenues were also used to buy trading goods. To collect taxes one must somehow be part of the government. Even if one hires native tax collectors to actually scoop up the revenue, one necessarily begins to govern. That is why this proposition was summarily turned down in 1759 by Sulivan and the rest of the directors. But after Clive returned to India in 1765, he was again offered the diwani. This time there was no Sulivan to restrain him, and he accepted. The nawab of Bengal retained, at least in theory, the police and criminal justice system, which meant that Muslim law applied to criminal as opposed to civil justice, which was the province of the British. This is what came to be called the "dual" system. But whatever you called it, the Company was now a different enterprise. Indeed, in 1769 the Bengal council stated to the Company's directors that "Your trade from hence may be considered more as a channel for conveying your revenues to Britain, than as only a mercantile system." As Edmund Burke later noted, "a very great Revolution took place in commerce as well as in Dominion."[10]

The dual system could function only if the people who actually carried out the tax collections were incorruptible, which, given the temptations, they weren't. This was one practical failure of Clive's administration, and there was another. Clive had the good intention of trying to end the practice of private trade by the lesser ranks of the Company's servants, which was often accompanied by the locals offering "presents"—bribes—to these people. But two factors impeded Clive's program. In the first place, the Company had not increased the salaries of these lower-level people, so they were not about to give up their perquisites without a fight. In the second place, Clive was hardly an example of self-deprivation. He had received more economic benefits than anyone else from the system he was now trying to abolish. In his attempts to reform the system he mainly aroused the anger of the people whose conduct he was trying to regulate.

All of this seems to have gotten back to the Company's directors in England, and in February 1767, after eighteen months in office, Clive resigned and left India forever. Five years later he was called upon to defend himself in Parliament on charges that the system he had introduced was corrupt. Outraged, he defended himself with great vigor. Among other things he noted that "A great prince was dependent on my pleasure; an opulent city lay at my mercy; its richest bankers bid against each other for my smiles; I walked through vaults which were thrown open to me alone, piled on either hand with gold and jewels! Mr. Chairman, at this moment I stand astonished at my own moderation."[11] After an all-night debate, he was voted a parliamentary commendation. By this time his health was failing; he was deeply addicted to opium and was suffering bouts of extreme depression. In November 1774 he committed suicide.

We can now return to Hastings, who is about to land in Madras and will soon have to deal with whatever chaos Clive left behind.

The Indiamen, when they reached Madras, were too large to dock close to shore. Madras was not a natural harbor. Fleets of cockleshell boats—*masulahs*—would come out to meet the big sailing boats and carry the passengers to shore. But even these did not come in all the way to shore. Indian men clad in *dhotis*—loin cloths—would wade through the surf and carry the women and children to the beach in seats, where possible. The men had to make it on their own, getting soaked in the process. It makes a delightful picture to think of Hastings and the baron immersed to their waists in water while the baroness was being carried ashore by a man in a dhoti. Going through this surf could be a dangerous business. Hastings tried during the two years he spent in Madras to explore the possibilities of a proper docking system for the Indiamen, but it was a century before there was a functional pier.

By the time Hastings made this landing, Madras and its surrounding communities had a population of a quarter of a million people. The British lived in a White Town and had their offices and the fort; everyone else lived in the Black Town, which was a racial fiesta—Europeans, every variety of Indian imaginable, and even a small seasoning of Jews. Hastings found a more rigorous caste system among the Indians, and greater social hierarchies among the British, than he had experienced in Bengal. As second in Council, he received 2,400 pounds annually, a very good salary. But he still kept his hand in private trading, much of it with Hancock, to whom he explained that he hoped to make enough so that he could give his "god-daughter" Eliza a decent dowry. As was his custom during his entire time in India, he lived moderately. He drank very little compared to most of the Company officials and spent the early hours of every morning riding one of his horses for exercise. He read widely. Books were sent to him on a regular basis from England. He also asked his brother-in-law to send him those issues of the *Annual Register* that contained letters from "Junius." These were biting, anonymous dispatches critical of all parts of the government, including the king. They were the sort of thing you would want to read if you wanted to keep up with the latest political gossip from home.

As second in command and governor-designate, Hastings had to deal with municipal questions such as finding a new water supply and paving the streets. There were also new military realities, which were to dominate the attention of the British all the way into the next century. In addition to the Marathas, always a potential menace, a new actor had appeared on the scene, a soldier of fortune named Hyder Ali. He had gone to school on British and French military tactics and had developed an army in uniform which posed the most serious threat the British had ever faced in India. In 1768 Hyder Ali's troops had come as close to Madras as the St. Thomas Mount, whose houses they sacked. Had he not accepted an alliance with the British to fight the Marathas, he might easily have taken the city itself. But the alliance would not last, and during much of the next decade Hastings would have to contend with Hyder Ali.

Hastings expected to succeed Du Pré shortly as president of the council in Madras. He was also greatly cheered by the news that his good friend Henry Vansittart was returning to Bengal to take up his old post as governor. Sulivan was in the process of cleaning house of Clive's old appointments. Vansittart and two other new councilors set sail for India in the fall of 1769 on the frigate *Aurora*. It, and its passengers, were never heard from again. Thus in December 1771 the directors in London appointed Hastings as the new governor of Bengal. With that appointment the defining phase of Hastings's career in India was about to begin.

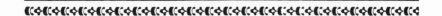

Five

HASTINGS IN BENGAL, 1772–1774

If in this or any other instance the governor-general's conduct, or the motives I attribute to him, should appear upon examination to imply a weakness and want of judgment in him that exceed probability, I can only say, with an appeal to your Lordship's future observation, that without denying him some little talents of the third or fourth order, we were as much deceived with regard to his abilities and judgment as to his other qualifications.

—Philip Francis to Lord North (1774)[1]

The first newspaper to have been published in India appears to have been the *Bengal Gazette,* which began publishing in 1780. It was followed by the *India Gazette,* and *Bengal Journal,* the *Oriental Magazine,* and the *Calcutta Journal.* But nothing quite matched the *Bengal Gazette.* It made its first appearance on Saturday, January 29, 1780, announcing that it was "A weekly political and commercial paper open to all parties but influenced by none."[2] The paper's publisher was James Augustus Hicky, apparently a printer who had done some work for the Company and had then come out from England. He drifted to Calcutta after disastrous trading ventures which landed him temporarily in jail. The paper began as a relatively harmless combination of political and social commentary with the odd joke tossed in. Typical of the various genres were such items as:

"Governor Whittal [sic] (Madras) [a reference to "Black Jack"

Whitehill, then acting governor of Madras, whom Hastings was shortly to fire] has acted with great judgment and spirit at this critical juncture ('Hyder Alli') [sic—referring to a new menace by Hyder Ali] by compelling the Armenians and rich dubashes to pay into the treasury at Madras a crore [ten million] of pagodas [a commonly used unit of money, worth about three rupees] at interest, a measure truly politic and justifiable, that those who derive their wealth under the liberality of the English should contribute during exigencies in return for the protection they receive. The banians [another spelling of *banyan*] here who are amassing incredible fortunes by imposition, usury, and extortion, might be made more useful instruments to Government than they are at present; they now in some degree resemble the drones, the rich abbots in England before the time of Henry VIII, that pucca Monarch."[3]

On a lighter note: *"April 1780.* A new Cotillon [sic] was danced at the last Harmonic [one of Calcutta's favorite taverns] to the great wonder and astonishment of many of the spectators. It is universally allowed that this exhibition was infinitely superior to anything known here of late. The merit of this performance is principally attributed to three young ladies lately arrived."[4]

The paper might have gone on indefinitely in this amiable vein except that it managed to cross Hastings. This happened when the proprietor of a rival newspaper apparently used his social connections to the baroness—now madam governor—to obtain special concessions at the post office. This outraged Hicky, who wrote that "there was something so sneaking and treacherous in going clandestinely to fawn and take advantage of a good-natured woman to draw her into a promise to getting that done which I know would be highly improper to ask her husband, though his unbounded love of his wife would induce him to comply. . . ."[5] While Hastings had a tolerant view of people macroscopically, on a microscopic level he had a rather thin skin, especially when it came to anything that concerned his personal dignity or, above all, that of his wife. Hicky was soon prohibited from circulating his paper through the general post office.

This does not seem to have stopped him for long. For the next round Hicky created a "Playbill" for a play which he entitled "Tyranny in Full Bloom, or the Devil to Pay," along with a farce called "All in the Wrong." The leading character in same was one Sir F. Wronghead, who was taken directly from a real play called "The Provoked Husband," about a husband whose wife was described as "thoughtless and extravagant." In a later version, Lady Wronghead was said to be "habited like a Tartarean [sic] princess, almost sinking under the weight of pearls and diamonds. The brilliancy of her dress was only eclipsed by her usual urbanity and vivacity." Despite the attempt to right the sinking ship of the first sentence by the ballast of the last, everyone understood that Lady Wronghead was the baroness, whose penchant for wearing jewels was well known. This sort of wit landed Hicky in jail, and the heavy fines that went with the jail sentences put his paper out of business. It published its last edition in 1782, and, after being released from jail, Hicky vanished.

Hicky's paper was basically concerned with the *ton*—the *bon ton*, or high society of Bengal.[6] I have seen no abstract from it that dealt with the lives of, say, village silk weavers. The *ton* resembled in many ways the passengers on the Indiamen that Macaulay so graphically described, except that here the sea was India itself. The life span of the *ton* in India was about the same as the lifespan of a typical Indiaman—about three years. In either case, if the "ship" was not sent back to England for repairs of its rotting timbers, it was no longer viable. The *ton* would have been as lost in an Indian village without a banyan, or some other intermediary, as a passenger alone on a lifeboat.

Since they were expecting a short "voyage," the *ton* lived high. Gambling for substantial stakes was common. Francis, for example, was said to have won thirty lakhs (three million) of rupees at whist while losing ten thousand pounds at backgammon. The difference in his favor enabled him, when he retired to England, to be independently rich. For the ladies the day was full. It began early in the morning with a ride or walk, followed by a light breakfast at no later than nine. As for dress, "The fashionable undress, except in the article of being without stays (and stays are wholly unworn in the East) is much in the English style, with large caps or otherwise, as fancy dictates. No care or skill is left unexerted to render the appearance easy and graceful (adds Miss Goldborne) [Sophia Goldborne had recently arrived in Calcutta; she was definitely one of the *ton*] as gentlemen in the course of their morning excursions continually drop in, who say the prettiest things imaginable with an air of truth that wins on the credulity and harmonizes the heart."[7]

"Dinner" was at two in the afternoon, a formal affair. The gentlemen wore white jackets, and the ladies, Miss Goldborne tells us, if they did not wear caps, had their hair done with an intermixture of artificial flowers. Powder, she informs us, was used in great quantities on the hair, and she goes on to say,

"To every plate are set down two glasses; one pyramidal (like hobnob glasses in England); the other a common sized wine glass for whatever beverage is most agreeable. Between every two persons is placed a decanter of water and tumbler for diluting at pleasure. Hosts of men on all occasions present themselves at dinner, but the sexes are blended (I will not say in pairs, for the men are out of all proportion to the female world), so as to aid the purposes of gallantry and good humor. . . . The attention and court paid to me was astonishing. My smile was meaning, and my articulation melody; in a word, mirrors are almost useless at Calcutta, and self-adoration idle, for your looks are reflected in the pleasure of the beholder, and your claims to first-rate distinction confirmed by all who approach you.

"After the circulation of a few loyal healths, &c, the ladies withdraw, the gentlemen drink their cheerful glass for some time beyond that period, insomuch that it is no infrequent thing for each man to dispatch his three bottles of claret, or two of white wine, before they break up."[8]

It is scarcely any wonder that so few of them lasted more than three years. Indeed, in the evening it began all over again. People came out for the cooler night air, either walking or riding in carriages imported from England on the one decent road that existed. Others went out on the river in small boats. Then there were housecalls to be made and possibly supper, followed by cards and, perhaps, music until midnight. All of them had uncountable numbers of servants. One family of four had 110! "One hundred and ten servants to wait upon a family of four," one commentator decried, "and yet we are economists! Oh monstrous! Tell me if this land does not want weeding!"[9] In 1757 the Company made it a rule that its junior employees should have no more than two servants and a cook, should not keep a horse, and should wear only plain clothes.

Some of these servants were slaves, quite literally. Poor people from the villages sold their children into service. The court records of the time are filled with descriptions of these slaves running away, being caught, and then being beaten with rattan canes. A curious form of beating was done with a slipper, which was considered even more demeaning. (Footwear has long been a form of defilement in India.) We will have many negative things to say about Philip Francis, so it is good to be able to say that from what he saw in India, Francis came to hate slavery. When he returned to England and entered Parliament, he became one of its most ardent opponents of the slave trade.

Hastings, as governor of Bengal and then as the first governor-general of India, which he became in 1774—the post had been created the year before by an act of Parliament—certainly had social obligations. His salary as governor-general was a princely 25,000 pounds a year, with another 5,000 pounds for expenses. He was notoriously careless with money. This was the year he gave an additional 10,000 pounds to Eliza Hancock. He did not marry the baroness until 1777, but he seems to have set her up in a house and then paid the baron 1,000 pounds as a divorce settlement. Hastings built a house with marble staircases. As Feiling remarks, "His scale was grand, his generosity as great, and his interests as wide as ever. [It was in the spring of 1774 that, at his own expense, he had sent Bogle to Tibet.] If his own brown coat was plain, his horses had silver-plated bits with his crest engraved. . . ."[10] There was a popular jingle in Hindustani:

Hathi par howdah, ghore par zin,
Jaldi bahar jata Sahib Warren Hastin.
Howdah on elephant [the saddle used to ride an elephant],
Saddle on horse.
Quickly sallies Sahib Warren Hastings.[11]

One thing the British in Calcutta did not do in broad daylight was to walk, let alone run. This was considered, in view of the heat, to be potentially fatal. All households came equipped with palanquins—litters with a small enclosed structure on the top. They were carried by bearers, who also were part of the household staff. Riding horses was reserved for the early morning—one of Hastings's favorite pastimes—or after sunset.

Hastings was sending money home to the aunt who had helped to raise him. While governor he was still engaging in private trade, some of it in opium and some in jewels. After he became governor-general he was still trading in diamonds. Once he married, entertainments were a feature at his house. One of the invitations to a concert and supper at the Hastingses asked that the gentlemen bring only their own "huccabadar"—a hooka-bearer. At dessert all the hooka-bearers came in with their masters' hookas, and "the consequent clamour and smoke filled the room."[12] In time, the ladies also took up the habit.

As one might imagine, the baroness, now the wife of the governor-general, attracted a good deal of comment. The wife of a barrister, Eliza Fay, who arrived in Calcutta in 1780 at the age of twenty-four, spent a day with her and commented, "Mrs. H____ herself, it is easy to perceive at the first glance, is far superior to the generality of her sex, though her appearance is rather eccentric, owing to the circumstances of her beautiful auburn hair being disposed in ringlets, throwing an air of elegant, nay almost infantine simplicity, on the countenance, most admirably adapted to heighten the effect intended to be produced. Her whole dress too, though studiously becoming, being at variance with our present modes (which are certainly not so), perhaps for that reason she has chosen to depart from them. As a foreigner, you know, she may be excused for not strictly conforming to our fashions; besides her rank in the Settlement sets her above the necessity of studying anything but the whim of the moment. It is easy to perceive how fully sensible she is of her own consequence: she is, indeed, raised to a giddy height, and expects to be treated with the most profound respect and deference...."[13] And from the estimable Miss Goldborne: "The Governor's dress gives you his character at once, unostentatious and sensible. His lady, however, is the great ornament of places of polite resort, for her figure is elegant, her manners lively and engaging, and her whole appearance a model of taste and magnificence."

From all this one might be tempted to assume that Bengal was a land of milk and honey, of balls and banquets. But keep in mind that in 1770 there was, as Bogle described graphically in the letter to his father, a famine in Bengal in which a third of the population either starved to death or succumbed to disease. People were living on roots and leaves and selling their children into slavery. The famine was not the fault of the Company—the monsoon had failed to bring rain—though it was accused of profiteering from the sale of food. It certainly had nothing to do with Hastings, who was in Madras. The real problem he faced when he returned to Bengal to become governor was that the Company was going bankrupt. Had it gone under it might have affected the entire British financial system. Understanding this is crucial to understanding the events that in the next decade led to Hastings's trial. For this we must return to England and to Fredrick, Lord North.

∽

FREDRICK NORTH was born April 13, 1732, which makes him some months older than Hastings, who was born the following December. He came from an aristocratic rural family. His father, Francis, had, after the death of his father in 1729, became the third Baron Guilford. North grew up in one of those stately English country homes of the kind, though probably on a grander scale, that Hastings's Daylesford must have been. When North was two, Baron Guilford became Lord North, and, unhappily, his wife, North's mother, died in childbirth. He soon remarried, the first of two subsequent marriages, each of which added to his already substantial estate. Young North was educated at Eton, but one of his stepbrothers, William Legge, the second Earl of Dartmouth, was at Westminster at the same time as Hastings (though I have found no evidence that they knew each other). Legge and North both matriculated at Trinity College, Oxford, in 1749, the year Hastings signed on to be a writer with the Company. North took his degree in 1751 and had acquired the reputation of being quite a competent classical scholar. The two stepbrothers then took the obligatory continental tour in the company of a chaperone, Mr. Golding. It was the only time in North's life that he left England.

Then, and for the rest of his life, North was singularly unprepossessing, but he was already beginning to show some of the qualities that eventually made him one of England's most important, albeit unlikely, eighteenth-century statesmen. As one description has it, "His figure was already beginning to round, his face had the chubby contours of a well-fed infant, his eyes were protuberant, his speech was thick and his pitch and volume badly controlled, and he stood with his feet apart as if braced against strong wind. His gestures were awkward, and he was extremely near-sighted. But these liabilities were countered by his affability, gentleness, wit, good manners, and morals. He never started and often ended an argument; his good sense impressed men of all opinions; his deference attracted and his modesty disarmed older men and women. Few young men had such integrity and seriousness and yet such humor."[14] In the latter he seems rather unique among the cast of characters in this story. Of wit they had great quantities, but of humor little or none. North could illuminate the darkest corners with a flash of humor. Late in his life— he died in 1792 at the age of sixty—he became blind. He would be led out for walks. On one of these he encountered an old political opponent, now also blind and also being led out. On being told who he was, North greeted him warmly with, "Though you and I have had our quarrels in the past, I wager there are no two men in England who would be happier to see one another today."[15] The other side of this humor, however, was a lack of decisiveness. For much of his life North deferred all judgments to his father, whose approval was essential. Even after he became independent of his father, he still had great difficulty taking strong, clear positions. People were not sure where he stood on important questions, and it is not clear if he knew himself. In the end this cost both him and his country dearly.

In 1754 both North and his stepbrother Dartmouth entered Parliament, Dartmouth in the Lords and North in the Commons. Both seats were "safe," that is, basically owned by an important family. Banbury, which North was to represent uncontested for the next 36 years, was owned by his father. It has been estimated that of the 205 borough seats in England at the time, 111 were controlled by a handful of patrons. The distribution of seats was highly erratic. London with a population of 700,000 was allotted 4 seats while Bath, which had only a population of 25,000, had 33. Scotland had 45, and most of these were carefully controlled. That is why the right kind of leverage applied in the right places by an entity like the East India Company could have such important effects.

During his first two years in the House, North never addressed his colleagues. In 1756 he married. His wife, Anne Speke, was no beauty and indeed North used to say jokingly that he and his wife

Lord North. (Painting by Nathaniel Dance)

were the ugliest couple in London. But they were one of the happiest. Like many young married couples, they soon ran into financial troubles. North asked his now very wealthy father not for money, not even for a loan, but to lend his name as a guarantor for a loan from a third party. His father never responded. North then asked his father to help him obtain a minor government post from which he could derive an income. This was successful, and in 1759 he received an appointment as a junior lord of the Treasury. Given North's disposition, it seems likely that if he had not had financial exigencies—if his father had been more helpful or if his wife's expected legacy had materialized—he would not have sought a ministerial post, even a very junior one. He had no interest in power in the abstract, and one can easily imagine him as a country squire, happy in the bosom of his family, coming to London periodically to do his service in Parliament.

After he moved up the ladder and became financially secure, and was on the short list for still higher offices, the question was always raised as to whether he could be persuaded to accept the job. This is part of what made him so attractive. The other part was that in financial matters, above all, he was extremely competent. Because he was still such a junior lord in the Treasury, he was not called upon to take clear positions on controversial issues, so his inability to do so when these became of great concern was not yet apparent. In so far as he did take a position, it was a somewhat unpopular one, such as avoiding a war with Spain. At one point he told the House, "In all my memory I do not remember a single popular measure I ever voted for. . . . I state this to prove I am not an ambitious man. Men may be popular without being ambitious, but there is rarely an ambitious man who does not try to be popular."[16]

In 1766 North accepted the position of joint paymaster general. Because of various political upheavals, he had been temporarily out of the government and was once again in financial difficulties, so this was a job he needed. A year later he became chancellor of the exchequer, a tribute to his growing recognition. About this time two of North's parliamentary colleagues were strolling in Hyde Park in London when one of them spotted him and said, "Here comes blubbery North!" To which the other observed, "North is a man of great promise and high qualifications, and if he does not relax his political pursuits, he is very likely to be Prime Minister."[17] North was not at all convinced he had the abilities even to be an adequate chancellor. Nonetheless in 1770 he did become prime minister. Most observers thought this was a caretaker appointment until someone more suitable could be found. But North remained prime minister for the next twelve years, during which time he had to deal with two of the most difficult problems that faced England in the eighteenth century, America and India.

Although each of these problems had its unique characteristics, there was at least one link between them: tea. As we have seen, tea was imported from China. It came to England or America on the Company's boats. It had been acquired from Chinese tea merchants, most often for the exchange of opium, which was exported from India. Strictly speaking, this opium trade was illegal in China, but this did not seem to inhibit it unduly. Over time Hastings ensured that the Company monopolized opium production in India.

The Company also had huge debts. Part of this had to do with reduced revenues from Bengal after the famine of 1770. Much of it also had to do with the fact that employees of the Company were siphoning off large sums of money for themselves by private trading in India; and still more of it had to do with the directors voting for larger and larger dividends, and the requirement, by the 1767 agreement, that the Company pay the government 400,000 pounds each year. Anyone who studied the balance sheets—and above all North, whose job it was to study balance sheets—could see that if something wasn't done, and soon, the Company would crash. In particular, by 1772 the king was strongly in favor of legislation that would strengthen the government's control over the Company's activities in India.

Worrisome too was that the Company used a good deal of the seasoned oak timbers in Britain in order to maintain its ships—timbers that were needed for ships of the Royal Navy. And there was competition for experienced sailors. The Company paid better than the navy; discipline was more benign on its ships; and when the voyage was over, sailors could go home. In short, an uncontrolled Company posed problems both in Britain and in India.

The American colonies too were part of the equation. In February 1765 the House of Commons had unanimously passed the Stamp Tax Bill. This entitled the British to collect stamp duties from the Americans, the kind that British subjects in England regularly paid. The imposition of this tax was resented—indeed more than resented—by the American colonists. Both then and later, the general attitude of the British government was that these colonists were behaving like rebellious children, and that a little dose of medicine—a few troops—would rapidly bring them to their senses. In 1769 the Massachusetts Bay Colony sent a petition to Parliament asking for the repeal of these taxes. North was now chancellor of the exchequer, so this petition, and a subsequent one from the General Assembly of New York, landed directly in his court. He opposed both of them, or so it seemed. When a more moderate view emerged that some of these taxes should be repealed, in particular the tax on imported tea, North seemed to favor that. The one consistent principle he held was that the government had the right to impose *some* tax on the colonies.

By 1772 both this tax situation and the imminent financial failure of the Company had reached a crisis stage. What gave the government leverage on the Company was that it needed a very large government loan for its survival. The question was how to use this leverage. Here there was a spectrum of views. At one extreme was the notion that the government should simply take over the Company, which appeared to be the view of the king. North's own view was that the government should exert enough control to force the Company to manage its affairs more reasonably. For example, it should not be allowed to declare dividends using money it did not have.

The Company took the position that if only the government would lend it the million and a half pounds it was requesting, all of its problems would take care of themselves. Curiously, Edmund Burke, whose obsessive prosecution of the Company and everything it stood for was to burst forth a decade later, took a position closer to that of the Company than to the government. That he was a Whig, and in opposition to the Tory government of North, had much to do with this. But Burke, his brother Richard, and his closest friend Will Burke (apparently no relation) all had a financial stake in the Company. This was part of the problem of trying to control it—too many members of Parliament were either directors of the Company or had financial ties to it.

Nonetheless by late 1772 North had persuaded the House to form a committee of ministers to examine the Company's affairs. Among other things, it would have the right to study to Company's books. In due course the committee learned that the Company had, along with its other debts, overdue bills of 1.6 million pounds. Its total obligations were over 9 million pounds, while its assets were less than 5 million. By March 1773 North was able to muster enough votes in Parliament to limit the Company's dividends to 6 percent as a condition for a loan of 1.4 million pounds. (It was in the course of this debate that Clive was accused of improprieties.)

At this point North had a brainstorm. For one reason or another—primarily because the Americans would not buy taxed tea—the Company had a surplus of tea in its warehouses in Britain. But if this tea were sold to the Americans at a price so low that it would appear untaxed, they would accept it. It had not yet dawned on North—it would later—that more was at stake here than the price of tea. From the Americans' point of view, unless the British gave up their right to tax, there could be no compromise. Nonetheless some of the tea was shipped to Boston, where it arrived in November 1773. Not only did the Bostonians refuse to pay for the tea, they dumped it into Boston harbor. In fact none of the colonies would buy this tea. Much of it rotted in the warehouses where it was stored.

Indirectly these financial matters were of concern to Hastings, but what affected him directly was the rest of North's so-called Regulating Act of 1773. This created the post of governor-general in India. Its occupant was to govern from Calcutta and rule over the affairs of Madras and Bombay as well. Hence whoever assumed this position would in fact be governor-general of India, or at least of British India. It came, however, with a price. The governor-general would be provided with four councillors, men appointed by the government. These councillors, who would be paid an annual salary of ten thousand pounds, would have an equal vote with the governor-general in all matters except in the case of a tie, when the governor-general would have the deciding vote. This might come into play—and did—if the Council was at any time not up to full strength. Thus, although the governor-general reigned, he did not necessarily rule.

In order to work, this system demanded a harmonious relationship between the governor-general and his councillors, and a governor-general willing to abdicate some of his powers. North, who had no real interest in power, and whose second nature was to compromise, seemed to feel that his Regulating Act had now put the Company on the right path. Instead, given Hastings's thin skin and strong sense of the power of his office, it was a recipe for disaster. To make matters worse, for reasons no one ever understood, North appointed as one of the councillors Philip Francis, who many people came to think was Junius, the letter-writing public critic of the government. Even if he wasn't, he was equally nasty. If ever there were two men designed to hate each other, it was Philip Francis and Warren Hastings. Having them both in the confines of the same council was like having two scorpions in a bottle. Trouble began as soon as the boat bearing the councillors arrived in Calcutta.

Six
HASTINGS, 1774–1785

This morning Mr. Hastings and Mr. Francis fought with
pistols; they both fired at the same time. Mr. Francis's ball missed,
but that of Mr. Hastings pierced the right side of Mr. Francis, but
was prevented by a rib, which turned the ball, from entering the
thorax. It went obliquely upwards, passed the backbone without
injuring it, and was extracted about an inch to the left side of it.
The wound is of no consequence, and he is in no danger.

—Sir Elijah Impey (1780)[1]

I: THE COUNCILLORS

When the Indiaman *Ashburnham* reached Madras in the late summer of 1774, Philip Francis found a letter of welcome waiting
for him which Hastings had sent from Calcutta. It is, as far as I can
see, the only cordial communication that ever passed between the
two men. The brief letter read, "I take the earliest opportunity of addressing you on your arrival in India, and congratulating you on your
appointment to a share of the administration of this government. I received with particular pleasure, a letter from General Clavering [one
of the other new councillors], wherein he unites with his own intentions an assurance of your disposition to co-operate in measures of
public utility. My hopes and wishes are equally sanguine, to concur

82

heartily in such measures as will most fully answer the intention of your appointment, and reflect honour on our councils. I shall impatiently expect your arrival here, both from the personal satisfaction I propose myself from it, and the desire of entering upon the several public measures which may be necessary for the discharge of the great trust confided to our joint direction. I am with esteem. &c."[2]

It is quite unlikely that before his arrival Hastings knew anything about Francis. The letter does not indicate that he did. It is not clear that when Lord North appointed him as one of the four councillors he knew much about him either. It is hard to imagine that he associated Francis with the vituperative letter writer Junius. While North was noted for his affability, it is difficult to believe that he would have countenanced something like the footnote Junius inserted in his letter of April 3, 1770, published in the *Public Advertiser*: "Lord North. This graceful minister is oddly constructed. His tongue is a little too big for his mouth, and his eyes a great deal too big for their sockets. At this present writing, his head is supposed to be much too heavy for his shoulders."[3]

Francis's passage to India was rather circuitous. He had been born in Dublin in 1740, son of the Reverend Philip Francis. The family moved to England when Philip Sr. became chaplain to the Fox family. One of the sons of Henry Fox (the first Baron Holland and an important man in his own right), Charles James Fox, became one of the most prominent parliamentary figures of his time. He figures in our story later.

Francis was educated at St. Paul's School, where he was a brilliant scholar. There is no question that he and Hastings were intellectual equals. Because of his father's connections to Henry Fox, Francis secured an appointment as a junior clerk in the secretary of state's office. In 1762 he was promoted to a principal clerkship in the war office. That same year he married Elizabeth Macrabie, a merchant's daughter. When he departed for India twelve years later, he left her in England to care for their six children. He dabbled at politics and after little success in the opposition to North's government, he decided that he wanted a job even if it was a governmental appointment. Indeed, he had been unemployed for a year before he was appointed a councillor. But why was he named to the Council? He had never been to India and did not seem to have any special knowledge of the country. Even his family was puzzled. An American cousin (Francis had some connections in America and even owned land there), a lawyer, wrote, "I have perused the Regulation Bill carefully, and am of the opinion that it will answer all your purposes effectually. It gives you vast powers and a vast salary. But how did you get this appointment? It is miraculous to me that a man should resign his office in 1772; and in 1773, without any change of ministry, be advanced so very extraordinary a manner.

"Your merit and abilities, I was always ready to acknowledge, sir, but I was never taught to think much of Lord North's virtue and discernment; his treatment of you has in some measure redeemed him in my opinion."[4]

Chances are that North, having created his regulating apparatus, and under great pressure with other concerns such as the American colonies and the constant worry about the French involvement there, made the appointment fairly haphazardly. Francis wanted the job. He was bright and came with references from the right sort of people—the king thought he would do—so the job was his. Needless to say, Hastings was not consulted, nor were the directors of the Company. When the nomination was brought to them they objected, but Francis was appointed anyway. Interestingly in view of what happened later, Edmund Burke had been offered the position but declined it. One marvels at the thought of Hastings and Burke actually trying to govern India together. They might well have discovered that at base they agreed about a great deal. As it was, Francis began communicating his discontents to Burke almost as soon as he landed in Calcutta. He despised India almost as much as he despised Hastings, but, paradoxically, he wanted nothing so much as to be its next governor-general.

He was not alone. On the *Ashburnham* with him were the other two newly appointed councillors from Britain, Colonel George Monson and General John Clavering. The other councillor, Richard Barwell, was already in India. He had attended Hastings's old school, Westminster, though he had been born in Calcutta. His father had been at one time its governor. He was thirty-one, some ten years younger than Hastings. He had served on the Bengal Council when Hastings was governor. At first the two men did not get along, since Barwell felt that Hastings wanted to do everything himself and take credit for whatever was done. But he soon came to realize how exceptional Hastings's abilities were, and in the course of the next decade he became his only true ally on the Council.

Monson, who at fifty-three was the oldest of the new appointees, had had Indian experience, but in the south. He had fought with Clive at Pondicherry, where he was badly wounded. He was not known for his radiant intelligence, but his appointment had the support of the king. He had an odd connection to Hastings which very likely did not improve his disposition toward him. Hastings's uncle Howard, the man who had sent him to Westminster, did general busywork for a nobleman, Lord Darlington. Monson had married Lady Anne Vane, Darlington's daughter. She was the source of a story—false—that Hastings was Howard's actual son. Howard had expected some sort of legacy from Darlington that was never forthcoming. There were bad feelings. Perhaps this affected the Monson-Hastings relationship, which was not very good, though in his letter of welcome to Monson, Hastings did send a greeting to Lady Anne: "As I understand that Lady Anne Monson is to be the companion of your voyage. I beg the favour of you to present my compliments to her in the hopes that I may have the honour still to bear a place in her remembrance."[5]

The final member of the Council, General Clavering, a Coldstream Guard, was fifty-one. He was again a choice of the king. He was not noted for his military prowess, though he had fought in Guadeloupe, but had been appointed commander-in-chief of the Company's army. This again was something that North cannot have thought through very clearly. In case of a military emergency, who was to be in charge, the governor-general or the commander-in-chief? The arrangement might have worked if Clavering had been a different sort of individual. He was bad-tempered, egocentric, and, as events were about to reveal, a stickler for protocol. Furthermore he seems to have been assured that *he* would be the next governor-general as soon as Hastings could be remaindered. He and Francis had a get-acquainted meeting in Clive's house in Shropshire, where Francis had ingratiated himself. Francis had decided that Clavering was a fool and that he, Francis, was the one to be the next governor-general. Both of them had been indoctrinated by Clive as to Hastings's flaws and came to India with an attitude.

Added to this witches' cocktail was another ingredient which, once again, North had not considered carefully. A parallel Judicature Act had created a Supreme Court with British magistrates who were to bring the benefits of British justice to one and all in Calcutta as well as to British subjects and Company employees elsewhere. Here there were two problems, both of which were to manifest themselves dramatically. The first problem was, would this court respect, for example, Hindu law, which was even older than Roman law? In a conflict between Hindu law and British law, which would be determinate? Britain was experiencing an outbreak of lawlessness, and to combat this several crimes had been made punishable by execution. You could be hanged for stealing a horse or, indeed, for shoplifting. Such a thing did not exist in Hindu law. And if you were a Brahmin, you were not subject to capital punishment under Hindu law. What would happen if a Brahmin were convicted by this British court and sentenced to be hanged for a crime that was capital in a British court of law but not in Hindu law? Which law would prevail?[6] A concrete example would soon arise. Furthermore, where did the final authority rest? With the court, with the governor-general, or with the Council? The Regulating Act did specify that the chief justice of the Supreme Court was next in authority to the governor-general—which did not please Clavering—but could the governor-general overrule him? This too became an issue.

Francis commented, "The natural conclusion in the mind of the native must be that the judicial is the first power, and the judges the first persons in the State."[7] On the positive side, from Hastings's point of view, was the fact that the first chief justice of the four-man Supreme Court was his old Westminster friend Elijah Impey. Here was someone he could at least communicate with. The judges of the court had sailed for India at about the same time as the councillors but on the Indiaman *Anson*. They all arrived in Calcutta together on October 19. The trip by boat from Madras had taken nearly a month, which illustrates just how difficult it was to coordinate the Company's jurisdictions. Bombay was even farther away than Madras from Calcutta.

Trouble began almost immediately. Francis had brought his young brother-in-law Alexander Macrabie[8] with him as his private secretary. Macrabie kept a diary which paints a vivid picture of the scene. He writes, "Exactly at noon, a comfortable season for establishing the etiquette of precedency [this surely must have been meant ironically; it is difficult to imagine any time of day less comfortable than high noon in Calcutta], the whole party are disposed in three boats, and both courts safely landed at the capital of their jurisdiction. The procession to the Governor's house beggars all description; the heat, the confusion, not an attempt at regularity. No guards, no person to receive or to show the way, no state."[9] The governor-general did not go to the pier to meet his fellow councillors. They came to his house, where he must have greeted them somewhat informally. Macrabie comments, "But surely Mr. Hastings might have put on a ruffled shirt!"[10] At this time Hastings was still a bachelor. One can rest assured that if he had been married to the baroness he would have worn a ruffled shirt! Indeed, in the only painting of the two of them together that I know of, done in 1883–1884 by the noted portrait painter John Zoffany, who spent six years in India, Hastings is a model of sartorial elegance.

The phrase "no state" in young Macrabie's diary refers to two breaches of protocol to which General Clavering in particular took great offense. On the one hand, no military parade or inspection had been laid on. On the other hand, the cannon salutes by which the councillors were received came up four guns short. Seventeen guns were fired whereas Clavering insisted that there should have been twenty-one. He must have felt strongly enough about this to have lodged a formal complaint, because on December 3 Hastings felt obliged to write a letter of explanation to the Court of Directors.

The letter is fascinating.[11] He begins by apologizing for disturbing the directors with a subject so "exceedingly frivolous." He goes on to explain the seventeen guns and the absence of a parade. All of this *is* "frivolous." What is not frivolous is the last paragraph, which is the heart of the matter. He writes, "Upon the whole, I must remark that I paid them higher honours than had ever been paid to persons of their rank in this country; as high even as had been paid to Mr. Vansittart and Lord Clive, when they came in the first station as Governors, men whose names will ever stand foremost in the memoirs of the people of this country, and who merited as much from their employers as any who have filled, or are likely to fill, that station. I wrote letters severally to the three gentlemen at Madras, bespeaking their confidence, as a measure necessary to the safety of the Company. The Board [one assumes this is a reference to members of the government then in Calcutta] sent their senior member down the river to meet them; and, as a mark of personal respect from me, one of the gentlemen of my staff attended them; the whole Council assembled at my house to receive them on their landing." (Clavering had complained that they should have met in the Council House, which would have been some sort of neutral ground.) But now come the concluding sentences, which say everything. "What more could I do without derogating from my own rank? But they seem to have considered themselves as the Government, and to have required honours done to it entire to be paid to their own persons, forgetting that they were only a part, and that it was from the head they expected such concessions." We are not talking here about a few cannon shots. We are talking about Hastings's authority as governor-general of India.

The day after their arrival, the councillors met in their first formal session, which Clavering insisted be devoted to what he said was the shoddy reception he had received. The meeting broke up acrimoniously. Between that meeting and the next, the weekend passed. During this period, as he tells us in the letter, Hastings contemplated resigning. "I was hurt at the extraordinary reduction of my authority . . . ," he wrote the directors. Why then didn't he resign? Different explanations have been offered. One suggested explanation is financial. While he had made some money in private trading and had been earning a good salary, he had also, as we have noted, spent a lot of money. If he returned to England, what would he live on, and would it be enough to support the baroness, whom he had not yet married but whose expensive tastes must have been clear? He certainly would not have had enough money to buy back his homestead, Daylesford. Indeed, what would he do with his life? He was just past forty, and the only employer he had ever known was the East India Company, for which he had worked since his teens. There is no reason to believe they would have hired him in England.

Had he resigned, and Clavering taken over, there is every reason to think the results would have been disastrous. The British might well have lost India just as they were in the process of losing America. Hastings had a great loyalty to the Company, and he probably felt an obligation to do his best not to let that happen. There was also un-finished, or partially finished, business. The two years in which Has-tings had been governor of Bengal had been very full ones. Between 1772 and 1774 he had accomplished a good deal and had also sown the seeds of things that would come back to haunt him.

✍

HASTINGS'S GOVERNANCE of Bengal can be examined as matters "domestic" and "foreign." Domestic matters occurred within the Company's territory in Bengal. Foreign matters did not occur within Bengal but involved the government of Bengal significantly. As often happens, these foreign affairs had more far-reaching consequences than the domestic ones.

On the domestic side the balance sheet seems almost entirely positive. Hastings created a postal service and sponsored the comple-tion of a geographical survey of the country, which he was able to aid from his own observations. He had a vision of a partially overland route to India through Egypt, even a canal. This route was already in use for some "fast" mail, though the risks were such that important dispatches were sent both by land and by sea in the hope that, one way or another, they would get through. Hastings began planning for a system of granaries to mitigate against famines. He unified the cur-rency system by establishing a sort of state bank in Calcutta. Most in-terestingly, he persuaded eleven Brahmin scholars to come to Calcutta to codify Hindu law, to set it down in written form. As he said, he thought the citizens of Bengal—of anywhere in India where there was a British government—should be ruled by laws that "time and religion had rendered familiar to their understandings and sacred to their affections."[12] This rendering was first done orally from San-skrit, which was then translated into Persian.

To make the translation into English, Hastings engaged the ser-vices of a newly arrived twenty-three-year-old writer named Nathaniel Halhed,[13] the son of a director of the Bank of England who had gone out to India as a writer in 1771. Halhed was a superb lin-guist who seems to have been the first employee of the Company who could carry out its correspondence in Bengali. It seems he was also the first person to point out the relationships between Bengali and Sanskrit. After publishing his translation of the laws—the *Code of Gentoo Laws*—in 1776, he prepared a *Grammar of the Bengal Language*, which he published in 1778. This required type characters in Bengali. With Hastings's encouragement, an equally young writer named Charles Wilkins, with the aid of a single Indian craftsman, made the fonts needed.

Halhed had been the best friend of the Irish-born playwright Richard Brinsley Sheridan. Both young men had applied together to come out to India as writers. But Sheridan had fallen in love and remained behind to get married. Eventually he went into Parliament and played an essential role in Hastings's impeachment trial. We will meet him again.

Hastings was also sensitive to the role of Muslim law in Bengal. As he wrote to the great British jurist Lord Mansfield, "With respect to Mohometan law, which is a guide at least on one fourth of the natives of this province, your Lordship need not be told that this is as comprehensive, and as well defined, as that of most states in Europe, having been formed at a time in which the Arabians were in possession of all the real learning which existed in the western parts of this continent. The book which bears the greatest authority among them in India is a digest formed by the command of the Emperor Aurungzebe [sic], and consists of four large folio volumes which are equal to nearly twelve of ours."[14]

The most difficult domestic matter for Hastings was the tax system. It may be recalled that Clive had accepted the diwani of Bengal—the right to collect taxes—from the ruling nawab. Local collectors were to collect these taxes and turn them over eventually to the Company. In practice this dual system had turned into a catastrophe, permeated by corruption at every level. What made matters worse was that since these tax collectors were in theory acting on behalf of the Company, they employed the Company's soldiers to enforce whatever tax collection they decided upon.

One of the first things Hastings did when he became governor was to leave Calcutta to see for himself what was happening in the rest of Bengal. He had already decided that the nawab had to be stripped of his powers and that, while he might be kept in place as a symbol, it was the British who would rule. "There can be but one government and one power in this Province," he wrote to an associ-

Tank Square in Calcutta, 1786. (Etching by Thomas Daniell)

ate.[15] The nawab in question was the minor son of the late Mir Jafar. The question was, who should be the child's guardian until he came of age? Hastings's selection, and its consequences, became another element in his impeachment trial. He chose not the young boy's mother but rather his stepmother, another wife of Mir Jafar, a woman named the Munni ("Pearl") Begum. She had been a dancing girl in Agra—some said a temple prostitute—and had caught the eye of the then elderly Mir Jafar. She had no children of her own. She was a shrewd woman of enormous vitality who, as it happened, outlived most of the other characters in this story. Her guardianship of the nawab was to be carried out in the nawab's capital, Murshidabad, where Hastings had served many years.

While he was there on this visit, Hastings took the first steps to modify the tax collection system. Local collectors would now be accompanied by an Indian official from Calcutta, and they would serve no more than two years in a given location. They would also not be allowed to engage in private trade while serving. In connection with tax collections, Hastings also made a stab at the difficult task of deciphering the ownership of land so that it could be taxed fairly. There was a continual and almost unresolvable difference of opinion as to whether taxes on the land were too low or too high. In order to bring the system under some semblance of control, Hastings transferred the collection functions from Murshidabad, the traditional capital of Bengal, to Calcutta. Thus for the first time a native province was ruled from a capital created by the British.

In foreign affairs, relations with the Bhutanese were a relatively minor problem, kept under control partly by small-scale military actions and partly by Bogle's diplomacy. The so-called Rohilla War was a very different story. It became one of the most difficult incidents for partisans of Hastings to defend. Although it never became one of the formal impeachment charges, it was constantly lurking in the proceedings.

It is difficult to find two historians or biographers who agree on the issues. As background, the history of India, up to the most recent period, has been characterized by strong but relatively small (compared to the local population) military powers coming in from the outside to dominate a territory with a vast number of people. They have maintained this dominance until some even stronger foreign power forces them out. That is why India is such a mosaic. The Rohillas were an Afghan clan, some fifty or sixty thousand strong—Muslim Pathans who came south from Khandahar. Their descendants now live on the northwest frontier of Pakistan. These are not people to be taken lightly. Early in the eighteenth century, when the Moghul Empire was disintegrating, this group took over a small northern territory of India that came to be called Rohilkhand. The largely Hindu native population that the Rohillas came to rule consisted of somewhere between one and two million people. On these facts there is no disagreement. Even Burke acknowledged that the Rohillas were a recent arrival in India. The British had preceded them.

The disagreement begins with an assessment of the Rohillas and of Rohilkhand itself. The spectrum of views is quite broad. Burke, for example, thought the Rohillas were people of great nobility and ancient tradition, something that was always very important to him. (He later vehemently opposed the French Revolution because nobility and tradition were being sacrificed.) He also regarded Rohil-

Traffic on the Hooghly River off the Bengali quarter, Calcutta, 1788.
(Etching by Thomas Daniell)

khand—which, needless to say, he had never seen—as a sort of Arcadia, whose standard of living widely surpassed those of its neighbors. Hastings, on the other hand, saw the Rohillas as "freebooters"—outlaws—who had invaded their neighbors' territory and were now exploiting the local population. Most modern students of the subject think that Hastings was closer to the mark.[16] But, in any event, this was not the real issue. The real issue was, what gave the British the right to meddle in the affairs of the Rohillas, whoever they were? In this respect the Company had given Hastings written instructions about all foreign entanglements. The problem was that the instructions were, perhaps deliberately, ambiguous. The operative sentence reads, "We [the directors of the Company] also utterly disapprove and condemn offensive wars, distinguishing, however, between offensive measures unnecessarily undertaken with a view to pecuniary advantages and those which the preservation of our honour, or the protection of safety of our possessions, may render absolutely necessary." Legions of grave diggers have dug the graves of soldiers killed preserving "honour." Where in this murky spectrum did the Rohilla War fit? First, what was it?

The geography is important. Rohilkhand, which was northeast of Delhi, had for its western neighbors a territory ruled by the Marathas, not the most desirable neighbors. To its east was Oudh, a state ruled by a nawab named Shuja-ud-Daula. He was said to have a harem that contained eight hundred women. This territory also had a boundary with Bengal, so its stability was of importance to the Company. For many years the Rohillas had either been in conflict with the Marathas or had conspired with them, possibly threatening Oudh and hence Bengal. Clive had negotiated a treaty with the nawab of Oudh some years earlier, but its provisions were now out of date and needed revising. In 1773 Hastings traveled from Calcutta to Benares to meet the nawab, with whom he found that, with patience, he could negotiate privately. Some territory was restored to the nawab for a large fee—fifty million rupees—and an arrangement was made to station some of the Company's soldiers in Oudh with the nawab paying the expenses.

Then there was the matter of the Rohillas. The nawab wanted to annex Rohilkhand, which he was too weak to do on his own. He wanted the help of the British troops stationed in Oudh, who theoretically were not allowed to participate in such actions unless they were actually threatened. But it was agreed that if such an action were to take place, the nawab would pay the Company an additional forty million rupees. Much of this was not written down in a precise way, and when Hastings returned to Calcutta it was vigorously debated by his Council before being reluctantly approved. It was surely Hastings's hope that the nawab would not call on the British troops in Oudh to fight the Rohillas, against whom he had no animus.

The only mitigating factor in favor of Hastings having engaged in such a nebulous and potentially explosive arrangement was the financial pressure he was under. Remember that this was the very time the Company in England was seeking to borrow 1.5 million pounds from the government to keep itself afloat. It was also a time when the Company was obliged to provide 400,000 pounds each year to the same government. This money had to come from India, and the nawab's 50 million rupees would cover the 400,000 pounds and more. As the decade unfolded, Hastings's economic initiatives paid off, at

Fort William, Calcutta, showing the factory and fortifications as redesigned after Siraj-ud-Daula's attack. (Engraving after Jan van Ryne)

least for a while, and the Company was able to send substantial sums back to Britain. This may well have helped to preserve North's government, which was spending heavily on both the American war and building up the fleet to ward off a possible French invasion. The notion that the nawab would refrain from taking over Rohilkhand when the conditions were right was wishful thinking. Hastings was too shrewd not to have understood this.

All of this became an issue in the impeachment trial where Burke, who was unable to get it approved as one of the articles of impeachment, nonetheless referred to it whenever he had the opportunity. He also added the notion that Hastings had taken a personal bribe from the nawab. This became part of his litany that Hastings had, like Clive, amassed a huge fortune in India, something that was certainly false. In any event, in February 1774, some seven months before the new councillors arrived in Calcutta, the nawab decided that the Marathas were in a state of disarray and that the time was ripe to move on Rohilkhand.

The conquest of Rohilkhand was accomplished in relatively short order. The Company's soldiers did take part in what one of them later called an "un-British" war. There were claims, later disputed, of atrocities, and certainly the nawab's soldiers did more looting than fighting. Hastings tried to protest this by instructing his resident in Oudh to "remonstrate with [the nawab] against every act of cruelty and wanton violence."[17] This was about as effective as trying to stop Niagara Falls with a sponge.

What happened to the Rohillas as a consequence of this operation is again a matter of dispute. Burke was to claim that what was involved was what we now know as "genocide"—that Hastings knowingly participated in a campaign of exterminating a sovereign people. (Much of the "exterminating," such as it was, was carried out by the local Hindu peasants, who were only too happy to get rid of the Rohillas.) Hastings, on the other hand, would claim that the action was more like what we would now call "ethnic cleansing." The large number of surviving Rohillas simply left Rohilkhand and joined the Marathas. The Company, incidentally, never got the forty million rupees it had been promised, though eventually some of the British officers who participated in the campaign were paid prize money. This happened only after Hastings, who vehemently objected, had left Bengal.

Meanwhile on Monday, October 24, 1774, five days after the new councillors had arrived in Calcutta, they had their second meeting. Francis, who had been in India for less than a week, had come prepared to challenge Hastings on his conduct of the Rohilla War—and, indeed, on every action he had taken while governor of Bengal. This story could not have a happy ending.

II: MRS. GRAND

When George François Grand married Noël Catherine Werlée on July 10, 1777, she was not quite fifteen. Her father was a functionary in the French settlement at Chandernagore, up the Hooghly from Calcutta. Mr. Grand, who was several years older, was a member of the Indian civil service. His family had emigrated to England from France during the reign of Louis XIV, and he had been educated in Lausanne. Using an aunt's connection, he had obtained an appointment as a cadet in the Company's army and in 1766 had landed in Bengal. (One of the other young men who had come out with him on the same Indiaman was William Makepeace Thackeray, the grandfather of the novelist.) After some years of service, Grand returned to England and then, in 1776, secured an appointment as a writer in Calcutta. He became a kind of private secretary to Hastings and seems to have become part of his household. With other writers, he used to spend some of his weekends boating on the river. On one of his upstream outings to Chandernagore he met Mademoiselle Werlée at a reception at the French governor's mansion. The French had been reestablished in Chandernagore during Clive's governorship of Bengal.

In a memoir of more than a hundred pages written many years later, Mr. Grand describes his courtship of Mademoiselle Werlée: "In one of these trips to the Presidency I formed an attachment to Miss Noël Catherine Werlée, the daughter of Monsieur Werlée, Capitaine du Port and Chevalier de Saint Louis, a respectable old man whose services had deservedly merited this mark of distinction from his sovereign. We were not long in expressing to each other our reciprocal inclinations and our engagement in matrimonial alliance took place, which we agreed should be solemnized as soon as I could obtain a situation which might enable me to commence housekeeping."[18] He discussed this matter with Hastings, who was nothing if not romantic. He was about to marry the baroness. He found the young man a position as secretary to the Salt Committee (the Company also traded in salt), which paid thirteen hundred rupees a month, enough to get married on. Mademoiselle Werlée was a Catholic while Grand was a Protestant, so they had two ceremonies. Mademoiselle Werlée was also by all accounts the most beautiful woman anyone had ever seen in Calcutta. She had extraordinary blond hair—one report says auburn—black eyebrows and eyelashes, blue eyes, and the figure of a nymph. A painting by Gérard, done nearly thirty years later when she was the Princesse de Talleyrand, takes your breath away. How she went from being the child bride of George François Grand to becoming first the mistress and then, in 1803, the wife of Charles Maurice de Talleyrand-Périgord, Napoleon's minister for foreign affairs, is a story you couldn't make up. Philip Francis was in the middle of it.

Francis kept a journal which is fairly laconic and mixes business with social matters. The entry for December 8, 1778, has the pithy sentence, after a description of his daytime professional activities, "At night the diable à quatre at the house of G. F. Grand, Esq."[19] Mr. Grand's memoir provides some of the details. The account begins, "On December 8th 1778, I went out of my house, about nine o'clock the happiest, as I thought myself of men; and between eleven and twelve o'clock returned the same night as miserable as any being could well feel. I left it prepossessed with a sense that I was blessed with the most beautiful as well as the most virtuous of wives, ourselves honoured and respected, moving in the first circles and having every prospect of speedy advancement. Scarcely had I sat down to supper at my benefactor, Mr. Barwell's society [Barwell, it will be recalled, was the one new councillor who took Hastings's part; he too had helped Mr. Grand], who required his friends to join him every fortnight at this convivial meeting [There were no wives, clearly. Mr. Grand, who wrote this memoir many years later, actually misremembered the locale of the dinner. It was at the house of a well-known restaurateur, a Mr. Le Gallais], than I was suddenly struck with the deepest anguish and pain. A servant who was in the habit of attending Mrs. Grand came and whispered to me that Mr. Francis was caught in my house, and secured by my jemidar [an upper servant exercising a certain authority over other servants]. I rose from the table, ran to the terrace, where grief, by a flood of tears, relieved itself for a moment. I there sent for a friend out, who I requested to accompany me; but the rank of the party [Francis was, after all, a councillor] and the known attachment which I was well aware, he held to him, however, he execrated his guilty action, pleaded his excuse with me." Grand, then and thereafter, assumed that Francis and his wife had been up to no good. He found another companion to return to the house with him and to lend him a sword. He planned to duel Francis, who was then thirty-eight, to the death.

Upon returning to his house Mr. Grand found not Francis but three of his accomplices, Francis having escaped in the ensuing scuffle. Mr. Grand then sent for his wife's sister and brother-in-law, and despite all of his wife's lamentations that she was only sixteen and was not responsible for what had happened, he ordered her out of the house. He challenged Francis to a duel to which Francis, who was not generally averse to the idea of sword dueling, did not respond. He claimed then, and later, that his tryst with Mrs. Grand had not been consummated. Mr. Grand then took him to court and sued him for 1.5 million rupees—160,000 pounds—a stupefying sum.

The transcripts of the trial, over which Elijah Impey presided, read like a novel. They reveal that this was not some spur-of-the-moment jape on the part of Francis but a campaign he had carefully planned. It goes without saying that the feelings of Mrs. Francis, who was in England tending to their six children, did not enter into the calculus, though later when she found out about it she explained the case by saying that poor Mrs. Grand had been married to a "dirty *old* sordid Frenchman."[20] The fact that Mr. Grand was English and younger than her husband did not seem to register. From her account, all Francis was doing was rescuing a maiden in distress. Young Mrs. Grand had an *ayah*—a lady's maid—whom she had asked from inside her bedroom to go fetch a candle. Upon returning fifteen minutes later, the ayah found the bedroom door locked. Puzzled, she went outside to discover a bamboo ladder leaning against the house and leading up to the window of Mrs. Grand's bedroom. She then went to fetch the jemidar, who was also surprised to see the ladder. While they were discussing it, Francis emerged from the house. He had been interrupted in his activities in Mrs. Grand's bedroom by the ayah's knocks on the door. The jemidar reported that Francis said to him, referring to the ladder, "Give me that thing. I will give you money. I'll make you great man."[21] By this time other servants had gathered at the scene, and Francis was confronted by what was turning into a posse.

Mrs. Grand appeared at the top of the stairs and asked the servants to let Francis go. (Incidentally, it appears that Mrs. Grand did not speak English very well. Her mother tongue was French, and she must have spoken to the servants in Bengali. Francis spoke French.) She was told in no uncertain terms to go to her room. This request would indicate to the suspicious mind a certain complicity on her part. Francis, who incidentally was wearing black so as to be less visible in the dark, was now joined by two of his friends who came from outside the house into the room where he was being held. A scuffle ensued, and Francis escaped. In the trial his accomplices testified that Francis had told them he was going to visit Mrs. Grand because he knew this was the night that Mr. Grand regularly had dinner with his friends. One of them also testified that Francis had had the ladder specially constructed for the situation. Clearly Francis did not have much of a case. On March 6, Judge Impey pronounced for the plaintiff, but the damage award was reduced from 1.5 million rupees to 50,000 thousand—about 5,000 pounds. Francis never forgave Impey for this decision, and when the opportunity arose some years later he helped to bring articles of impeachment against him.

There were aftershocks. Hastings was displeased, to put it mildly, by what Francis had done with the wife of what was after all, one of his young protégés. To Francis's annoyance, he brought the matter up before the Council. Considering Hastings's affair with the baroness, Francis thought that Hastings had no right to moralize. About three months later Francis established the former Mrs. Grand in a house in Hooghly, a town upstream from Calcutta. His journal records frequent visits. The liaison appears to have lasted until at least the end of 1779. Francis himself left India late in 1780. When he returned to England he resumed his married life with his wife and six children. Mr. Grand left Calcutta soon after the trial and had a not very successful career elsewhere in India. He stayed in the country until 1799. For the rest of his life he sought additional redress from Francis with no success. He seems never to have recovered from his wife's affair.

Not a great deal seems to be known about the immediate trajectory of Mrs. Grand. She certainly returned to France, where she may have been visited by Francis, and came to marry Talleyrand.

It did not take the episode with Mrs. Grand to initiate Hastings's feeling of contempt for Francis. It merely added to the quotient. Hastings certainly did not like Monson and Clavering, but with Francis it was something else. Contempt is probably the right word. The tensions began immediately. Francis had learned enough about the Rohilla War before arriving in India that he had planned to attack Hastings over it even before his boat docked in Calcutta. In this he had someone he thought was a useful ally—Colonel Alexander

Champion, who had taken part in the campaign and who expected to be awarded prize money. When he didn't get it, he began discussing the "atrocities" that he had not actually seen but had information on through "reliable" sources. When the British officers who had been present in the field contradicted him, Francis backed off. But then the majority on the Council began systematically dismantling the reforms Hastings had instituted. They did away with the state bank. Francis developed a tax system which in essence revived Clive's old dual system with all its faults. They revoked many of Hastings's senior appointments and blocked the advancement of the junior people he had carefully trained and nourished. Even Bogle was not immune, In March 1776 he wrote to his father, "Mr. Hastings bears this attack [of the Council majority] with calmness and equanimity, which raises his character in the eyes of everybody; and although to pay court to him is the sure way to give umbrage to his opponents, who are possessed of all power, yet the respect that is felt for his character preserves his levées, now when he is stripped of power, as crowded as ever. [These are presumably the public sessions that Hastings used to have to hold periodically to address complaints and problems.] As regards myself, fidelity is, in my opinion, a virtue of all others the most indispensable, and there is only one *beau chemin* to take. Thus you will observe that my fortune depends on Mr. Hastings. If he succeeds I have everything I hope for. If he falls I must betake myself to some other line, more independent of the Supreme Council."[22]

Not long after the arrival of the new councillors, letters began flowing to Lord North. Francis's letters were highly critical of Hastings. While Hastings may have shown "calmness and equanimity" to Bogle, the letters he wrote to North show rather the opposite. The first one, written on December 4, 1774, less than two months after the councillors arrived in Calcutta, is fairly typical of the genre. It is a very long letter, really a dispatch. It begins with remarks about his appointment.

"My Lord—I esteem it an especial duty to acknowledge, by the earliest opportunity, the receipt of the letter with which your Lordship was pleased to honour me by General Clavering [Clavering must have brought it with him by ship]; and to mark, at the same time, the strong, the unaffected feelings of my heart, on the kind and handsome manner in which you were pleased to notify me of the part you took in my late appointment. Being an entire stranger, without either personal or political connexion with your Lordship, I must look on the favour shown to me as the most incontrovertible token of your Lordship's approbation of my past conduct. . . ."[23] As far as Hastings was concerned, this resolved the doubt in his mind as to whether his appointment had been on merit or whether the new Regulating Act required *someone* to be governor-general and that he was, accidentally, at hand. But Clavering had been told that he would be the next governor-general as soon as Hastings could be brought home decently. So either Hastings had read North's letter too naively, or he wanted to put his interpretation of it in writing in order to force North to acknowledge it. He knew that North was receiving complaints from Francis and the rest of the Council, so he wanted to make it clear that he was the best man for the job. Indeed, he goes on to say that his "temper and views are moderate with respect to fortune, and many of common objects of life, but I own, I possess a more than ordinary degree of ambition to act in an elevated sphere under the auspices of my sovereign, and to recommend myself more and more in his favour." While North understood this sort of ambition in the men that surrounded him, he did not share it. He was at this time writing almost monthly to the king, asking to be allowed to resign as first minister.* Whatever ambitions North had "to act in an elevated sphere" had pretty much evaporated.

Hastings's letter then turns to the fractious situation that had developed in the Council. He writes, "The public despatches will inform you of the division which prevails in our council. I do not mean in this letter to enter into a detail of its rise and progress, but will beg leave to refer to those despatches for the particulars, and for the defence both of my measures and opinions. I shall here only assure your Lordship that this unhappy difference did not spring from me, and that had General Clavering, Mr. Monson, and Mr. Francis, brought with them the same conciliatory spirit which I had adopted, your Lordship would not have been embarrassed with the appeals of a disjointed administration, nor with the public business here retarded by discordant councils."

*North did not like the term "prime minister" and referred to himself as first minister.

Having said that he would not enter into the specifics, Hastings proceeded to do so: "The cause assigned for these differences, your Lordship will observe, is the Rohilla war. I own I looked for praise rather than blame from this measure, because no visible consequence could be derived from it in the situation which these gentlemen found it, but such as was every way advantageous to the Company; but had they disapproved of it, I still think that if their dispositions were to promote harmony and to maintain the credit of the Government, free from inconsistency, they ought to have afforded me the means of receding, without fixing a mark of reprobation on my past conduct. . . ." This of course is just the point. The new councillors had no interest in promoting "harmony" with Hastings. If they had, why would they bring up a war that had been fought eight months before they arrived? Doing so was part of a strategy, which seems to have been carefully calculated by Francis, to make things so unpleasant for Hastings that, even if he was not recalled, he would resign.

One does not know exactly what North made of these letters, which he received five or six months later. North was notorious for not reading his mail, especially if it might concern a disagreeable subject that might call for a decision. In his memoirs, North's fellow member of Parliament, Nathaniel Wraxall, a great admirer of North, noted that "A Letter of the first political importance, addressed to him by the King, which he had lost, after a long search, was found wide open in the water-closet."[24] Some of the letters from India were later found in his office with their seals unbroken. He had certainly hoped that his Regulating Act would be a successful compromise between the Company's view that no regulation should be imposed and the king's view that the Company should be taken over by the crown. These dispatches were the last thing he wanted to read.

It soon became clear to the new councillors that Hastings was a tougher nut to crack than they had thought, so they escalated their operation. They attempted to impeach Hastings for what they claimed were criminal acts of accepting bribes and embezzling money that belonged to the Company. On at least one of these charges Hastings had left himself vulnerable. This was the matter of accepting what were known as "presents." It was customary in India that when a company delegation made an official visit to a provincial capital, the local authorities would make an offering in cash or kind.

One way of viewing this was that these delegations incurred expenses during their visits, and the presents were a form of reimbursement. On the other hand, if the local authorities wanted something from the visiting delegation, such an offering could not hurt. It was not expected that such a present would be refused; nonetheless Hastings did refuse some of them. The Regulating Act prohibited the taking of these presents; still, both before and after the passage of the act, Hastings did accept some. His argument was always that they were not accepted for himself but for the Company, and that the sums involved went on the Company's books. The problem was that he was a notoriously sloppy bookkeeper. The accounts were muddled. If one wished to see something conspiratorial in this, one could—as Burke later did in the impeachment trial—do so fairly readily.

On his tour of inspection in 1772, after he became governor of Bengal, Hastings accepted a present equivalent to fifteen thousand pounds—a rather substantial sum—from the Munni Begum. This particular present, which Hastings never denied accepting, became one of the issues in his impeachment trial a decade later. But the new councillors who were trying to rid themselves of Hastings in 1774 needed something at hand that represented an actual criminal act—a clear bribe, for example. By this time it had become known among the local populace that Hastings was in trouble and that the real power lay with the Council majority. People who were more pragmatic than scrupulous came forward with "evidence" that would indict Hastings and thereby gain points for themselves with the new power base. Foremost among these was a Brahmin, now approaching his seventieth year, named Nand Kumar, whom we briefly mentioned earlier.

Of all the descriptions of Nand Kumar I have read, only one presents him with any redeeming features. This is in a play written in the late 1920s by the well-known German playwright and novelist Lion Feuchtwanger. The play, written in collaboration with no less a figure than Bertolt Brecht, and containing pretty muddled history, is called *Warren Hastings*.[25] Closer to the norm is a famous passage in Macaulay's essay on Hastings. This has, apart from its racist tone, a particular value because Macaulay had no sympathy with Hastings's role—or at least what he claimed was Hastings's role—in the real drama that was about to unfold. To make his point it would have been simpler if Nand Kumar had been a more sympathetic figure. Macaulay wrote, "Of his [Nand Kumar's] moral character it is difficult to give a notion to those acquainted with human nature only as it appears in our island. What the Italian is to the Englishman, what the Hindoo is to the Italian, what the Bengalee is to other Hindoos, that was Nuncomar to other Bengalese." Macaulay then goes into a rapture of insults about the Bengalee. "What the horns are to the buffalo," he writes, "what the paw is to the tiger, what the sting is to the bee, what beauty, according to the old Greek song, is to woman, deceit is to the Bengalee. Large promises, smooth excuses, elaborate tissues of circumstantial falsehood, chicanery, perjury, forgery, are the weapons, offensive and defensive, of the people of the Lower Ganges." That having been established, Macaulay notes that "In Nuncomar the national character was strongly and with exaggeration personified. The Company's servants had repeatedly detected him in the most criminal intrigues. On one occasion he brought a false charge against another Hindoo, and tried to substantiate it by producing forged documents. On another occasion it was discovered that, while professing the strongest attachment to the English, he was engaged in several conspiracies against them, and in particular that he was the medium of a correspondence between the court of Delhi and the French authorities in the Carnatic. For these and similar practices he had long been detained in confinement. But his talents and influence had not only procured his liberation, but had obtained for him a certain degree of consideration even among the British rulers of his country."[26]

Hastings's acquaintance with Nand Kumar dated from the late 1750s when Hastings had been Clive's emissary in Murshidabad. For some reason Clive had made Nand Kumar the revenue collector for a small part of Bengal, near where Hastings was stationed, which was a license to steal. Hastings watched Nand Kumar's illicit activities in a state of helpless fury. His next contact with the Brahmin came when Hastings was governor of Bengal, at a time when the Company had decided to take up the revenue collections in Bengal. Hastings was informed of this from London and was told to arrest the collector for those lands owned by the Munni Begum and to replace him. He was instructed to use Nand Kumar to collect evidence. Hastings hated this arrangement but was obliged to obey instructions. He did, however, install Nand Kumar's son, who was on bad terms with his father, as the new collector.

In early March 1775, Nand Kumar charged that Hastings had taken a bribe of 350,000 rupees from the Munni Begum. This was the reason, he claimed, why she had been awarded the guardianship of the young nawab. This accusation did not refer to the relatively modest "present" Hastings had accepted, which at least could be defended legally. The claim was that Hastings had performed a criminal act—the taking of a bribe. On March 13 the Council majority proclaimed itself a kind of Star Chamber and summoned Nand Kumar to present his evidence, with Hastings now in the role of defendant. Hastings was justifiably outraged, and, after a violent argument, he and Barwell walked out. Nand Kumar was then called in to give his "evidence," which consisted of a transparently forged letter from the Munni Begum. She later denied that she had ever written such a letter. Nand Kumar claimed that Hastings's banyan, Krishna Kanta Nandi, who was known as Cantoo, had been the instrument by which the Munni Begum's bribe had been transmitted to Hastings. The next day Clavering ordered that Cantoo be put into stocks. Hastings made it clear that Clavering would have to deal with him first, with pistols of necessary. Clavering backed off. But the Council declared on the basis of their evidence that Hastings was guilty and would have to return to the Company the money he had allegedly stolen.

Hastings refused to have anything to do with this verdict. He did, however, write to Lord North to explain what had happened. In his letter of March 27 he writes, "Your Lordship will have perceived that in the endeavours of General Clavering, Colonel Monson, and Mr. Francis, to condemn the measures of the late administration, and in the pains taken to attribute them wholly to myself, their aim was to destroy my credit at home, while their public measures served to proclaim the annihilation of my power abroad. To effect both purposes in the most complete manner, agents, chosen from the basest of people [Nand Kumar]—and none but the basest would have undertaken such an office—have been excited to bring accusations against me of receiving presents in the course of my former government. These accusations, true or false, have no relation to the measures which are the ground and subject of our original differences; but my opponents undoubtedly expect, that if they can succeed to lower my private character in the opinion of the world, the rectitude and propriety of my public conduct will be overlooked, and their credit will rise in proportion as mine is debased. How far with the people, who are ever prone to receive allegations for proof, and to suppose that everything must be criminal which is delivered as a charge, they may prevail to raise a clamour against me until the truth be fairly known, I cannot pretend to foresee, but I am confident they will not succeed with your Lordship, or those who are to be effectual judges between us. . . ."[27] This was not a letter that, if he read it, would have pleased North at all.

All of this turmoil had an effect on Hastings. How could it not? He had, when the trouble with the Council began, dispatched a Colonel Lachlan MacLeane[28] to Britain to act as his agent—to defend his interests—along with an assistant named John Graham. MacLeane hand-delivered Hastings's letter to North when he arrived in England. On March 27 Hastings wrote a letter to Graham which reflected his state of mind but which later caused all sorts of mischief. It read:

"My dear Graham—I think it necessary to give both you and Colonel MacLeane this separate notice, lest you should be at a distance from each other when the packet arrives [mail sent in the returning Indiamen], of a resolution which I have formed, to leave this place and return to England on the first ship of the next season, if the first advices from England contain a disapprobation of the treaty of Benares [the treaty that Hastings had negotiated with Shuja-ud-Daula], or of the Rohilla war, and a mark of evident disinclination towards me. In that case I can have nothing to hope, and shall consider myself at liberty to quit this hateful scene before my enemies gain their complete triumph over me.

"If, on the contrary, my conduct is commended, and I read in the general letters clear symptoms of a proper disposition towards me, I will wait the issue of my appeals.

"I have imparted this resolution to no other person on your side of the water, and I leave it to your discretion and MacLeane's to make such use of it as you see proper. . . ."

It was the last sentence that caused the mischief. It put Graham and MacLeane in the position of being able to tender Hastings's resignation based only on what they could observe of the politics of the Company and the government in England, without knowing what was actually happening in India. In the several months before the next mail packet might arrive, dramatic changes could have taken place which would alter everything. In fact this is what happened. One involved Colonel Monson, and the other Nand Kumar.

In 1769, upon the death of a native banker, Nand Kumar had produced what he alleged to be a bond showing that the banker had owed him a substantial sum of money. The money was thereupon paid from the banker's estate. About half the estate went to settle this alleged claim. The documents supporting it went to the court of probate and were found to have been forgeries. A man named Mohan Prasad then brought suit against Nand Kumar in the civil court. Under instructions not to interfere with Nand Kumar, Hastings had interceded in this procedure and blocked the suit. Now, in May 1775, at the very time the Council majority had accused Hastings of bribery on the basis of Nand Kumar's forged evidence, Mohan Prasad brought criminal charges of forgery against Nand Kumar. These involved the same bond and were brought in the Supreme Court, where Hastings's school friend Elijah Impey was chief justice. Was this a coincidence? On this matter Macaulay, for one, is categorical, and everyone who has ever tried to write about this subject has had to confront his challenge. Here is Macaulay: "Of a sudden, Calcutta was astounded by the news that Nuncomar had been taken up on the charge of felony committed, and thrown into the common jail. The crime imputed to him was that six years before he had forged a bond. The ostensible prosecutor was a native [Mohan Prasad]. But it was then, and still is, the opinion of everybody, idiots and biographers excepted, that Hastings was the real mover in the business." But was he?

Neither Macaulay, nor anyone else, has ever produced documentary evidence that Hastings had anything to do with the timing of Mohan Prasad's complaint. Many people have remarked that it is odd that it came up seven years after the original offense. But this ignores the fact that the Supreme Court had come into being only a few months before Mohan Prasad sought its jurisdiction. Before that time he could have brought such a case only in lower courts. Since Nand

Kumar was a very powerful individual in his community, what native judge or junior Company official would have dared to go against him? Furthermore, why would Mohan Prasad have any interest in helping Hastings, the very man who had denied him his due in court in the first place? It seems to me that the timing was probably related to the fact that charges of bribery and forgery were in the air.

In any event, the charge was brought and a trial scheduled. This was a very serious matter because, according to the prevailing English law, which would be determinant, forgery was a capital offense. In short, a Brahmin was about to be put on trial in a British court for an offense—forgery—that could lead to his execution, something unheard of in Hindu law.

Nand Kumar now went on a hunger strike, claiming that he could not eat in a place—his jail cell—where a Muslim or a Christian might have been, or might someday be, without losing his caste. He also demanded to be allowed to bathe once a day in the Ganges. (The Hooghly, which flowed past Calcutta, was a branch of the Ganges.) The matter was brought to the attention of General Clavering, who in turn brought it to the attention of Judge Impey. He in turn dispatched various pandits to visit Nand Kumar in his cell to pronounce on the religious situation. The first batch of four pandits ruled that Nand Kumar could perform his functions in the jail cell provided that he did a certain number of penances to purify himself. Nand Kumar then insisted that another group of pandits, of even greater reputation, be consulted. This was more than Impey could deal with, so he granted Nand Kumar the privilege of having a private tent pitched for him within the prison walls. There he received a variety of visitors, including the aide-de-camp of General Clavering. Messages of condolence were received from various quarters, including Lady Anne Monson. Nonetheless, on June 8 the four British justices began the trial before an all-British jury of twelve.

This was the period just before the arrival of the monsoon, and the heat and humidity were almost unbearable. The judges felt obliged to wear their red robes and heavy wigs. It was said that Impey and the other judges retired three or four times a day to change their linen during the trial.

The first issue to arise was the matter of interpreters. The interpreter of choice was a young man named Alexander Elliot, who was fluent in both Hindustani and Persian. As he was a friend of both Hastings and Impey, there was a wrangle over whether this might be of significance. The jurors insisted they needed someone of Elliot's skills to make any headway with the testimony and evidence. Elliot was selected.

After the indictment was read, one of the justices—Robert Chambers, who had been a professor at law at Oxford and had come to India with a warm personal letter of recommendation to Hastings from Samuel Johnson—argued that forgery had been made a capital felony in England in the reign of George II. The conditions that produced this draconian penalty, he said, did not apply to Bengal. He asked that the felony case be dismissed. He was overruled by Impey and the two other justices.

On the second day of the trial Nand Kumar requested a private meeting with his British counsel with only an interpreter present. Nand Kumar told the counsel that he had decided he would be convicted in any event and wished to stop his defense. By this time documents in various languages had been placed in evidence. Nand Kumar thanked his advocate warmly for his efforts but said the members of the court were clearly his enemies and that it was pointless to go on. This was conveyed to the justices. Justice Chambers, who had been against the proceedings in the first place, personally assured the defense that the questions would be fair. On midnight, June 15, the defense rested its case, and the following morning Impey summed up for the jury. Impey's summation was later severely criticized, but, given the dubious nature of the whole proceedings, it seems not unreasonable.[29] The jury deliberated all night, and the next morning, at 4 a.m., they pronounced Nand Kumar guilty as charged. He was then sentenced to hang. A date of Saturday, August 5, was chosen, allowing the defense and its allies a few weeks to try to reverse the sentence.

Some commentators on the trial believe that Hastings should have commuted the sentence. But this assumes that Hastings, like the governor of a modern American state, had the power to commute. The act establishing the court gave the governor-general no such right. An attempt to commute would have created a constitutional crisis over something that, as distasteful as it was, did not threaten the stability of the state. And why would Hastings have intervened to save Nand Kumar, the very man who had presented evidence to his enemies which, had it been valid, would have subjected Hastings to the same sort of trial?

If there was to have been an intervention, it should have come from the Council majority. Their behavior was abominable, considering that Nand Kumar had been serving their interests. A petition was circulated by some of the British residents in Calcutta to have the sentence reviewed. Such reviews by the Privy Council in London— the Supreme Court—were envisioned in the Judicature Act. Clavering and Monson, however, refused to associate themselves with such a petition, though Francis showed some interest. It evaporated. Nand Kumar wrote a letter of appeal to Clavering, who did not even open it until after the execution. Most commentators agree with Macaulay that Impey's behavior was inexcusable. Macaulay writes, "A just judge would, beyond all doubt, have reserved the case for the consideration of the sovereign. But Impey would not hear of any mercy or delay."[30] The sentence never should have been handed down, and Impey should have insisted on a review. A terrible wrong was done.

Whatever his many flaws, Nand Kumar went to his death with great dignity. The full account of his last hours—again one of the classic bits of literature from this period—was written by Alexander Macrabie, Francis's young brother-in-law, who was the sheriff appointed to carry out the execution.[31] He visited Nand Kumar the night before the hanging. "Upon my entering his apartments in the jail," he wrote, "he arose and saluted me in his usual manner. After we were both seated, he spoke with great ease and such seeming unconcern that I really doubted whether he was sensible of his approaching fate. I therefore bid the interpreter inform him that I was come to show him this last mark of respect, and to assure him that every attention should be given the next morning which could afford him comfort on so melancholy an occasion; that I was deeply concerned that the duties of my office made me of necessity a party in it, but that I would attend to the last to see that every desire that he had should be gratified; that his own palanquin, and his own servants should attend him; and that such of his friends who, I understood, were to be present should be protected.

"He replied that he was obliged to me for this visit; that he thanked me for all my favours, and entreated me to continue it to his family; that fate was not to be resisted, and he put his finger to his forehead—'God's will' must be done. He desired that I would present his respects and compliments to the General, Colonel Monsoon [sic] and Mr. Francis. . . ."

The following morning at seven, Macrabie was informed that everything was in place for the execution. He again went to Nand Kumar to find his cell filled with the "howlings and lamentations" of the people who had come to pay their last respects. Nand Kumar himself appeared perfectly serene and again presented his compliments to the general, the colonel, and Mr. Francis. After some final prayers, Nand Kumar and his executioners went outside, where there was a vast crowd of orderly people in attendance. "Upon my asking him," Macrabie writes, "if he had any more friends he wished to see, he answered he had many, but this was not a place, nor an occasion, to look for them." His hands were then tied, and a cloth handkerchief supplied by a sepoy officer, who was a Brahmin, was tied over his face. "He had some weakness in his feet," Macrabie reports, "which, added to the confinement of his hands, made him mount the steps [to the gallows] with difficulty; but he showed not the least reluctance, scrambling rather forward to get up." Then it was over. Many in the crowd immediately went and bathed in the Ganges to purify themselves. The body was delivered for burning. No native in Bengal ever testified against Hastings again.

This was the first event that changed the situation in Bengal for Hastings. The second involved deaths from natural causes, if you acknowledge the murderous climate, the tropical diseases, and the excesses of food and wine that most of the colonials in Calcutta indulged in as natural causes. The first death was that of Lady Anne Monson in February 1776. This was followed by that of her husband, Colonel Monson, the following September, and then that of Alexander Macrabie in November. Both Barwell and Clavering too were beginning to show the effects of the climate, and Francis was wondering why he himself had remained alive. Hastings, who now had the casting vote in the Council, would, Francis was sure, never die a natural death.

III: THE INSURRECTION

The most graphic description of the duel that Philip Francis and Hastings fought at sunrise on Thursday, August, 17, 1780, was written by his second, Colonel Pearse, the commandant of artillery at Fort William. Francis was seconded by Colonel Watson, the chief engineer at the fort. Although he was the challenger, Francis had never fought a pistol duel. Indeed, it appears that until that morning he had never fired a pistol. Hastings had never fought a pistol duel either, but in the course of his military service he had used a pistol a few times.

The first issue to be settled was the time. Watson noted that it was half past five, but Francis said it was close to six. Watson noted that he had used his astronomical clock to set his watch to solar time. Then the place for the actual duel had to be agreed upon. The first site suggested was deemed not suitable because it was on a public road. Hastings rejected a path leading off the road because he said it was too dark. Finally they located a spot agreeable to all parties. Pearse now takes up the story:

"As soon as the suitable place was selected, I proceeded to load Mr. Hastings's pistols; those of Mr. Francis were already loaded. When I had delivered one to Mr. Hastings and Colonel Watson had done the same to Mr. Francis, finding the gentlemen were both unacquainted with the modes usually observed on these occasions, I took the liberty to tell them that, if they would fix their distance, it was the business of the seconds to measure it. Colonel Watson immediately mentioned that Fox and Adam had taken fourteen paces, and he recommended the distance. [A Mr. Adam and a Mr. Fox had fought a pistol duel in Alipore in November 1779, the news of which had just come to Calcutta. Mr. Fox was slightly wounded.] Mr. Hastings observed it was a great distance for pistols; but as no actual objection was made to it, Watson measured and I counted. When the gentlemen had got to their ground, Mr. Hastings asked Mr. Francis if he stood before the line or behind it, and being told behind the mark, he said he would do the same, and immediately took his stand. I then told them it was a rule that neither of them were to quit the ground till they had discharged their pistols, and Colonel Watson proposed that both should fire together without taking any advantage. Mr. Hastings asked if he meant they ought to fire by word of command, and was told he only meant they should fire together as nearly as could be. These preliminaries were all agreed to, and both parties presented; but Mr. Francis raised his hand and again came down to the present; he did so a second time, when he came down to his present—which was the third time of doing so—he drew his trigger, but his powder being damp, the pistol did not fire." One of the jobs of the seconds was to bake the powder for their respective duelists.

The colonel continues: "Mr. Hastings came down from his present to give Mr. Francis time to rectify his priming, and this was done out of a cartridge with which I supplied him upon finding they had no spare powder. [The colonel was *Hastings's* second!] Again the gentlemen took their stands, both presented together and Mr. Francis fired. Mr. Hastings did the same at the distance of time equal to the counting of one, two, three distinctly, but not greater. His shot took place. Mr. Francis staggered, and in attempting to sit down, he fell and said he was a dead man. Mr. Hastings hearing this cried out, 'Good God! I hope not,' and immediately went up to him, as did Colonel Watson, but I ran to call the servants."[32]

Francis was carried to a nearby room in town. Hastings sent his own surgeon to look after his wound. That day Hastings asked to see Francis, but Francis said he would see him only in future Council meetings. Hastings had arranged to turn himself in to Impey for prosecution if, in the course of the duel, he actually killed Francis. When it was over he felt obliged to report it to Laurence Sulivan, who was once again chairman of the Company's directors. He wrote, "I hope Mr. Francis does not think of assuming any merit from this silly affair. I have been ashamed that I have been an actor in it, and I declare to you upon my honour that such was my sense of it at the time, that I was much disturbed by an old woman, whose curiosity prompted her to stand by as a spectator of a scene so little comprehended by the natives of this part of the world, and attracted others of the same stamp from the adjacent villages to partake in the entertainment."[33] His wife, "Marian" as he called her, had gone for a rest in Chinsura, a town upriver from Calcutta. She had not known about the duel. He

Philip Francis, 1810. (Painting by James Lonsdale)

wrote her three letters, two on the day of the duel and the third the next day. That one began, "MY DEAR MARIAN—I have received yours. You must not be angry; perhaps it is best that what has passed has passed, and it may be productive of future good." Hastings's future was to be one of impeachment and disgrace, and Francis would be at the center of it.

Short of one of their deaths, or their recall, it is difficult to see how there could have been anything but an eventual duel between these two men. The remarkable thing is that it took six years from the time of Francis's arrival in Calcutta for it to happen. They were born to be antagonists. Hastings had at his core a block of impenetrable steel. You can see it in his eyes in the paintings done of him after he became governor-general. None of his associates felt they really knew him. Francis was a brilliant dandy. Portraits show him with his aquiline nose sniffing at what he felt was the foul air of India. His nickname was "King Francis." None of his writing tells us anything about the sights and sounds of the India Hastings loved and knew better than almost any man who ever lived. Having them together was like the constant striking of sparks when a hammer hits an anvil. That the ultimate duel took so long to materialize can, I think, be traced to two things. On the one hand, for at least part of the time Francis was part of a majority in the Council that could do pretty much as it liked; and, on the other, even when he was no longer in the majority there was good reason for Francis to believe that Hastings would be recalled.

The first serious attempt to recall Hastings occurred in the spring of 1776. In April an Indiaman arrived in England with the news of Nand Kumar's execution which had occurred the previous August. This seems to have created a scandal. It is not clear why. Probably Francis had persuaded his allies in England that where there was the smoke of Nand Kumar's bribery charges, there must be some fire of truth. In any event, by a vote of 11 to 10 taken on May 9, the Court of Directors of the Company voted to recall both Hastings and Barwell. Parliamentary approval might have been required, but it never came to that, because the Court of Proprietors voted on May 18, by a huge majority of 107, to retain both of them and thus overruled the directors.

It is interesting to note who came to the proprietors' meeting and voted for Hastings. There were several members of Parliament, all of whom had financial stake in the Company. Among them was Charles Watson-Wentworth, the second Marquis of Rockingham. He had inherited his father's title in 1750 and the next year took his seat in the House of Lords as a Whig. Like North's father, Rockingham controlled a number of parliamentary seats. Their occupants were known as the "Rockingham Whigs," the most famous of whom was Edmund Burke, who had been Rockingham's secretary. Ultimately the Rockingham Whigs, most of whom did not come from Rockingham's pocket boroughs, came to dominate the party. While not (at least not yet) proposing independence for the American colonies, all during this period the Rockingham Whigs opposed North's government's hard-line policy toward them. These Whigs were anathema to the king, who wanted the American war pursued at any cost. Later they would be the engine that drove the Hastings impeachment trial.

But Rockingham, like Burke, had a financial stake in the Company's prosperity in India. The blood of money—as it often does—ran thicker than the water of high principle, so, Nand Kumar or not, they voted for Hastings as the best person available to maintain their investment. When news of the proprietors' vote in support of Hastings got back to India, Monson and Clavering prepared to resign. But before that happened, Monson was dead.

His death occurred on September 25, 1776. One of the first things Hastings did, now that he had the deciding vote in the Council, was to begin promoting the young people whose careers he had developed—and whom the majority had kept from advancing because they were "Hastings's people." Bogle, for example, was now appointed to an office that was to examine the status of expiring leases on land in the provinces. In early November he was able to write his father that "It is a work which will engross my whole time, and require my greatest exertions to execute my part in it."[34] On the larger issues, however, Hastings had decided to proceed cautiously. By this time he was well aware that the Court of Directors had voted for his recall and that Lord North's government was under pressure to keep a restraining eye on the Company's activities in India. Indeed, on September 26, the day after Monson died, Hastings wrote a letter to North which begins, "My Lord—It is my duty to give your Lordship the earliest information that Colonel Monson departed this life at Hugly yesterday evening after a severe illness of more than two months.

"This event has thrown me into a situation which, while our disputes [Hastings's disputes with the Council majority] in England remain undecided, I could have wished to avoid. It has restored to me that constitutional authority of my station; but without absolute necessity I shall not think it proper to use it with that effect which I should give it were I sure of support from home. Thus circumstanced it is my wish to let the affairs of this government remain in their present channels, and to avoid alterations which in the course of a few months may possibly be subject to new changes, and introduce weakness and distraction into the state. This line I am resolved to follow as far as it depends on myself, but much will depend on the incidents of business, and on the temper of my associates. I should dissemble with your Lordship were I to pretend to be insensible of the injuries which I have received. These, however, shall not break in upon the line of my public duty. The long course of business in which I have been engaged, and the various, and often divided councils in which I have sat have taught me moderation, and I believe few men can easier govern their resentments than I can, or totally sacrifice them to the interests of the public...."[35] One wonders what North made of the last sentence, if he read it.

Hastings was, of course, also aware that as soon as word of Monson's death reached London a replacement would be named. Depending on who it was, Hastings's situation might change dramatically. He might once again find himself in an embattled minority. On the day he wrote to North, he also wrote to one of his agents in London, John Graham: "My dear Sir, —An event which has been expected these three weeks is at length come to pass, and has occasioned a kind of revolution in our Council. Colonel Monson, after an illness of ten weeks, died last night, and a letter has been written to the Court of Directors to advise them of it. They, I suppose, will receive it in the month of March, while Parliament is sitting, and in the height of their own despatches. Of course I conclude that an immediate choice will be made of a successor to fill up the vacancy, and I much fear, from its being made at such a time, that it may prove equal to a decision against me. It will be impossible to nominate a neutral man, and I have no ground to hope that the appointment will fall on any friend of mine. If it should, there will be an end put at once to all contention, the majority being so clear on the side which ought constitutionally to take the lead. If a friend of Clavering's is sent out to reinforce his party, I must in that case either quit the field, or resolve to remain and have new warfare perhaps more violent than the last encounter. The first is a wretched expedient, which I will never submit to. Having gone through two years of persecution, I am determined now that no less authority than the King's express act shall remove me, or death...."[36]

This letter, as Hastings suggested, would arrive only the following March. To understand the somewhat confused sequence of events that followed, a kind of chronological tour is necessary. What makes this material difficult to follow—indeed, what makes biographies of Hastings and other figures in this story difficult to follow—is not only the unfamiliarity of the material but the time delays of many months while different actors on different continents were playing out their dramas, unaware that they were often working at cross-purposes to one another.*

In August 1775 Nand Kumar was executed. News of this, when it reached London in April 1776, prompted the directors to vote for Hastings's recall, which was overturned by the proprietors. It also caused North to decide that this kind of factionalism in the Council in India could not go on, and that one side or the other would have to leave the scene. But Hastings's agents in London, Graham and MacLeane, had a letter from him that seemed to authorize them to tender Hastings's resignation under suitable, though not very well-defined, circumstances.

Thus in late summer, sensing this might be a good moment to offer Hastings's resignation, MacLeane opened negotiations with the Company. The object, of which Hastings was totally unaware, was to secure the most favorable terms for Hastings in return for his agreement to resign. These would include, MacLeane assumed, an honor from the government (perhaps an eventual peerage) as well as suitable recompense from the Company in the way of a retirement pension. When asked by what authority he was acting, MacLeane produced Hastings's letter, which, under the circumstances, the directors were only too happy to accept without further examination. The letter, as we saw, was scarcely a formal resignation, but that did not seem to trouble the directors. They immediately nominated Edward Wheler, who at one time had been chairman of the Court of Directors, to succeed Hastings. None of the parties had any idea that, in September, Monson had died and that as a consequence Hastings's whole situation had changed.

When the gazette announcing Wheler's appointment to succeed Hastings appeared, it also contained an announcement that *Clavering* had been awarded the Order of the Bath, the very sort of honor that MacLeane assumed would be given to Hastings. Thus

---

*In our "information age" it is difficult for us to recreate what this must have meant. I, for one, find myself often saying—absurdly—why don't they just pick up the phone and talk things over? The modern equivalent might be that of space travelers in the far reaches of outer space receiving communications from Earth about events that occurred months, or years, or even decades, earlier.

MacLeane, feeling he had been double-crossed, wrote immediately to Hastings to tell him *not* to resign. Of course, Hastings was totally unaware that he *had* resigned.

This takes us to the spring of 1777. By that time, news of Monson's death had reached London. Being unsure of what this meant with respect to his status, Wheler had himself reappointed as *Monson's* successor rather than Hastings's. In May he set sail for India on the *Duke of Portland*. By the time he got there, there had been further dramatic changes.

During the spring of 1777 Clavering's behavior appeared to grow more and more erratic. He was not well, and at times his body was covered with boils. Hastings's relations with Francis, whom he referred to as "This man of levity . . . this vilest fetcher and carrier of tales . . . without one generous or manly principle,"[37] were growing, if anything, worse. In June the dispatches finally reached Calcutta from London with the news that Hastings had "resigned" and that Wheler had been appointed. In mid-June, Clavering, who had temporarily left Calcutta for his health, received urgent word from Francis to return.

The dispatches announcing Hastings's resignation seemed to give Francis and Clavering a green light, so on Friday, June 20, Clavering declared himself governor-general. He summoned Barwell to a meeting of the new Council. He also addressed a note to "Warren Hastings Esquire," ordering him to surrender the keys of the Treasury and the fort by noon. Barwell refused the summons, and Hastings consulted with his loyal young colleagues, including Bogle, as to what should now be done. The first step was to contact the officers of the Company's army to instruct them to obey no orders but those of Hastings. It is a measure of the loyalty that the army felt for Hastings that, despite the fact that Clavering was its commander-in-chief, they stood firmly behind Hastings. The next step was to ask the judges of the Supreme Court to adjudicate the dispute. This put into play the full ambiguity of North's Judicature Act. Push had now truly come to shove. Hastings said he would abide by the decision of the court; Francis, who probably figured that one way or another Hastings would be gone soon, persuaded Clavering to do likewise.

The justices met in the evening at Impey's house. The next morning they delivered their unanimous verdict that Hastings had not resigned and was still governor-general—or at least that Clavering was not governor-general. They argued that the letter Hastings had written to his agents in London did not constitute a letter of resignation but rather an expression of possible intent, given a certain set of circumstances—and now the circumstances had changed.

On June 29 Hastings wrote a most remarkable long letter to North, stating the situation graphically. The second paragraph begins:

"By letters received from my confidential friends in England, I have been informed that Colonel MacLeane had made a declaration in writing to the Court of Directors of my desire to resign the government, that this offer had been accepted, and that Mr. Wheler had in consequence been nominated to succeed to the seat of the youngest councillor [in terms of seniority and not age] whenever it should become vacant by my actual resignation, and that his nomination had received the final sanction which the law required of his Majesty's approval. It was added that one condition of this accommodation, made with your Lordship's knowledge and participation, was that the time of my resignation was left to my own choice."

The letter then goes on to discuss the "unexampled and extravagant conduct" of General Clavering. "Instead of waiting for the natural period of its [Hastings's supposed resignation] accomplishment, and without any intimation to me of his intention, he at once attempted to seize the government by force, took possession of the council-chamber, demanded from me the keys of the fort and treasuries, took the oath of Governor-general, held a Council as such with Mr. Francis, and I presume would have proceeded to the last extremities of violence, had not the timely measures which were taken by myself and Mr. Barlow entirely disabled him; for he had written and signed a letter to the commandant of the fort requiring his obedience, a proclamation was written and formally recorded on their proceedings notifying his admission to the government, and a resolution to send them with circular letters to all the commandants of the military stations and to the Provincial Councils."

In short, all the elements were in place for a civil war. Hastings then describes how the justices were consulted, noting that in the last analysis it was their superiors in England who must ultimately resolve this conflict. He goes on, "This, my Lord, is an epitome of the transactions of this Government during a convulsion of four days, which might have shaken the very foundation of the national power and interests in India; nor is it yet safe. The spark of sedition, though latent, will break out, and with a blaze, which the same prudence, the same vigilance, and moderation may prove ineffectual to extinguish."

He now explains the circumstances of his "resignation." "My Lord, I was not pleased with the engagement made for me by Mr. MacLeane; I will candidly own. But I held myself bound to it, and was resolved to ratify it. This was my resolution; but General Clavering himself has defeated it, by the attempt to wrest from me by violence what he could claim only as a voluntary surrender, by persisting in asserting his pretensions to all rights and functions of my office from a time already passed, and independent of my option; and by his incapacity to possess the government, after having by his own acts and declarations vacated the place from which alone he could legally ascend to it.

"Thus, circumstanced, I think myself not merely absolved from this obligation which has been imposed on me, but bound by every tie of duty to retain my ground, until I can honourably quit it. . . ."

The letter ends with a two-paragraph *cri de coeur*. "I do not expect to be confirmed by this government," Hastings writes. "I have long since given over all hopes of it. Let me be removed from it, but suffer me not, my Lord, to be dragged from it like a felon, after the labour of seven and twenty years dedicated to the service of the Company and the aggrandizement of the British dominion.

"And now forgive me, my Lord, if I may appear to have expressed myself with a warmth either unbecoming an address to your Lordship, or inconsistent with the temperance of my own character. What I have written, I have written from my heart, not heated by resentment, but warmed with the conscious sense of my own integrity, and with respect for your Lordship which I shall ever retain, because I am assured that if I must suffer injustice from the hands of others I shall yet obtain every relief from you, which it shall be in your power to afford me. I have the honour to be, with the greatest respect, my Lord, your most obedient and most humble servant."[38]

By the time North received this letter, General John Burgoyne had surrendered his British troops in Saratoga on October 17, and war with the French was under way. North must have had other things on his mind than a factional quarrel in Calcutta. He also would not have known about another event—the death of Clavering—which had occurred that summer. This is described in a letter that Bogle sent his father. He writes, "You will have learnt the consequences which the unexpected accounts of Mr. Hastings' resignation produced in this settlement; the assumption of the government by General Clavering; the refusal of Mr. Hastings to relinquish it; the appeal of both parties to the Judges; their opinion in favour of Mr. Hastings; the General's suspension of his claim; the apparent quiet that succeeded, and, finally, the death of General Clavering, on the 30th of August. This event has relieved Mr. Hastings from a great part of the opposition to which he had so long been exposed. How far it will give stability to his government must depend on the supreme power in England. Independent of partiality, if I can divest myself of it, I hope for the sake of the British nation, that Mr. Hastings will be confirmed and his hand strengthened. He is possessed of talents which it may be difficult to equal, and of a mind more just and disinterested than is commonly to be found in a man who has passed so many years in public business. The remaining member of the majority, Mr. Francis, is of a more pliant discipline than General Clavering, and regulates his conduct more from policy and less from passion."

In a final gesture of animosity, Clavering had left instructions that in case of his death Hastings was not to be informed until after he was buried. Bogle lived a year past the time that Hastings and Francis fought their duel. One wonders if he had changed his mind about the "pliant discipline" of Francis.

IV: THE DUELS

On January 10, 1784, Hastings's beloved "Marian" set sail for England on the Indiaman *Atlas*. Hastings described why in a letter to Major John Scott, his new representative in England—the replacement for the unfortunate Colonel MacLeane. He wrote, "Mrs. Hastings's declining health required her instant departure. She was not afflicted with any severe attack of sickness in the last rainy season, but I was alarmed with daily symptoms, and could only attribute her escape [from severe illness] to the weakness, not to the strength of her constitution. I was told too, that another season might prove fatal to her. I consented to part from her, nay, I urged her departure, nor even in the painful hour of trial do I repent it. I will follow her within the present year, nor shall any consideration detain me beyond it. Indeed my own constitution is much impaired, and I shall expect another attack in the next rains, though I shall be as much as possible upon my guard against it."[39]

By the next day the full impact of her departure had hit him, and he wrote her a letter which he hoped somehow might reach her ship before it left the Cape of Good Hope. He writes, "MY BELOVED WIFE— . . . I left you yesterday morning. I followed your ship with my eyes till I could no longer see it [Hastings had accompanied his wife downriver as far as the sea], and I passed a most wretched day with a heart swol'n with affliction, and a head raging with pain. I have been three tides making this place, where I met my budgerow [a type of oared vessel with cabins that plied the Indian rivers], and in it a severe renewal of my sorrow. The instant sight of the cabbin [sic], every object in it, and beyond it, brought my dear Marian to my imagination, with the deadly reflexion that she was then more than 200 miles removed from me, and still receding to a distance which seems, in my estimation, infinite and irretrievable. In the heavy interval which I have passed, I have had but too much leisure to contemplate the wretchedness of my situation, and to regret (forgive me, my dearest Marian, I cannot help it) that I ever consented to your leaving me. It appears to me like a precipitate act of the grossest folly; for what have I to look forward to but an age of separation, and if ever we are to meet again, to carry home to you a burthen of infirmities, and a mind soured, perhaps with long and unabated vexation. Nor is it for myself alone I feel, though I have been possibly more occupied than I ought to have been by the contemplation and sensation of my own suffering. . . . Yesterday, as I lay upon my bed, and but half asleep, I felt a sensation like the fingers of your hand gently moving over my face and neck, and could have sworn that I heard your voice. O that I could be sure of such an illusion as often as I lay down! And the reality seems to me an illusion. Yesterday morning I held in my arms all that my heart holds dear, and now she is separated from me as if she had no longer existence. O my Marian! I am wretched; and I shall make you so when you read this. Yet I know not why, I must let it go; nor can I add anything to alleviate which I have written; but that I love you more by far than life, for I would not live but in the hope of being once more united to you. O God grant it! and grant my deserving my blessed Marian['s] fortitude to bear what I myself bear so ill, conduct her in health and safety to the termination of her voyage, and once more restore her to me with everything that can render our meeting completely happy. Amen, amen, amen, Yours ever, ever affectionate, W. HASTINGS."[40]

One of the reasons that Hastings was so concerned about his wife's voyage is that when she left India she was pregnant. She wrote him on August 3, just after her safe arrival in England, that she had had a miscarriage. When he received her letter telling him of this, he replied on December 26, "My beloved Marian,—I have received your letter of the 3rd August informing me of your safe arrival in England. . . . Whether I was happy or unhappy in reading it I cannot tell you. I fear my disappointment on one subject equaled my joy for your safety, the close of your perils, and the promise that you would soon be as well as you ever had been at any period of your life. . . ."[41] The Hastings never succeeded in having children of their own.

The period from the death of Clavering in August 1777 until February 3, 1785, when Hastings left India for the last time, was the most complex of his entire service. It was a time when the British came close to losing their foothold in that country. It was a time when Hastings made a number of decisions and took a number of actions that certainly saved the British Raj but which, in the years that followed, cost him dearly. In order to trace these out, we must look more carefully at the other British enclaves in India—Bombay and Madras and their surroundings, and Fort St. David, near the French settlement at Pondicherry, which was more readily defensible than Madras. The Company had occupied Fort St. David since 1688. It is remarkable, incidentally, that if one compares British India in, say, 1769, when Hastings returned to Madras, to 1785, when he left the country, there is almost no change in the territories the British occupied. The great expansion came in the next century. Hastings's concern was to hold on to what the British had.

As noted earlier, the island on which Bombay was built had been ceded to Charles II by the Portuguese as part of Catherine of Braganza's Indian dowry. It was then acquired by the Company. By the mid-eighteenth century the authorities in Bombay had begun seriously eyeing the neighboring island of Salsette (where the present Bombay international airport is located). The only value of this island was strategic. (One could, in the same vein, argue that the only value of Bombay was its harbor. During this period it was the least economically productive of the Company's enclaves.) Salsette was the last stepping-stone to the mainland territory of the Marathas, whose capital, Poona, was not far to the southeast on the Deccan Plateau. In principle the government in Bombay was subservient to the Council in Calcutta, but because of the distances involved the Bombay government could engage in independent activities without the authorities in Calcutta being aware of it for some time. In this instance the government concluded a treaty with a disaffected Maratha pretender to the throne in Poona named Raghunath Rao, who was generally known as Ragoba. In return for helping Ragoba reclaim his throne, he would cede, once it was conquered, Salsette to the British. But the Bombay government jumped the gun and occupied Salsette immediately upon signing the treaty.

At the end of May 1775 the Council in Calcutta, in a rare show of unanimity, upon learning of the treaty ordered that it be abrogated. Hastings wanted to give the government in Bombay some discretion in implementing this retreat so that it could be achieved without a total loss of face, while the majority, which prevailed, wanted it to be abrogated unconditionally. In any case, this difference turned out to be academic since, unaccountably, the Company in England overruled the Calcutta Council, and two years later even renewed the treaty with Ragoba. It is also remarkable that the directors approved the provision in the treaty that required the Company to furnish a minimum of 2,500 soldiers in return for a guarantee by Ragoba that he would pay for their maintenance. This was the very sort of arrangement that had led to British participation in the Rohilla War, for which Hastings and the Company had been soundly rebuked. One wonders whether the directors in London, 15,000 miles away, had a clear idea of the Marathas' military power. This was not an ineffective band of Afghan marauders but a major military establishment. As it turned out, Ragoba was a fragile reed on which to lean. The impending disaster became evident early in 1778 when the Marathas were able to enlist French officers to command their troops, now that the British and French were once again at war with each other in Europe.

On December 11, 1777, when the new councillor Edward Wheler arrived in Calcutta, both Hastings and Francis attempted to coopt him. The efforts included even a Christmas dinner served by Marian—then a relatively new bride—which was attended by all the principals. With characteristic grace, Francis described it as a "wretched shabby dinner."[42] Hastings had hoped for Wheler's neutrality, but it soon became clear that he and Francis would vote in a bloc against Hastings and Barwell, with Hastings having the deciding vote.

An immediate issue over which the Council split was the course of action with respect to Bombay. While Hastings thought that Bombay had enough in the way of forces to defend itself from the most likely assault by the Marathas, which he was sure would come by land and not sea, some sixth sense told him that the colony would nonetheless be in deep trouble. He proposed to send reinforcements from Bengal.

The conventional way to have done this was by sea. Hastings had a different idea: he would send the reinforcing army overland. If you look at the map of India you will find Bombay southwest of Calcutta on the opposite coast. If you draw a straight line from Calcutta to Bombay you will see, more or less, the route Hastings was suggesting. It is about a thousand miles long but considerably shorter than the sea route. It ran through territory, however, that no British army—quite possibly no European—had ever entered. This fact certainly must have appealed to Hastings. It did not appeal to Francis and Wheler. Apart from the route, Francis thought such an invasion could be considered an act of aggression which might provoke a confrontation with the Marathas and their French allies. Hastings, on the other hand, wanted this confrontation to take place sooner rather than later, when the French-Maratha alliance would be still more powerful. And he had the deciding vote. So by late spring of 1778 an army of six thousand sepoys, under the command of one Colonel Leslie, was on the march toward Bombay.

Colonel Leslie and his column ambled at a leisurely pace across India. The officers in the field were served by a vast array of bearers, animal and human. There was no common mess, so each officer had his own supply of table linen as well as stocks of wine, brandy, and gin and a hamper of live chickens. He also had a barber, a grass-cutter, and a cook.[43] For a brief moment it looked as if the Marathas might not attack, so the Council in Bombay tried, unsuccessfully, to flag Leslie off. By June, news of Burgoyne's surrender at Saratoga reached Calcutta. Francis felt that Leslie's troops should be recalled for the eventual defense of Bengal. Hastings disagreed. He felt that Bengal was in no immediate danger and that now it was more imperative than ever to show the British flag in India. All during this period he regarded it as part of his mission to balance the losses Britain was suffering in America by retaining its hold in India.

In the first week of July, news came via the Suez overland route that France and Britain were now at war, and a little later there was news that the French were sending an armada east. Hastings reacted by seizing the French outpost at Chandernagore. Its governor, Chevalier, the very man in whose mansion Mr. Grand had met his future wife, and who was now apparently plotting with the elements of the French in the south, escaped southward. He was later captured and returned to Calcutta. Hastings also ordered the army at Madras to begin an attempt to take Pondicherry. Calcutta was placed on a wartime basis with an increase in the number of sepoys and the raising of a volunteer militia of a thousand Europeans.

Some months passed while Colonel Leslie seemed to be getting no closer to Bombay. The Council unanimously voted to replace him, but before the order could be served, Leslie took ill and died. He was replaced by his second-in-command, a Lieutenant Colonel Goddard, whom Hastings regarded as one of the best officers in the army. Goddard was instructed to proceed west, obeying no one's orders except those that came from Calcutta.

Meanwhile the authorities in Bombay, contrary to every instruction, decided to make a unilateral attempt to restore Ragoba to the throne he claimed was his. They launched an invasion into the rugged, hilly Maratha territory with a force of five hundred Europeans and two thousand sepoys. These were supported by a herd of nineteen thousand bullocks.*

Twenty-five hundred soldiers was an absurdly small invasion force against the Marathas. The assumption was that the local population would arise to embrace Ragoba. It did nothing of the sort. The expedition was doomed from the start.

The Marathas made a strategic retreat toward Poona, burning everything in their path to keep it from being used by the British. It was a trap, and when the British were some sixteen miles from Poona they found themselves surrounded by an army of fifty thousand Marathas. The only issues to be disputed were the terms of surrender. On January 17, 1779, the British signed the so-called Convention of Wargaum. This restored all the territory they had seized and also handed over Ragoba. In addition, two British hostages were taken. What was left of the army was allowed to return to Bombay. In the treaty the British also agreed to the retreat of Goddard's advancing army. When Hastings heard of the defeat and the treaty he was both furious and mortified. His response was to order Goddard to march as rapidly as possible toward the coast. His army covered the last three hundred miles through difficult territory in twenty days, arriving in late February 1779 at the coastal town of Surat, north of Bombay. This extraordinary feat of British arms appeared to have impressed the Marathas. They made no attempt to attack, and Bombay was saved.

---

*These transport animals in the thousands were a fixed feature of all the British wars in India. They hauled field pieces, ammunition, and supplies. "Bullock contracts" were a big business. Hastings was later accused of showing various kinds of nepotism in awarding these very lucrative contracts.

༄

THE COUNCILLOR who replaced Clavering played a key role in the events at Madras. He had the remarkable name of Eyre Coote, and when he arrived in Calcutta in March 1779 he was Lieutenant General Sir Eyre Coote and had been appointed commander-in-chief of the army. Coote, the son of a clergyman, was born in 1726 near Limerick, Ireland. The army was his life. He became a captain of the first British regiment (as opposed to the private Company army) to be sent to India, in 1756. After Clive, he was arguably the most distinguished British officer in the subcontinent. Following the battle of Plassey, he led a detachment of troops who pursued the French for four hundred miles. He was said to have been lean and lantern-jawed and greatly admired by his men. In 1761 he was put in command of the army in Bengal, but the next year he returned to England. In 1769 he was once again back in India, again in command of the army. But he soon quarreled with the authorities and again returned to England. His personal behavior had struck a negative chord with Hastings. In February 1772 he had written to Laurence Sulivan, "Your sentiments with respect to General Coote's powers, though such as I expected, afforded me great satisfaction. May success and honour attend him in any other part of the world, but God forbid that he should ever return to any part of India again." Coote was childish and irascible, as well as vain and venal, and now, in 1779, he was back in Bengal. But this time Hastings was desperately in need of Coote's military expertise. The situation in Madras was turning catastrophic, and Hastings was determined to do whatever was necessary to keep the general happy.

Lining Coote's pockets was essential. Hastings arranged a special field allowance for him which brought his annual salary up to eighteen thousand pounds, much more than any other councillor had ever been paid, including Clavering.*

---

*This later became an issue in the impeachment trial. At one point in the trial Hastings explained to the Lords sitting in judgment, "My Lords, it was impossible for Sir Eyre Coote's allowance to be settled *at home* to be sufficient in the field, if the same sum was not too much for General Clavering in Calcutta. . . ." He had earlier noted, with some derision, that General Clavering had never left Calcutta to go into the field with the army. He then concluded by saying, "But my Lords, it was not a

Coote appeared determined to stay out of the factional politics that had split the Council. His concern was with its military affairs. This seemed to unnerve Francis, who now also realized that he would not become governor-general when Hastings left. He turned some of his venom on Coote. "I despise him from the bottom of my spirit," he wrote, "and the moment it is in my power I shall treat the wretch as he deserves."[45] With even the best of intentions, Hastings found Coote all but impossible to deal with. Soon after Coote's arrival he wrote to a colleague, "Sir E. Coote quarreled with me. I made no return. He became when we met my fast friend, and has broke out into violent invective against me since, and upon my honor I know not for what cause. . . . This I know, that it is absolutely impossible for him to be on terms of peace with any man living who possesses a power either superior or equal to his own, unless the latter is forever at his elbow, and coaxing him into good humor. If you doubt this, try him, and you will be convinced." As if this were not enough, Barwell had announced that he intended to resign and return to England. His health had not been good. His young wife had died, and the news from England indicated there would once again be drastic changes in how the Company was run. Barwell's resignation would have meant—with Coote's abstention in all but military matters—that Hastings would once again have been in the minority on the Council. It took all of Hastings's powers of persuasion to persuade Barwell to stay on, at least until the matters involving Madras could be decided.

The problems Hastings faced in dealing with these circumstances would have overwhelmed anyone else. In the first place there were the Marathas. Part of the British agreement with them involved giving up Ragoba. Hastings had no problem with this. The trouble was that Ragoba had escaped and sought asylum with the British. The Marathas regarded this as a breach of their understanding and were again on the warpath. To this end they sent envoys to try to form an alliance with that archnemesis of the British in the south, Hyder Ali, who it may be recalled had come close to capturing Madras some years before. To make matters worse, the governor of Madras, one

time to cavil with Sir Eyre Coote about field allowances: I never was more convinced of the truth of any hypothesis than of this; namely, that if Sir Eyre Coote had resigned in disgust, which he might have done, the Carnatic [the region of India that included Madras] had been infallibly lost to this country, *for ever.*"[44]

Thomas Rumbold, chose this time to alienate the nawab on whose territory Madras rested by entering into a negotiation with the nawab's brother on matters of close concern to the nawab without either informing him or, indeed, the governor's nominal superiors in Calcutta. Thus the nawab too wanted the British out of Madras. Added to this was the fact that the French fleet was expected off the coast at any time, and the directors in London were issuing mutually conflicting instructions which, in any event, often arrived after the fact. By this time Hastings had concluded that nothing he did would pacify the directors, so he decided to ignore them. This conglomeration of unfavorable events provoked Hastings into taking rash actions. The most significant involved, on the one hand, Francis, and on the other, money—money to fight the war. First Francis.

∽

HASTINGS REALIZED that Barwell really wanted to leave. He decided that the only way this could happen without destroying his authority to fight the war was to come to an accommodation with Francis. To this end, in January 1780 he began negotiations with Francis through intermediaries. This resulted in a dinner for the two principals on February 4, which Marian hosted. Terms were put into writing, though they were never converted into a formal document signed by both parties. The essence was that Francis would give Hastings carte blanche in fighting the war, and, in return, Francis would be allowed to appoint a number of his own people to various lucrative positions of patronage. The spirit in which Francis entered the agreement can be gathered from a letter he wrote: "When I speak of a pacification with Mr. Hastings," he notes, "I mean literally what I say. It is *not* a union. It is *not* an alliance. . . . In short, it is more like an armed truce than anything else; for it is to endure no longer than October next."[46] The Company's charter was to expire in October 1780, and Parliament would once again have to take up the entire matter of its governance. It is not clear that Hastings acknowledged a time limit to his agreement with Francis. In the event, it was academic, for that August they fought the duel that could well have killed one or both of them.

Soon after this agreement was drawn up, Barwell resigned and departed for England. This meant that Hastings now depended entirely on Francis's word that he would stay out of military affairs. Things started well. Goddard had made good progress against the Marathas. Hastings's idea was to give the Marathas enough of a fight so that he could come to some accommodation with them and head off their alliance with Hyder Ali. But by May, as the season in Calcutta grew hotter and as both men had problems with their health, the inevitable began. By June, Francis was taking the position that there should be no military expeditions beyond Bengal, something that Hastings regarded as a clear violation of their understanding. By July, Hastings had decided that he would have to kill Francis—or die trying. This plan he kept to himself. He told no one, above all not his wife, who in early August he escorted to Chinsura for a small respite from the weather in Calcutta. On the evening of August 14, Francis was handed a copy of a minute that Hastings would present formally to the Council the next day. It read in part,

"I did hope that the intimation conveyed in my last minute would have awakened in Mr. Francis's breast, if he were susceptible of such sensations, a consciousness of the faithless part which he was acting towards me. I have been disappointed, and must now assume a plainer style, and a louder tone. In a word, my objections do not lie in the special matter of his minutes, to which I shall separately reply, but to the spirit of opposition which dictated them. I have lately offered various plans for the operations of the war. These have been successively rejected as I have successively amended and endeavoured to accommodate them to Mr. Francis's objections. I had a right to his implicit acquiescence. I have lately proposed a service requiring immediate execution, and I have freed from it the only objection formally made to it. In truth, I do not trust to his promise of candor, convinced that he is incapable of it, and that his sole purpose and wish are to embarrass and defeat every measure which I may undertake, or which may tend even to promote the public interests, if my credit is connected with them. Such has been the tendency and such the manifest spirit of all his actions from the beginning. Every fabricated tale of armies devoted to famine or to massacre have found their first and ready way to his office, where it was known they would

meet the most welcome reception. To the same design may be attributed the annual computations of declining finances and an exhausted
treasury, computations which, though made in the time of abun-
dance, must verge to truth at last, from the effect of discordant government, not a constitutional decay."

He goes on, "I judge of his public conduct by my experience of
his private, which I have found to be void of truth and honor. This is
a severe charge, but temperately and deliberately made from the firm
persuasion that I owe this justice to the public and to myself, as the
only redress to both, for artifices of which I have been a victim, and
which threaten to involve their interests, with disgrace and ruin. The
only redress for a fraud for which the law had made no provisions is
the exposure of it. . . ."[47]

It is important to emphasize that this was an official document
once it was presented to the Council, and not some sort of private
reprimand. Hastings wanted this document to serve as an unavoidable challenge to Francis's honor. He would either have to confront it
or leave India branded as a coward. In fact, after the Council meeting
of the 15th, Francis took Hastings aside privately and challenged him
to a duel. This became the duel the two men fought on the morning
of August 17th. Hastings was quite prepared to die in it. Indeed, on
the 16th he had written a letter to his wife which was to be delivered
to her only in the event he was killed. It read,

"MY BELOVED MARIAN,

My heart bleeds to think what your sufferings and feelings must
be, if ever this letter shall be delivered into your hands. You will soon
learn the occasion of it. On my part it has been unavoidable. I shall
leave nothing which I regret to lose but you, nor in my last moments
shall I feel any other affliction. Let it be a consolation to you to know
that at this moment I have the most grateful sense of all your past
kindnesses, and of the unremitted proofs which you have daily and
hourly afforded me of your affection. For these may God reward you!
I know not how. How much I have loved you, He only knows. Do
not, my Marian, forget me; but cherish my remembrance to the latest
hour of your life, as I should yours were it my lot, and my misery to
survive you. I cannot write all that I feel and that my heart is full of.

"Adieu, my best wife, and most beloved of women. May the God of Heaven bless you and support you. My last thoughts will be employed on you. Remember and love me. Once more farewell.

Your

WARREN HASTINGS."[48]

The original of this letter—which ends with a P.S. instructing Marian as to where she may find his will—is preserved in the British Library. As one looks at its darkened sweeps and occasional emendations, one can only wonder what sort of consolation it would have been had it ever been delivered.

Immediately after the duel, Francis wrote to his friends in England. If his letter had genuinely reflected a change of mind, it might have made a difference in the events that were to unfold in the next decade. He wrote, "I consider this event as a quietus to all personal hostility between Mr. H, and me, and I desire that you and all my friends *will speak and act accordingly.* This injunction goes to everything. It would be irregular and unbecoming in me *now*, as well as useless in every respect, to suffer the public quarrel to lead me into anything that could bear the appearance of personal animosity to him. Let him be condemned or acquitted by the evidence that exists of his whole conduct. As I lay bleeding on the ground and when I thought the wound was mortal, I gave him my hand in token of forgiveness. From that moment to the end of my life, I am neither his friend nor his foe."[49]

One wonders how calculated the hypocrisy in this letter was. To mention only one item, recall it was *Francis* who refused Hastings's offer of a visit after the duel. A month later Francis was again attending Council meetings and again attempting to interfere with Hastings's prosecution of the war. But by this time events on the ground had taken precedence. While the British were doing well in their war with the Marathas in the west, Hyder Ali was laying waste to the Carnatic, the gateway to Madras. It was clear—at least to everyone but Francis—that the only hope was to send reinforcements from Bengal. Thus, when this matter came before the Council, both Eyre Coote and Wheler voted in favor of it. This turned Francis against Wheler, whom he now accused of being Hastings's dupe. In early October, Francis decided to resign, sending a letter to the directors which stated that only he and Clavering had kept the peace in India, a peace that Hastings was in the process of destroying. *Après moi, le déluge.* In December he left India forever and returned to England to begin his campaign to destroy Hastings.

But before leaving, Francis had one more opportunity to cause trouble. The problem that arose was once again related to the imprecision in North's Judicature Act. It nearly destroyed the friendship between Hastings and Impey. The question, which had been simmering under the surface for some time, was the proper domain of the Supreme Court. This was never spelled out clearly in the act, probably because North and his advisers had relatively little understanding of actual circumstances in India. Thus the court began taking jurisdiction over matters that the Council felt belonged to it. The court had been created to function with justices appointed by the crown and not by the Company; its primary function was to administer justice to servants of the Company. It was not supposed to have police power. But at this time a number of the Company's tax collectors were getting out of hand. It was clear that something had to be done about this, and without consulting the Council, the Court began arresting people, something it had no authority to do. This produced a situation of near anarchy which threatened to paralyze the government. Hastings was forced to take a strong position in opposition to Impey. This disturbed him so greatly that he wrote to Laurence Sulivan, "I suffer beyond measure by the present contest, and my spirits are at times so depressed as to affect my health. I feel an injury done me by a man for whom I have borne a sincere and steady friendship during more than thirty years, and to whose support I was at one time indebted for the safety of my fortune, honour, and reputation, with a ten-fold sensibility."[50]

Some commentators have taken this as a reference to Impey's role in the Nand Kumar trial and have used it to link Hastings and Impey in this affair. More likely it refers to Impey's role in suppressing Clavering's attempt to take over the government. In any event, Hastings continues his letter without adumbrating: "And under every consciousness of the necessity which has influenced my own conduct, and the temper with which I have regulated it, I am ready to pass the most painful reproaches on myself on the least symptom of returning kindness from him. . . . We are both of us unhappily situated and associated; myself linked in the same cause with a man equally his enemy and mine. . . ." This last is presumably a reference to Francis.

To deal with this crisis, Hastings proposed a unification of the criminal and civil courts with the chief justice, whomever he might be, administering the whole apparatus. He also commissioned Impey to begin formulating the jurisdictions that would govern the court and the Council. All of this required a vote of the Council, and even with such a vote it was not clear that a plan could be made consistent with the Judicature Act. The Council vote was split, with Francis and Wheler voting against, Coote voting for, and Hastings casting the deciding vote. One of the features of this expanded position for the chief justice was an expanded salary. Impey, knowing there had been opposition to this in the Council, decided not to begin collecting the added salary until he had explicit written approval from the Company in London. This turned out to be irrelevant, because in 1781, the year following this debate in the Council, Parliament amended North's Regulating Act. In 1782 Impey was recalled and an impeachment process, in good measure fueled by Francis, was begun. It failed, but the issues had their resonance in Hastings's own impeachment trial. The restructuring of the court that Impey had begun to formalize took place only in the middle of the next century.

MONEY TO FIGHT THE WAR was Hastings's other chief problem. It will be recalled that the Council had voted to send a relief army to Madras to try to save it. This would cost money—tens of thousands of pounds to pay the sepoys, who were after all mercenary soldiers, to say nothing of all their supplies and transport—those thousands of bullocks. Hastings's government simply did not have the money at hand, and there were no prospects of getting it from the Company in London. Hence the governor-general resorted to measures that were debatable and, indeed, have been debated ever since.

The first measure involved a nawab Chait Singh and took place in the city of Benares. Benares, on the Ganges River, was, and is, in a sense the religious capital of India. It lay to the west of Bengal and thus outside the territory of the Company. Nonetheless, because it was a gateway to Bengal, it held immense strategic importance for the Company, and it was essential that the Company remain on good terms with its ruler. From 1738 to 1770 the ruler had been a man named Balwant Singh. Nominally he was a vassal of the nawab of Oudh, but in practice he functioned as an independent entity. When Balwant Singh died he was succeeded by his son, Chait Singh. In 1775 the nawab of Oudh, Shuja-ud-Daula (the man for whom the British had launched the Rohilla War), died, and the Council decided that its arrangement with him for the governance of Benares had died with him. A new arrangement would have to be negotiated. Over Hastings's objections, the Council majority decided that the Company would now take over Benares. But Hastings managed to persuade the Council to allow Chait Singh a good deal of autonomy, provided certain conditions were met. In particular, a British Resident would be the power behind the rajah and would receive the annual dispensation on behalf of the Company—2,340,249 rupees, a little more than 23 lakhs—which is what Chait Singh had formerly paid to the nawab of Oudh.

The issue now arose under what circumstances, if any, could this arrangement be changed. In particular, were there circumstances under which the annual revenue could be increased? Hastings took the position that, in the case of an emergency such as a war, he had the right to demand additional payments. Furthermore the Resident, a man named Thomas Graham, the younger brother of John Graham, who had been one of Hastings's agents in London, had been attempting to usurp more and more of Chait Singh's authority. In short, the seeds of a rebellion were being sown in Benares.

In the years 1778 and 1779 Chait Singh paid, with considerable reluctance, a "war tax" of an additional five lakhs of rupees over and above the annual twenty-three that he was under treaty obligation to pay the Company. But in 1780, when the military situation looked quite menacing, Coote proposed to the Council that Chait Singh be required to furnish two thousand mounted soldiers in addition to the revenue. When Chait Singh failed to reply, the Council reduced the number to one thousand. Negotiations continued until January 1781, when Chait Singh finally said he would furnish five hundred foot soldiers and five hundred mounted ones—though in fact he never furnished any. Hastings, his patience exhausted, decided to pay a visit to Benares. Meanwhile Chait Singh had offered Hastings a "present" of two lakhs of rupees. In retrospect Hastings would have been wise to have refused it altogether. Instead he accepted it and deposited the sum in the Company's account to pay for the war effort. He would also have been wiser, given what he might have surmised about Chait Singh's state of mind, to have gone to Benares with a strong military escort.

In July 1781 Hastings left Calcutta with a body of five hundred soldiers and a few personal aides. This might have been adequate for a friendly visit to a neighboring potentate, but it was an absurdly small company with which to confront an angry ruler with a large army. Before the group left, Chait Singh had offered an additional twenty lakhs to buy Hastings off. But Hastings decided, rightly or wrongly, that this sum was much too small and that the rajah would have to be disciplined. On August 12 the company reached the frontier of Chait Singh's domain, where he was waiting with an army of two thousand. After unsatisfactory negotiations, Hastings decided that the only thing he could do was to put Chait Singh under arrest. He sent two companies of sepoys to Chait Singh's palace in Benares to do the job.

For reasons unknown, these sepoys were without ammunition. A melee broke out with the palace guard and the sepoys were cut to pieces. Chait Singh, meanwhile, had climbed down the wall of his palace using a rope made of turbans, and was gone. These events provoked a full-scale rebellion in the city. Hastings now had a remaining force of only four hundred sepoys, so he sent for the nearest British troops, at Chunar, some twenty miles away. It took two weeks to assemble sufficient forces to begin to crush the rebellion, and another two months to complete the effort. In the end, Chait Singh had left the area with most of his fortune.

Hastings had given orders which seemed to be an invitation to plunder. They read, ". . . It will be your part to secure the fort and the property it contains for the benefit of yourself and detachment."[51] It is not clear what Hastings could have been thinking when he gave this order. In 1781 the Bengal government was in debt by 1.7 million pounds and the war had hardly begun. It needed every last rupee it could find. The troops to whom the order was addressed looted Chait Singh's fort and ignored Hastings's demand that they give the money back. It was never recovered. Also lost was the economic viability of Benares. The administration that was installed to replace Chait Singh increased the annual revenue the province was required to pay to a level it could not really afford.

Hastings does not come off well in this episode. His only excuse was his desperate need to find money to fight the war—money he felt the Company was entitled to collect from Chait Singh. This was not an excuse that the people who later impeached him were prepared to accept. Chait Singh lived another thirty years, a broken man without a real home in India.

The second incident in 1781 involved the begums of Oudh, a province north of Bengal. It had been ruled by Shuja-ud-Daula, who had died in 1775. He was succeeded by his son Asaf-ud-Daula. About the best one can say of him is that he was pliable; he did pretty much what the Company asked him to. He seems to have collected watches and clocks. A portrait of him by Zoffany makes him look like an overstuffed cushion. He was said to have fifty barbers and four thousand gardeners. Both his mother and his grandmother—the two begums in question—despised him. They lived in luxury in a *zenana* (a woman's quarter into which nearly all men were forbidden to enter) in Fyzabad, a city in Oudh. Part of their wealth came from a hoard of jewels said to have been worth two million pounds, and part from estates they rented out. Much of this fortune had come by inheritance after the death of Shuja-ud-Daula. Asaf-ud-Daula, son of the younger begum, had inherited the large debts—about a million and a half pounds—his late father owed the Company. He did not have the money to pay them.

What gave Hastings the rationale he needed to confiscate the begums' fortunes was their conspiracy with Chait Singh and the other leaders of the rebellion in Benares. To take one example, some of the begums' soldiers were actually seen in Chait Singh's garrisons. Nonetheless, Hastings did not feel he was in a position to act on his own. He wanted any action to at least appear to have been initiated by Asaf-ud-Daula, who needed money for his debts. Hastings was quite sure there would be questions from the Company in London, perhaps even from the government, and he tried to cover himself as carefully as he could. For one thing, he asked Elijah Impey, who happened to be in the region, to take testimony to the effect that the begums had been collaborating with forces that were attempting to rebel against the English. In view of the interests of the parties who testified, it is not clear that any of this testimony had much value.

Asaf-ud-Daula, meanwhile, was showing no signs of initiating action against his mother and grandmother. This seems to have had less to do with filial piety than with his reluctance to initiate anything, and with his attempt to use this reluctance to extract as many concessions from the Company as he could. He was still paying for the garrisoning of a large contingent of the Company's troops in Oudh, and he wanted the numbers reduced. The Company finally agreed to pay for its own troops in Oudh, and the British agreed to return to Asaf-ud-Daula the estates that had been confiscated by his mother and grandmother, on the condition that he pay them the income they would have earned. In early January 1782, under the nominal aegis of the nawab, troops moved into the begums' capital at Fyzabad.

They captured the fort with basically no resistance. Despite the flamboyant impeachment rhetoric of Burke and Richard Sheridan, which we will have a chance to sample later, there is no evidence that the begums themselves were molested in any way. The troops did not enter their quarters, and they managed to hold on to a sizable percentage of their fortune. But their two senior councillors—eunuchs—were captured. No matter how one chooses to look at it, the treatment of these middle-aged gentlemen was inhumane. Whether Hastings had any responsibility for this is debatable. Essentially the eunuchs had information that Hastings's agents insisted on having—they knew where in the fort and its environs some of the begums' fortune was stored. They refused to say, so they were put in irons and confined. They may well have also been beaten. Those who defend this action argue that by the standards of treatment of prisoners in these Indian wars, the eunuchs were treated mildly. Perhaps, but it is not a pretty picture.

After nearly a year of this, the British decided they had learned all they were going to learn about the location of the fortune, and the eunuchs were released. About fifty-five lakhs were recovered. This money, which went on the Company's books, turned out not to be the windfall Hastings might have expected. It just made up for the loss in revenue from Oudh due to droughts that struck the province in 1781 and 1782. The junior begum, Asaf-ud-Daula's mother, lived until 1816. In 1813 she valued her property at seventy lakhs, substantially more than had been confiscated some thirty years earlier. Meanwhile there was the war.

⌇

IN JULY 1780 Hyder Ali led an army of eighty thousand soldiers trained by French officers into the Carnatic, the gateway to Madras. They burned everything in their path, leaving Madras isolated, and reached the sea near Pondicherry in September. A large part of a force of British soldiers sent in relief were annihilated; the rest retreated in panic to Madras, leaving their guns and stores in the field. This encouraged both the local nawab and the Marathas to begin their own campaigns. While the Marathas captured and sacked Delhi, the French fleet was approaching the coast.

Now Hastings showed his iron resolve. News came of the capture and massacre of the British troops on the weekend of September 23. Hastings decided on two essential principles: under no circumstances should Madras be surrendered, and some accommodation must be reached with the Marathas to keep them from forming an alliance with Hyder Ali. He was sure that if he could not achieve these two aims, Bengal would be the next to be attacked and the British might well be driven out of India.

Hastings realized that the only person who had a chance of saving Madras was Eyre Coote. Coote had been ill, which did not improve his disposition. But Hastings knew him well enough to flatter his vanity and appeal to his patriotism. There was opposition in the Council—Francis was still in Calcutta—to doing anything that might weaken the defenses of Bengal, but it was outvoted. An emergency fund of fifteen lakhs of rupees stored in the fort—a pitifully small sum—was given to Coote to finance his expedition. It left Calcutta on October 13 and arrived in Madras on November 5. The first thing Coote did, on Hastings's order, was to sack "Black Jack" Whitehill, the acting governor of Madras, who was generally regarded as both corrupt and incompetent. Coote found the military situation bordering on desperate. It took him until January 1, 1781, to assemble a sufficient military force to take the field. There followed a series of engagements which resulted in Pyrrhic victories for the British—with each one of them they lost men and materiel they could not readily replace. Hyder Ali realized this and avoided open combat, expecting simply to wear the British down. Meanwhile the French fleet, anchored off Madras and in position to blockade the city, unaccountably weighed anchor and sailed away, allowing Madras to be provisioned by sea. A sort of uneasy stalemate had been reached.

By July 1781 the treasury in Calcutta was barren, and Hastings had embarked on his expedition to Benares and Chait Singh to try to replenish it. On another front, the war with the Marathas showed progress. What had always prevented the Marathas from conquering India was their tendency to factionalize; now it was happening again. One of the Maratha leaders, a man named Scindia, seemed to be breaking away from the others. He had treated his British prisoners with special kindness and had even spoken of some day fighting as an ally of the British. In the spring of 1781 the British had scored a military victory over Scindia's troops which, it was hoped, would enhance the prospects of coming to terms with him. It was October before an accommodation was reached—an uneasy accommodation—which at least served to forestall an alliance between the Marathas and Hyder Ali.

The following May the British completed a treaty with the Marathas in which the British agreed to give up all the territory they had conquered since 1775. Part of the treaty, which turned out to be difficult to deliver on, provided that Hyder Ali relinquish the territory he had taken from the British in the Carnatic. It might never have happened but for Hyder Ali's death in December 1782.

This was a fortunate bit of timing. Coote had suffered what was described as an "apoplectic stroke" while still in the field. He continued campaigning while being carried on his palanquin. That September he had returned to Bengal, an invalid, to recuperate. The following April he had courageously started his return to Madras. He came within sight of the coast when four ships were spotted that turned out to be French. There followed a harrowing chase during which Coote suffered a grave stroke. He was taken ashore where he died. Whatever his faults, Coote was a great soldier. His widow, Lady Coote, who was in England at the time of her husband's death, insisted that his body be disinterred and shipped back to England where it could be reburied in the family vault.

In the spring of 1783 the British and the French signed a treaty of peace in Versailles, news of which reached India in late June. The French had meanwhile allied themselves with Hyder Ali's son Tipu, who was carrying on his father's war against the British and continued to do so even into the next century. With the peace treaty the French withdrew their troops, and within a year the British had temporarily subdued Tipu. The last two years of Hastings's regime in India were thus relatively peaceful. It was in England where the war against him was being organized.

⸎

BEFORE TURNING to these dark and controversial matters, it is worthwhile to touch upon a subject about which there seems to be little controversy: Hastings's contribution to the dissemination of the culture of the Indian subcontinent to the English-speaking world.[52] We have already seen how he subsidized Bogle's expedition to Tibet in 1774 and then Halhed's translation of a compilation of Hindu law in 1776, followed by his *Grammar of the Bengal Language*. Hastings wanted the Company to purchase a thousand copies of the *Grammar;* Francis got the number reduced to five hundred. But Hastings was able to create for young Charles Wilkins, who had made the Bengali type that enabled the printing of the *Grammar*, the post of printer to the Company. Wilkins subsequently studied Sanskrit, thanks to Hastings encouraging and paying the pandits to teach it to him. Sanskrit had been a language largely inaccessible to foreigners. Until this time most of what was known in Europe about Indian culture and history had come through abridgments commissioned by Muslim rulers, which had been translated into Persian. The great Hindu religious literature, such as the *Bhagavadgita*, had never been translated. This was the task that Wilkins, with Hastings's sponsorship and encouragement, carried out.

Hastings also sponsored a second expedition to Tibet. Had he lived, Bogle would have led it. It was commanded instead by Captain Samuel Turner, a cousin of Hastings.[53] It left India in January 1783 and returned in March 1784. The other two British members of the expedition were a doctor, Robert Saunders, and Lieutenant Samuel Davis, an artist as well as a soldier. For some arcane reason, Davis was not allowed to enter Tibet, so his wonderful drawings depict only Bhutan.[54]

The new expedition followed Bogle's route. After a stay in Bhutan, prolonged for three months because of a rebellion against the ruler, Saunders and Turner proceeded to Tibet. They finally reached Shigatse toward the end of September. Unfortunately Bogle's beloved Panchen Lama had died of smallpox on a visit to Peking in November of 1780. (Bogle himself died in Calcutta on April 3, 1781.) But there was an infant reincarnate, and the Panchen's brother was his regent. The reincarnate lived in a monastery about two days' journey south of Shigatse, and Turner visited him on his return voyage to India. He was eighteen months old.

There is, incidentally, nothing in the Tibetan religious tradition that requires the reincarnate to be identified immediately after the death of the inhabitant of the previous body, so the lapse of time here is not especially unusual. What is more surprising is that Turner, who probably knew little or no Tibetan, claimed to have had a "conversation" with the infant reincarnate. Turner "explained" to the infant that Governor-General Hastings deeply regretted the passing of the previous body but welcomed with joy his reincarnation. Turner later claimed that the baby studied him carefully during this discourse, occasionally nodding its head in apparent agreement. In any event, the baby eventually grew into a much-revered Panchen Lama who died in old age. That is more than one can say of the British relations with Tibet. This was the end of diplomatic missions to Tibet until the beginning of the twentieth century. When they recurred, it was only with force of arms.

Hastings's concern for Indian culture can be seen in an eight-page letter he wrote in October 1784 to Nathaniel Smith, who was then the chairman of the East India Company.[55] In reading this letter one should bear in mind that Hastings was preparing to leave India. He had intimations, though by no means a complete understanding, of the situation in England. Yet the letter has nothing to do with these political matters. It is rather an introduction to Wilkins's translation of the *Bhagavadgita*. At one point in the letter Hastings describes himself as "an unlettered man." He seems never to have forgotten that he was not allowed to graduate from secondary school, let alone go to a university. His vast cultivation, especially on all matters relevant to the Indian subcontinent, was self-taught. In this letter he explains to Smith what the *Bhagavadgita* is and what it represents. Of the *Gita* he tells Smith, "Many passages will be found obscure, many will seem redundant; others will be cloathed with ornaments of fancy unsuited to our taste, and some elevated to a track of sublimity into which our habits of judgment will find it difficult to pursue them; but few which will shock either our religious faith or moral sentiments."

Further in the letter are three paragraphs so prescient that they could almost serve as Hastings's epitaph, let alone that of the British in India. He begins, "I have always regarded the encouragement of every species of useful diligence, in the servants of the Company, as a duty appertaining to my office; and have severely regretted that I have possessed such scanty means of exercising it, especially to such as required an exemption from official attendance; there being few emoluments in this service but such as are annexed to official employment, and few offices without employment." (This probably refers to the difficulty of finding funds to allow "servants of the Company" to pursue these cultural activities. It was exceptional that in December 1783 Hastings managed to persuade the Council to allow Wilkins a leave of absence at full pay to study Sanskrit in Benares.) He goes on, "Yet I believe I may take it upon me to pronounce, that the service has at no period more abounded with men of cultivated talents, of capacity for business, and liberal knowledge; qualities which reflect the greater lustre on their possessors, by having been the fruit of long and laboured application, at a season of life, and with a licence of conduct, more apt to produce dissipation than excite the desire of improvement."

In the next two paragraphs he gets to the heart of the matter: "Such studies, independently of their utility, tend especially when the pursuit of them is general, to diffuse a generosity of sentiment, and a disdain of the meaner occupations of such minds as are left nearer to the state of uncultivated nature; and you, Sir, will believe me, when I assure you, that it is in the virtue, not the ability of their servants, that the Company must rely for the permanencey of their dominion."

Then comes the following remarkable declaration: "Nor is the cultivation of language and science, for such are the studies to which I allude, useful only in forming the moral character and habits of the service. Every accumulation of knowledge, and especially such as is obtained by social communication with people over whom we exercise a dominion founded on the right of conquest, is useful to the state: it is the gain of humanity: in the specific instance which I have stated, it attracts and concilliates distant affections; it lessens the weight of the chain by which the natives are held in subjection; and it imprints on the hearts of our own countrymen the sense and obligation of benevolence. Even in England, this effect of it is greatly wanting. It is not very long since the inhabitants of India were considered by many, as creatures scarce elevated above the degree of savage life; nor, I fear, is that prejudice yet wholly eradicated, though surely abated. Every instance which brings their real character home to observation will impress us with a more generous sense of feeling for their natural rights, and teach us to estimate them by the measure of our own. But such instances can only be obtained by their writings: and these will survive when the British dominion in India shall have long ceased to exist, and when the sources which it once yielded of wealth and power are lost to remembrance."

One can only marvel at the last sentence. I have no doubt that Hastings meant it—and he was right.

In September 1783 Sir William Jones arrived in Bengal as a newly appointed justice on the Supreme Court. He was already famous both as a jurist and an orientalist. He belonged to the Royal Society and the even more exclusive Literary Club, the men who gathered around Samuel Johnson. He knew Persian and Arabic and had translated from them. He began learning what he could about India before his arrival and had drawn up a plan of study that he planned to follow once he got there. He found in Hastings an extremely receptive and knowledgeable colleague. Indeed, it was Hastings who introduced Jones to the *Gita*, and Jones then sought out one of the most learned Sanskrit pandits who could further instruct him. This tuition enabled Jones to begin his own program of translations from Sanskrit. He got the idea of forming an "Asiatick Society," an association of English residents in India who like himself were interested in Indian history and culture as well as the science—flora and fauna and the like—of the Indian subcontinent. He suggested that Hastings be its first president, but Hastings deferred to Jones. The Society began a publication, *Asiatick Researches*, which was printed on the Company's press. Jones's own articles and translations were printed in *Astatick Researches* and were widely read both in Britain and on the Continent. Jones remained on in India after Hastings left, and one of his translation projects was continued after his death in 1794. All of this too must be weighed as part of Hastings's legacy in India.

ళ

WE NOW TURN to the dark clouds that were forming in Britain—the prelude to Hastings's trial for "High Crimes and Misdemeanours." I approach these complex and controversial matters by offering you a quotation. I will not tell you who its author is until you have read it. I will tell you only its date, which is December 1, 1783. In light of what you have read so far, I ask you to guess from whom it comes. The reference is to India. It reads:

"My next inquiry to that of the number [the number of inhabitants of British India, which the author estimated to be about thirty million, more than four times the population of Britain] is the quality and description of the inhabitants. This multitude of men does not consist of an abject and barbarous populace; much less of gangs of savages, like the Guarnaries and Chiquitos, who wander on the waste borders of the River of Amazons or the people of the Plate; but a people for ages, civilized and cultivated—cultivated by all the arts of polished life, whilst we were yet in the woods. There have been (and still the skeletons remain) princes once of great dignity, authority, and opulence. There are to be found the chiefs of tribes and nations. There is to be found an ancient and venerable priesthood, the depository of their laws, learning, and history, the guides of the people whilst living and their consolation in death; a nobility of great antiquity and renown; a multitude of cities, not exceeded in population and trade by those of the first class in Europe; merchants and bankers, individual houses of whom have once vied in capital with the Bank of England, whose credit had often supported a tottering state, and preserved their governments in the midst of war and desolation; millions of ingenious manufacturers and mechanics; millions of the most diligent, and not the least intelligent, tillers of the earth.

Here are to be found almost all the religions professed by man—the Braminical, the Mussulman, the Eastern and Western Christian."

At first glance, without being told the source, one might well be tempted to attribute these remarks to Hastings himself. He certainly would have endorsed them heartily. But in fact they are due to Edmund Burke. They occur in one of Burke's most famous parliamentary speeches about India.[56] The occasion was the debate over whether to send what was known as the Fox East India Bill to the next stage toward its passage by Parliament. The bill was almost entirely written and inspired by Burke, and introduced in November 1783. It proposed to create a commission, responsible to Parliament, to replace the Company's Court of Directors and its Court of Proprietors. In short, the Company would now be run by the government. It was not the intent of the bill to destroy the Company. Nowhere does Burke say that there should not be such an entity operating in India. Quite the contrary. The intent of the bill was to impose direct parliamentary supervision over the Company's activities and thus curb its perceived abuses. If the bill had passed, the process by which the Company became formally the British Empire would very likely have occurred a half-century earlier than it did.

Burke's address in favor of the bill shows him at the height of his oratorical powers. Here is an often quoted paragraph which concerns the men—or "boys almost"—whom the Company sent to India: ". . . Our conquest there, after twenty years, is as crude as it was the first day. The natives scarcely know what it is to see the gray head of an Englishman. Young men (boys almost) govern there, without society and without sympathy with the natives. They have no more social habits with the people than if they still resided in England—nor, indeed, any species of intercourse, but that which is necessary to making a sudden fortune, with a view to a remote settlement. Animated with all the avarice of age and all the impetuosity of youth, they roll in one after another, wave after wave; and there is nothing before the eyes of the natives but an endless, hopeless prospect of new flights of birds of prey and passage, with appetites continually renewing for a food that is continually wasting. Every rupee of profit made by an Englishman is lost forever to India. With us are no retributory superstitions, by which a foundation of charity compensates, through ages, to the poor, for the rapine and injustice of a day. With us no pride erects stately monuments which repair the mischiefs which pride had produced, and which adorn a country out of its own spoils. England has erected no churches, no hospitals, no palaces, no schools; England has built no bridges, made no highways, cut no navigation, dug out no reservoirs. Every other conqueror of every other description has left some monument, either of state or beneficence, behind him. Were we to be driven out of India this day, nothing would remain to tell that it had been possessed, during the inglorious period of our dominion, by anything better than the orang-outang or the tiger."[57]

Reading this, I thought at once of a few sentences in Macaulay's essay on Hastings. They deal with Burke. Macaulay writes, "His knowledge of India was such as few, even of those Europeans who have passed many years in that country, and such as certainly was never attained by any public man who had not quitted Europe."[58] One must understand that Macaulay's admiration for Burke was almost boundless. The fact that Burke "had not quitted Europe" was, as far as Macaulay was concerned, quite irrelevant, for "His reason analyzed and digested those vast and shapeless masses; his imagination animated and colored them. Out of darkness, and dulness, and confusion, he formed a multitude of ingenious theories and vivid pictures. He had, in the highest degree, that noble faculty whereby man is able to live in the past and in the future, in the distant and in the unreal."

But did he? No churches? Didn't he know that when Bogle came back with a commission from the Panchen Lama to make a Buddhist center in Calcutta, it was done at once? Burke might have had the tact to mention that the Anglican Church in Calcutta was destroyed in 1756 when Siraj-ud-Daula sacked the city. Ironically, its successor, St. John's, was beginning to be constructed in 1783, about the time Burke gave this speech. The church was finished in 1787. No schools? Didn't he know that in 1781 Hastings had founded the Moslem College, the famous Calcutta Madrassa? No monument? Isn't Calcutta a monument? Didn't Burke understand that the Company had taken a few mud villages a century earlier and turned them into one of the greatest cities in Asia? Even in 1750 it had an estimated population of 120,000. Living in the future? Burke, of course, could not imagine that the meager museum collection of the Asiatick

Society would turn itself in the next century into the Indian Museum in Calcutta, one of the most important in India, or that the Writers Building would come to house the entire government of West Bengal.[59] Burke couldn't imagine these things, but the contemporary commentators who simply accept Burke's polemic as if it were historical fact show a depth of ignorance that appalls.

And what about his blanket characterization of all the men who came to work for the Company? Does it apply to those young men such as Halhed and Wilkins who disseminated to the English-speaking world what Hindu religion and law were about? Does it apply to Jones, a man of Burke's age who, like Burke, was a member of Samuel Johnson's Literary Club? Does it apply to Bogle? In fact, does it apply to Hastings? Would Burke have said what he said, in the way he said it, if he had ever visited India? One, of course, does not know. I, for one, doubt it. But Burke did not arrive all at once at the extreme views he expressed in this speech. A decade earlier they were the polar opposite. In order to understand this evolution we must begin to try to understand Burke. He is about to take center stage.

Burke was born in or near Dublin on New Year's Day, 1729. This makes him a little older than Hastings but of the same generation. His mother was a Catholic and his father a Protestant. As some biographers of Burke have noted,[60] the religion of his parents has a special meaning in the context of eighteenth-century Ireland and England, and it had an essential resonance in Burke's life. Burke's father was in fact a Catholic who had converted—"conformed" is a better word—to the state Protestant religion so that he could practice law. His wife, Mary Nagle, never stopped practicing her religion. When Burke was six he was sent to live with his maternal uncle in the countryside at Ballyduff. A very likely reason for this was that here, where most of the people were Catholic, he would have a chance to be educated in the Catholic religion. This was done illegally in what were known as "hedge schools"—classes that were taught in the open air by priests so they could readily disperse if they were discovered. Historians and biographers are not sure how much of a Catholic education Burke had, because once he himself had conformed, he drew a veil over this part of his life. It was too dangerous.

When he was twelve, Burke's introduction into the Protestant world began. He was sent to a school run by a Quaker. Henceforth his overt life was lived as a conformist, though the fault lines of his Catholic heritage always lay close to the surface. Not only did he try to lift the legal burdens off the backs of the Catholics in Ireland, but it gave him an urgent sensibility to ethnic suppression wherever he perceived it. It accounts, certainly in considerable measure, for the fury—the rage—of his polemics concerning India. In 1744 he entered Trinity College in Dublin. He seems to have thrived there. He founded and wrote most of a paper he called *The Reformer*. Due to the influence of his father he was heading for a career in the law, so at age twenty-one he traveled to London to apprentice in the Middle Temple.

Biographers and historians all note that this period of Burke's life, which lasted until the summer of 1757, is an informational "black hole." During most of Burke's life correspondence abounds, but from these seven years there is essentially nothing. This has led to all sorts of conjectures. One possibility, which has the ring of plausibility, is that Burke experienced a religious crisis which might have led him back toward Catholicism. One knows that he fell in love with Jane Nugent, the daughter of an Irish Catholic physician. Perhaps she or her family attempted to reintegrate Burke into his childhood faith. One does not know. One does know that he married her in 1757—a very happy marriage that lasted for forty years—and that she continued to practice her faith. We also know that once Burke became a public man he was dogged by innuendo that he was secretly "popish" or "Romish."

In 1759 Burke made his first entry into politics. He became assistant to a young parliamentarian named William Gerard Hamilton. Two years later Hamilton became chief secretary for Ireland and Burke became his private secretary. He went to Dublin for sessions of the Irish Parliament and tried to exert an influence on improving the legal status of Catholics. In 1765 Burke and Hamilton had a falling out over these issues, but Burke soon found another patron, Charles Watson-Wentworth, the second Marquess of Rockingham. Of Rockingham, Macaulay writes, with his usual flair, that he was "a man of splendid fortune, excellent sense, and stainless character. He was indeed nervous to such a degree that, to the very close of his life, he never rose without great reluctance and embarrassment to address the House of Lords. But, though not a great orator, he had in high degree some of the qualities of a statesman. He chose his friends well; and he had, in an extraordinary degree, the art of attaching them to him by ties of the most honorable kind. The cheerful fidelity with which they adhered to him through many years of almost hopeless opposition was less admirable than the disinterestedness and delicacy which they showed when he rose to power."[61]

As it happened, this was a time when the government was in crisis. The king had been confronted by his own ministers and in desperation sought to form a government with the opposition Whigs. Rockingham took the Treasury. He also made one of the most important decisions in his career—to hire Burke. It is somewhat puzzling how he found Burke. Macaulay writes that Burke ". . . had, some time before, come over [from Ireland] to push his fortune in London. He had written much for the booksellers; but he was best known by a little treatise, in which the style and reasoning of Bolingbroke were mimicked with exquisite skill, and by a theory, of more ingenuity than soundness, touching the pleasures which we receive from the objects of taste. [Macaulay refers to Burke's first two books, *A Vindication of Natural Society*, published in 1756, and *A Philosophical Enquiry into the Origin of Our Ideas of the Sublime and Beautiful*, published in 1757.] He had also attained a high reputation as a talker, and was regarded by the men of letters who supped together at the Turk's Head [where Johnson's Literary Club met] as the only match in conversation for Dr. Johnson. He now became private secretary to Lord Rockingham, and was brought into Parliament by his patron's influence. [In December 1765 Burke was elected to represent the Borough of Wendover, a "pocket" borough "owned" by Ralph, Lord Verney.] These arrangements, indeed, were not made without some difficulty. The Duke of Newcastle, who was always meddling and chattering, adjured the first lord of the treasury [Rockingham] to be on guard against this adventurer, whose real name was O'Bourke, and whom his Grace knew to be a wild Irishman, a Jacobite, a Papist, a concealed Jesuit. Lord Rockingham treated the calumny as it deserved; and the Whig party was strengthened and adorned by the accession of Edmund Burke." While the specifics of Newcastle's charges may have been calumny, he had come close to the bone, something that Burke never forgot.

The alliance of the Rockingham Whigs with King George III was an unnatural one, and like many unnatural alliances it did not last long—a year and twenty days. The proximate cause of the rupture was the Whig government's successful repeal of the so-called Stamp Act. This act, as noted earlier, had been adopted in 1765 under the previous government of George Grenville. It claimed the right to impose a tax on the American colonies in the form of stamps on legal documents. Such a tax was standard in Britain, and Grenville and his party felt that the colonies should also pay. Of course the colonists were not consulted, nor did they have representation in Parliament. They protested—indeed, more than protested: they introduced a successful boycott of British goods.

Even before he entered Parliament, Burke realized that this American unrest might become dangerous. He did not propose freedom for the colonies (that would come much later), but as he said in a noted speech he delivered on the subject in 1766, "Govern America as you govern an English Corporation which happens not to be represented in Parliament."[62] One is struck by the fact that if you replace "America" by "India" in the above quotation, it might have come from one of the speeches Burke delivered on India a decade or two later.

With the repeal of the Stamp Act came a Declaratory Act that confirmed the right of Parliament to make laws for the colonies. Without it the Stamp Act would not have been renounced. It did not solve the problem of the status of the colonies, it merely put it off. Nonetheless the Stamp Act repeal caused the fall of the Rockingham government. From that time until 1782, when Rockingham was called back finally to make peace with the Americans, the Whigs were the party in opposition.

In considering Burke's evolving views on India, one question inevitably arises: what connections did Burke and his family and intimate friends have with the Company, and did these play any role in Burke's ultimately extremely hostile attitude toward both the Company in general and Hastings in particular? The answer involves the figure of William ("Will") Burke.[63] The precise family relationship of Will Burke to Edmund, if any, is not clear. Burke did refer to Will as "my cousin," but there seems to be no documentary evidence that they were in fact cousins. Many commentators on Burke assume that they were related—that they were literally cousins—but for our purposes it does not matter. Will Burke, who was a year older than Edmund, came from a well-to-do English Anglican family. He and Edmund apparently met in the Middle Temple in 1750, when both were apprentices at law. Indeed, they shared rooms and became inseparable. Among other things, they wrote poetry to each other. How much else is to be read into their relationship is conjectural.[64] It was sufficiently close that when Burke married, Will shared the house with the Burkes. Also living in the house was Edmund's younger brother Richard and the couple's son, also called Richard, who was born in 1758.

Edmund aside, no commentator, contemporary or otherwise, has much good to say about Will Burke. It was Will, apparently, who first attached himself to Lord Verney and was offered both the seat in Parliament and the opportunity to become secretary to Rockingham, which he gave up in deference to Edmund. Verney seems to have been a rather disreputable character in his own right. He had come across Will when, after 1759, Will was turning out pamphlets for the government, touting the prospects of getting rich quick by investing in Guadeloupe. This appealed to Verney, who was always trying to get rich quick. In the next decade all the Burkes, as well as Verney, invested in stock in the East India Company. Initially they made a great deal of money, enough so that Edmund could buy a twenty-thousand-pound estate called Beaconsfield. But in 1769 the Company's stock collapsed, putting everyone, including Verney, in deep financial trouble. It seems that Edmund had to borrow heavily to maintain his estate. By 1777 Will Burke was in such debt that he more or less had to flee the country—to India—to repair his fortunes. If anyone suited Burke's description of fortune hunters in India as "birds of prey and passage," it is Will Burke.

Strangely, Will Burke came out to India with a letter of recommendation from Edmund to Philip Francis; "strangely" because, as we shall see, four years earlier Burke had led the Whig opposition to North's Regulating Act which had created the position that Francis was now occupying. But Burke had gradually changed his mind and had begun to correspond with Francis. In his letter of June 9, 1777, he writes to Francis of Will, reminiscing of their days together in the 1750s: "These thoughts occur to me too naturally, as my only comforts in parting with a friend [Will], whom I have tenderly loved, highly valued, and continually lived with, in an union not to be expressed, quite since our boyish years. Indemnify, my dear Sir, as well as you can, for such a loss, by contributing to the fortune of my friend."[65]

Possibly in response to this letter, Francis wrote to Burke on November 21, ". . . I could give you a History of myself and the Slavery I have gone thro', which I am sure would affect you sensibly, if your own Conduct did not convince me, that you deem no man unhappy, who is conscious of doing his Duty. Whatever your Ideas may be of political Characters in England, you have Men to contend with at the worst, and many of them honourable—but these are Devils. I am the last and perhaps not the least considerable of the Difficulties they have to remove. —The Climate, however, is not very adverse to me, and if I have fair Play at home, I think the Victory is only delayed." And then, "You and I, Sir, seem to be travelling up opposite sides of a steep Hill—but I hope we shall meet near the Top of it. It is reserved for us, I trust to look back from Stations not too widely separated, to the weary Steps we have taken—to compare the Difficulties we have surmounted, and to descend into the Vale of Life together. Are these Things possible, or do I suffer myself to be flattered by a sanguine delusive Imagination. —Whatever may happen hereafter it is my immediate Interest to encourage such Hopes—for how could I endure my Present State, if no prospect of future Honour and Happiness were open to me!"[66] The "steep Hill" was the destruction of Hastings.

From the tone of Francis's letter it is clear that by 1777 he was sure that in Burke he could find a sympathetic audience. As noted, this would not always have been so. When Burke came into Parliament there was a fixed Rockingham position on India, namely that the government should keep its hands off the Company. Indeed, Burke's first recorded parliamentary speech on India, on May 16, 1767, opposed what was known as the East India Dividend Bill, which imposed the annual levy of 400,000 pounds on the Company. There were several motives for the Rockingham position. Of course it opposed the government's stance. The Whigs were also against anything that strengthened the hand of the king and the court. It must also be said that if you were an investor in a company on which the government was about to impose a very large tax, you might object too. It does not seem that, to this point, Burke had given much deep thought to India.

In 1769 when the Dividend Bill came up for renewal, again the Rockingham Whigs opposed it, and again Burke spoke against it. But evidence shows that his views had begun to moderate. Clive had recently been elected to Parliament, and he spoke vigorously for reform of the Company and for reigning in its officers. A cynic might well have asked where Clive had been when he himself was engaging in the practices he now objected to and, employing them, managed to extract hundreds of thousands of pounds from India. But Burke, though he still argued against reforms, seemed to be impressed by what he heard from Clive. Three years later he was still defending the Company in India, but on the curious grounds that it could not be blamed for the fact that its directors in London had not anticipated the changes needed to transform a purely commercial enterprise into one with actual governance over a foreign territory. This was the time when Burke was offered the opportunity of going to India, as head of a commission of three supervisors which the Company was sending to investigate its Indian enterprise.

In the debate of 1773 over North's Regulating Act, the Rockingham Whigs were again in opposition and again Burke spoke more than once. But in his speech of April 5, one paragraph as reported in the press (there were no verbatim accounts) seems express Burke's real feelings. The paragraph contains a warning about the liability of the East India Company, as it was presently constituted, both to the North government and to Britain itself—a warning that on its face is totally incompatible with Burke's opposition to the very reforms the government was proposing. The report reads:

"... The East-India Company tied about their necks [those of North's government] would, like a mill-stone drag them down into an unfathomable abyss; that it was well if it dragged not this nation along with them, for that for his [Burke's] part, he always had had his fears, and would now venture to prophecy his apprehensions, that this cursed Company would at last, viper, be the destruction of the country which fostered it in her bosom. . . ."[67]

Since this is not a transcript of Burke's speech, one is not sure of the entire context, but it is clear enough. It must have been clear enough to his contemporaries. Francis had visited Clive before he left for India, but he had also visited Burke. As Burke had voted against the act that had created Francis's position, for Francis to have visited him, one would think, showed some notion that Francis would get a sympathetic reception. Moreover, Clive's former secretary, a man named Henry Strachey, had advised Francis to include Burke among the recipients of his letters from India so "that he may remember you in any opportune compliment in the House of Commons."[68]

෴

FRANCIS BEGAN WRITING letters of complaint from India almost as soon as his boat docked in October 1774—letters to Clive, to North, to anyone else who might be interested. They vary in length but not in tone. To Strachey he writes on December 7, 1774, "By the next Ship I believe we shall send you such an Account of the internal State [of Bengal] as will make every Man in England tremble. . . ."[69] A year later, November 30, 1775, he writes to his friend Edward Hay, Earl of Kinnoull, ". . . You cannot but have heard of the unhappy Situation of Affairs here. On our Arrival we found everything diametrically the reverse of what we had reason to expect. An Acquiescence in the System established would have secured to us personally a quiet Life and an ample Fortune, but they must have been purchased at the Expense of Honour and Integrity and of the probable Ruin of Bengal. [As noted, Francis managed to secure a more than ample fortune before he returned to Britain. Bengal was not "ruined" by his activities.] The Line we took has involved us in all the Distress and Confusion naturally incident to divided Councils, Factions, Oppositions and personal Animosities. The Labour and Vexation I have undergone must still endure for several Months until a Decision and new Arrangement can come from England are really inexpressible. If we have not done our Duty we have been amply punished for it already. . . ."[70] Whatever word Francis awaited from England—presumably to remove Hastings—did not come, and they remained trapped like scorpions in a bottle until Francis's departure in December 1780.

Hastings knew that Francis had been writing letters to England that were highly critical of him. He did not seem fully to understand the depth of the opposition that was developing, but he understood enough so that he dispatched Major John Scott to try to counteract the returning Francis. After an especially long voyage, Francis landed in Britain in October 1781, where he was followed a month later by Major Scott. Scott comes off badly in most biographies of Hastings. Feiling, for example, calls him an "unmitigated disaster."[71] He was indefatigable to the point of annoyance. He was compared to a grasshopper jumping and chirruping about, interrupting people's work with his pamphlets and lectures as to the merits of Hastings. He also wrote long letters to Hastings containing misguidedly optimistic evaluations of the darkening political scene in England. In fairness, this was not entirely his fault. Some of his information came from North, who was telling both Hastings and his opponents whatever he thought they would like to hear. And Scott was expensive. Again Feiling: ". . . the Major was an expensive luxury. After a bare year at home, he had spent on Hastings account 3843 [pounds] of which some 1200 had gone on special messengers. His bill for 1783 rose to 5664 [pounds]. He explained how he must dine with ministers, keep a carriage, and take a furnished house in Holles Street [very close to where Francis lived on Harley Street]; there were also appearances to think of; 'I sit under a confounded barber's chair in great pain, one hour at least every day.' In a later stage he was provided with the eligible parliamentary seat of West Looe, at a cost (to Hastings) of apparently some 4000 [pounds]."[72]

Francis landed at Dover on October 19, 1781. On the 20th he was in London and had written to the Court of Directors of the Company to inform them of his arrival. He then went calling on Laurence Sulivan, once again the director, who was not at home. This appears not to have been a coincidence since, remarkably, the deputy director, on whom Francis called next, was also not at home. When Francis finally pinned Sulivan down, Sulivan told him that, because of a letter he had had published in the newspapers, the Company would not receive him unless he made a written request which was approved. This happened, and on November 19 Francis was allowed to have his say. He was, as one would imagine, scathing about Hastings, which split the directors into a faction that supported Hastings and a faction that didn't. Francis also called on North and the king and claimed to have had a favorable reception.

Things now began to take a dramatic course. On January 15, 1781, nearly a year before Francis's arrival, North had set up two committees of the House to deal with matters arising from India. A Select Committee aimed to make a public investigation of the supposed misconduct of leading figures there. Members of North's own party were not terribly interested in serving on the committee. It consisted mostly of opposition members, including Burke. By the time Francis arrived in England, Burke had become the acknowledged authority on India among the Rockingham Whigs. When commentators argue that Francis was not responsible for instigating Burke's now definitely formed hostile attitudes about the Company and Hastings, they appear to be correct. But once Burke and Francis began to collaborate, what had begun as a relatively modest breeze turned into a hurricane.

Francis soon became the star witness before the Select Committee. More than that, he became Burke's guide and mentor. Consider the following letter written from Burke to Francis on March 12, 1782: "May I beg the favour of seeing you as soon as you can with convenience this morning. I wish to talk the plan over with you, in order to settle something about the line of examination. I have read the papers; but cannot enter into them in a manner as intelligent as I could wish to do without your interpretation."[73] The "examination" referred to here is very likely of a witness who might give favorable testimony for Hastings. Such witnesses were given a very hard time by the committee. The work of the committee resulted in several reports, the most important of which were written by Burke. Reading them, one can see the outlines of the articles of impeachment that were to be drawn up against Hastings a few years later.

As if this were not enough, North's second committee, called the Secret Committee, consisted largely of people loyal to the government and focused on the Company's corporate affairs. It was presided over by Henry Dundas, the lord advocate for Scotland. It too used Francis as its main witness. It is not clear why the committee was called "secret," since it regularly published pamphlets of its proceedings (nine detailed reports in all). But it decided that Hastings had been the cause of the war in the Carnatic that involved Hyder Ali. On May 22, 1782, Dundas managed to push a resolution through Parliament condemning Hastings and demanding that the directors of the Company dismiss him. This prompted a meeting of more than a thousand proprietors who quashed the idea on the grounds that Parliament had no right to dictate the management of the Company's affairs. To Dundas and his allies, it became clear that the only way they were going to control the Company was to change its charter and strip the proprietors of their power.

These machinations, while interesting, were really a sideshow to the main event. On Sunday, November 25, 1781, North had learned from reliable reports that General Charles Cornwallis had surrendered to Washington at Yorktown. When he heard the news, which was brought to him at his residence in Downing Street, he was reported to have said, "O God, it is all over."[74] Britain, he was convinced, had now lost the war with the American colonies. The only person in power who refused to accept this prospect was the king. North was still under his sway and thus tried to continue to muster parliamentary support for financing the war. But he was swimming against very heavy water, to say nothing of reality. North knew that the Americans would accept nothing but total independence from Britain, something the king would not hear of. By early spring North was again trying to resign as first minister since he could no longer support the king's policy. This time the king began to take him seriously. He authorized his lord chancellor, Edward Thurlow, to try to form a new ministry.

Thurlow was an interesting man. He was born in 1731, making him slightly older than both Hastings and Burke. He was a dyed-in-the-wool Tory and a good friend and patron of Dr. Johnson, also a stout Tory. It is remarkable that Dr. Johnson's circle could include both a Whig like Burke and a Tory like Thurlow. Considering the strongly held views of these people—and their caustic wits—there must have been some understanding that they would check their politics at the door. The portrait of Thurlow done by Thomas Phillips shows him to be a man with a massive head and a formidable gaze. Wraxall notes that he was "Of a dark complexion, and harsh, but regular features, with a severe and commanding demeanor, which might be sometimes denominated stern; he impressed his Auditors with awe, before he opened his lips. Energy, acuteness, and prodigious powers of argument, characterized him in Debate. His comprehensive mind enabled him to embrace the question under discussion, whatever it might be, in all its bearings and relations."[75]

In trying to form a coalition government, Thurlow ran into an ineluctable problem: the Rockingham Whigs—no doubt fortified by Burke—refused to budge on the question of independence for the American colonies. They refused to accept peace terms without it. The king was so adamantly against independence that he was prepared to abdicate. He had even prepared an abdication message, the last paragraph of which read, "In consequence of which Intention [the intention of Parliament to agree to the independence of the American colonies] His Majesty resigns the Crown of Great Britain and the Dominions appertaining therto to His Dearly Beloved Son and lawful Successor, George Prince of Wales, whose endeavours for the Prosperity of the British Empire he hopes may prove more successful." A profound constitutional crisis was avoided when the king changed his mind.

On March 18 North submitted his resignation, only to receive a petulant letter from the king of the sort that earlier would have intimidated North from carrying through his intention. This time it didn't. Six days after North's resignation was accepted, a new government was formed with Rockingham as its first minister. This gave Hastings's enemies in Parliament—now the Whigs—a relatively free hand and led to Dundas's May 22 resolution condemning Hastings. In the new government, Burke became paymaster-general, and his brother Richard, who was bankrupt, secretary to the Treasury; a sinecure was created for Will—deputy paymaster in India.

Somehow Major Scott managed to put a positive spin on these events. Toward the end of June 1782 he wrote Hastings a very long letter in which he said, among other things, "The season is now so very far advanced and the ministry so divided among themselves, and the Marquis of Rockingham so dangerously ill [he died on July 1] that I think the Houses of Parliament will be up before any thing can possibly be done, and the gentlemen who composed the secret and select committees, finding it to be the determined sense of a great majority of the Proprietors, that none of them shall be permitted to go out to Bengal, are now grown very lukewarm in the prosecution of this business. Mr. Burke, too, has lost his popularity, and the unworthy motives by which he was actuated in his illiberal persecution are now very fully understood. Nothing can be certain in this country, but to judge from present appearances, I should think you will be left in the undisturbed possession of your government for some time longer. Yet, my dear Sir, how greatly inadequate is that to what you have a right to expect. No support—no confidence—no communication with the confidential servants of His Majesty, and a resolution of the Commons [that of Dundas] remaining upon their journals as unjust, in point of fact, as it is illiberal in expression. I hope to God you will not suffer this resolution to give you uneasiness. Consider it, as it really is, the work of a party, and be assured, my dear Sir, all good and impartial men will join with that respectable body of Proprietors, who are determined to defend you against the violence, the injustice, and the folly of a small part of that branch of the Legislature, or to give up their charter. The shameful manner in which those resolutions did pass, the evidence your greatest enemies so unwillingly bore to your abilities and integrity at the very time they accused you of sacrificing the national honour, have rendered their votes a public jest, I do assure you. Many of your friends and the friends of the public are exceedingly uneasy lest, in consequence of what has happened, you should quit the government in disgust, but they earnestly hope you will remain on every account public and private. Never man, I assure you, obtained such a triumph as you have done, and let me again tell you what Lord Mansfield told me yesterday, that beyond all doubt you were the most wonderful man of the age. He earnestly wishes that you may not think of giving up the government."[76]

It is not clear what Hastings made of this report when he received it some months later, but by this time events in the British government had begun to move inexorably toward his ultimate downfall. Rockingham, until his death, had shared the government with William Fitzmaurice Petty, and second Earl of Shelburne (the first Marquess of Landsdowne). Between his followers (called the Shelburne Whigs) and those of Rockingham, there was a good deal of hostility. Rockingham did not trust Shelburne, whom he thought of as a Tory in disguise. That is why during the negotiations with the king about American independence, he would not have Shelburne representing the Rockingham Whig position. After Rockingham died, the question was how to compose the new government. Charles James Fox now became the nominal leader of the Rockingham Whigs, though Burke continued to supply the intellectual fuel. Fox insisted that he should succeed Rockingham as first minister, but the king chose Shelburne. Fox then resigned. Shelburne brought into his ministry young William Pitt. Pitt had been born in 1759 and was therefore in his twenties throughout this period. He was obviously someone to watch.

The Shelburne government was an unstable vessel wanting only a moderately strong wind to blow it over. This was soon supplied by disagreements over the peace treaties with the French and the Americans that the death of Rockingham had left to Shelburne to complete. The Shelburne government could not hold together without the support of at least some of the Tories, since the Rockingham Whigs would not support it. North returned from his summer vacation to find that he held the balance of power because of his still strong following in Parliament. His spirits had also risen to the point where he wanted to be back in the government. It was generally assumed that he would ally himself with Shelburne, who seemed to be more compatible politically. The other choice was Fox. But Fox had said things in Parliament about North that were much nastier than anything even Junius had thought of. Furthermore Fox had a bad reputation personally. He was an inveterate gambler, capable of losing thousands of pounds in a single evening. A longtime friend of his commented, "Charles is unquestionably a man of first-rate talents, but so defficent in judgement, as never to have succeeded in any object during his whole life. He loved only three things, women, play [gambling], and politics. Yet, at no period did he ever form a creditable connection with a woman. He lost his whole fortune at the gaming table; and with the exception of eleven months, he has remained always in Opposition"[77] Thus when in February 1783 it was announced that North and Fox would form a collegial government, the news was greeted with general stupefaction. Later North admitted that he was not sure why he had done it either. One reason was that a union with Shelburne turned out to be impossible since Pitt would not serve with North, and Shelburne would not serve without Pitt. The king was beside himself, but, as events were to prove, he was quite capable of getting back his own. As it was, he did everything he could to keep the new ministry from being seated. Finally, on April 2, 1783, he gave in.

In the new government, North dealt mainly with affairs in the House of Commons. His relations with the king were never restored to their previous cordiality and intimacy. It was Fox, as secretary of state for foreign affairs, who dealt directly with the king. On these matters he found that he had more agreement than he expected. One of the things the two men seemed to agree upon was the need for a new relationship between the East India Company and the government. Fox and Burke began crafting the legislation noted earlier. The new coalition government had to deal urgently with the fact that the Company was again on the verge of bankruptcy and needed an immediate government loan of a million pounds to meet its expenses. And the temporary extension of the Company's charter was about to expire, so a six-month extension was agreed to.

On November 11, 1783, Fox introduced two East India Bills that bore his name, though they were largely written by Burke. One had to do with the government at home, and the second with the government in India. It was on December 1 that Burke delivered his famous speech from which we have already quoted. Another paragraph from it discusses one of the bogies that drove this debate. This had to do with the Englishmen who returned from India seemingly with large sums of money and appeared to be buying their way into everything, including the government. Nabobs, they were called. One of Burke's consistent concerns was the maintenance of what he regarded as the proper social order. In India he thought he saw in the nawabs and viziers the sort of noble princes who should govern the state, whose rightful places the British had taken. Whether he would have changed his mind if he had actually visited the country and observed a few of them in action, we do not know. Here is what he said about the nabobs:

"There is nothing in the boys we send to India worse than in the boys whom we are whipping at school, or that we see trailing a pike or bending over a desk at home. But as English youth in India drink the intoxicating draught of authority and dominion before their heads are able to bear it, and as they are full grown in fortune long before they are ripe in principle, neither Nature nor reason have any opportunity to exert themselves for remedy of the excesses of their premature power. The consequences of their conduct, which in good minds (and many of theirs are probably such) might produce penitence or amendment, are unable to pursue the rapidity of their flight. Their prey is lodged in England; and the cries of India are given to seas and winds, to be blown about, in every breaking up of the monsoon, over a remote and unhearing ocean. In India all the vices operate by which sudden fortune is acquired: in England are often displayed, by the same persons, the virtues which dispense hereditary wealth. Arrived in England, the destroyers of the nobility and gentry of a whole kingdom will find the best company in this nation at a board of elegance and hospitality. Here the manufacturer and husbandman will bless the just and punctual hand that in India has torn the cloth from the loom, or wrested the scanty portion of rice and salt from the peasant of Bengal, or wrung from him the very opium in which he forgot his oppression and his oppressor. They marry into your families; they enter your senate; they ease your estates by loans; they raise their value by demand; they cherish and protect your relations which lie heavy on your patronage; and there is scarcely an house in the kingdom that does not feel some concern and interest that makes all reform of our Eastern government appear officious and disgusting, and, on the whole, a most discouraging attempt. In such an attempt you hurt those who are able to return kindness or to resent injury. If you succeed, you save those who cannot so much as give you thanks; but they show its necessity too. Our Indian government is in its best state a grievance. It is necessary that the correctives should be uncommonly vigorous, and the work of men sanguine, warm, and even impassioned in the cause. But it is an arduous thing to plead against abuses of power which originates from your own country, and affects those whom we are used to consider as strangers."[78]

As usual in Burke's polemic rhetoric, there are nuggets of truth which must be extracted from veins of hyperbole. There is also, if one dares to say so, hypocrisy. Burke's own estate was "eased" by money he earned from his shares in the Company and borrowed from Verney and others, who also earned their money from shares in the Company. One also notes in all of Burke's rhetoric no critique of Clive, who was, after all, king of the nabobs, to say nothing of his friend Will Burke, who was trying to pry as much money out of India as rapidly as he could. Furthermore the direct influence of the returning nabobs was grossly exaggerated.[79] Only a tiny handful of members of the House of Commons had served in India during the Hastings era. Three more, sympathetic to him, were elected in 1784. The India bloc never voted cohesively, even on the matter of Hastings's impeachment. Most of the returning servants of the Company severed their relations with India, and most of them found that remitting money to Britain while they were in India was a slow process taking years. The Company's ships would not in general transport private trading cargo for Company employees, so that Indian fortunes were taken back to England either in jewels such as diamonds or by lending money to the Company in rupees and then redeeming the bills in England, which could also be a slow process.

Part of Burke's problem was that he was trying, in 1783, to defend something he had attacked with the same eloquence ten years earlier when he argued that government control of the Company violated the liberty of chartered merchant companies. Now he was arguing that, because the Company derived its charter from Parliament, Parliament had every right to change it. In any event, Fox's bill changing the governance of the Company passed the House of Commons by a large majority a week after Burke's speech. Nothing had prepared Burke and his colleagues for what then happened.

This is described in a fascinating letter from Major Scott to Hastings on December 20, when some of the dust had settled. Scott was on the scene, but his interpretation of events is the mirror opposite of Burke's. It is as if both men had taken photographs of the same object and emerged one with the positive and the other with the negative image. After a preamble in which he describes the vote counts on Fox's bill in the House,[80] where it passed overwhelmingly, Scott writes: "Our next resource was the House of Lords, and here we hoped to make a firm stand. Lord Thurlow sent for me the day before the Bill had finally passed the Commons; he took very great pains to obtain complete information on the subject, and he lamented very sincerely that I had been so long in England at so critical a period without obtaining a seat in the House of Commons [that would come later], where such bold and infamous assertions had passed uncontradicted, merely for want of some person to speak to matters of fact. I had the pleasure to meet Lord Thurlow and Lord Temple several times before the business came on in the House of

Peers. [Thurlow we have already met. George Nugent Temple Grenville was the second Earl Temple and first Marquess of Buckingham. He had been born in 1753, the son of the author of the Stamp Act. Temple had ingratiated himself with the king, and the relationship would play a significant role in what followed.] They both expressed the highest regard for you, and the firmest conviction of the importance of your services to the public. Lord Temple in particular made use of the following remarkable expressions:—'You must know, Major Scott, perfectly well, that if the present Bill should be lost in our House, we shall turn out the Ministry; in that case we wish most cordially to support Mr. Hastings, and I hope to God he will not think of quitting Bengal. I have taken great pains to make myself acquainted with the transactions in Bengal during his administration, and I find the deeper I go the more reason I have to admire the conduct of Mr. Hastings.'" In short, the fate of Hastings and his tenure as governor-general were now a matter of party politics.

Scott goes on: "On the 9th [of December] instant the Bill was read for the first time in the House of Peers, when Lord Thurlow made one of the finest speeches ever uttered in Parliament, to which I have attempted, though in vain, to do justice in the printed account of the debates which will accompany this letter. I sent the speeches to the press, as they were so miserably given in the newspapers. The King was certainly very much alarmed when he thoroughly understood the drift of Mr. Fox in bringing his Bill. Lord Temple had a conference with his Majesty on the 11th and the consequences which have resulted from it are most important. All those noblemen who are denominated the friends of our constitution, and who have strenuously defended the King's prerogative, came up to town, and when the Bill was read a second time on the 15th, the House of Lords was fuller than it has been known during the present reign. Our counsel opened the business with wonderful ability, and defended the Company with great success. The Minister [the Fox-North coalition] lost the question that night at twelve o'clock by a majority of eight."

Scott has put his usual cheerful spin on these events. The king had never gotten over his anger at what the Rockingham Whigs, abetted by North, had done for American independence. He was biding his time to get even, and now it was at hand. Fox and Burke were sure that, since their bill had passed the Commons with such a large majority, it would have no trouble getting through the Lords. The king had even given the impression that he favored the bill and would not oppose it. Meanwhile he was doing everything within his power to defeat it. He considered vetoing it if it did pass the Lords— which again would have provoked a profound constitutional crisis. In the event, he provided Temple with a message to be read, if necessary, at the height of the debate. This happened on the 17th, then Temple rose and read from a card, which he said had come from the king, "His Majesty allowed Earl Temple to say that whoever voted for the India Bill was not only not his friend but would be considered by him as an enemy; and if these words were not strong enough, Earl Temple might use whatever words he might deem stronger and more to the purpose."[81]

To the peers, the implications were clear. The king still had a great deal of patronage to offer, both in honorifics and simple money. To vote for the bill would assure that a peer would be excluded from any of them while the king reigned. None of this had anything to do with the merits of the bill, or even attitudes toward Hastings. These had now been lost. The final vote on the Fox bill in the House of Lords was 95 to 76 against. The bill was finished, and so was the government. In the early morning hours of December 19, North was awakened by a messenger from the king who demanded his seals of office. That same morning Pitt became first minister with a cabinet that had been selected in advance. North was told that his services would no longer be required in any form. He never again served the crown. Despite Scott's optimism about what the new government would do for Hastings, the new cabinet contained people like Henry Dundas who, as we have seen, had been chairman of the Secret Committee and was the prime mover in the House of Commons vote on the resolution that condemned Hastings and his governance of India. Hastings's days in India were now numbered.

V: THE FINAL DAYS IN INDIA

On December 29, 1784, Hastings wrote to his wife, one of the last letters he sent to her before he left India the following February. It explains his reaction to Pitt's India Bill (whose contents we will discuss shortly), which had been passed on August 13. Telling her that he was now resolved to leave India, he writes, "Mr. Pitt's bill, and the injurious reflections which he has cast upon me, are the grounds of this resolution; not as they excite my resentment, for I have not suffered a thought of myself to influence me, but as they are certain indications of his acquiescence in my return according to the terms which I have constantly stated as those which should determine it. [We shall shortly see the meaning of this somewhat arcane statement.] . . . I have said nothing to Scott about Mr. Pitt's bill, because I should hurt his feelings, and I know that he was not aware of its malignity; yet I must say to you, but to you only, that his support of it astonishes me, for an act more injurious to his fellow-servants, to my character and authority, to the Company, to the proprietors especially who alone have a right to my services on the principle of gratitude, and to the national honour, could not have been devised, though fifty Burkes, Foxes and Francises had clubbed to invent one."

Then the letter takes a more personal tone: "I am well, but keep myself so by attention which would be misery to another. But what care I for society. My days pass in incessant writing, reading, hearing and talking, and even close with weariness and little headaches which sometimes grow to great ones. If I am doomed to remain another year, and survive it, I must carry witness of my identity, or return like Ulysses an old man and beggar to $\frac{my}{his}$ [sic] Penelope, and with only one scar, which cannot be seen, to convince you that I am your husband. . . ."[82] "Doomed to remain another year" sounds, in view of what was happening, like whistling past the graveyard.

We have a witness to how Hastings appeared to people who did not know him very well in these last years in India. In 1784 a young lawyer named William Hickey returned to India to resume his law

practice. He had been shipped off to India by his father, a distinguished barrister who had given up on him, some years earlier. This
didn't take, so he had then been shipped to Jamaica. That didn't take
either, so he was now back in Calcutta practicing law, this time with a
common-law wife and an enhanced dedication to sobriety. It had
taken the couple a sea voyage of eighteen months to get there.*

William Hickey's closest personal contact with Hastings came
about because, like Hastings, he had attended Westminster. Hastings, after becoming governor-general, had taken to giving an annual
dinner for the "Westminsters," and this continued in the absence of
his wife. Hickey writes, "Mr. Hastings, who was by nature uncommonly shy and reserved, always unbent upon these occasions and became playful as a boy, entering with great spirit into all the laugh and
nonsense of the hour, himself reciting a number of ridiculous circumstances that occurred in his time. His health being precarious, he was
necessarily abstemious both in eating and drinking, and therefore
when he was obliged to give toasts, had a mixture of weak wine and
water prepared for himself, with which beverage he went through all
the ceremonies announcing the standing toasts with great regularity
and precision. After filling the chair until past midnight, by which
time a majority of the company were incapable of swallowing any
more wine, he vacated his seat and retired unnoticed, leaving a few of
us to continue our orgies until a brilliant sun shone into the room,
whereupon we rose, staggered into our palankeens [palanquins], and
were conveyed to our respective homes."[84]

*If ever one wishes to learn what it was like to travel from Europe to India in one
of those sailing vessels, reading Hickey's memoirs in a must.[83] Hickey and his wife
could not book passage on a Company Indiaman since they were not Company employees or dependents, so they went to Lisbon and booked passage on a Portuguese
ship. Nearly everything went wrong. They were hit by terrible storms that almost
wrecked their vessel, which was finally captured by the French. They had a lengthy
sojourn as prisoners of the French in Ceylon, which enabled Hickey to get to know
many of the French naval officers. When they finally reached Calcutta, Hickey found
that his license to practice law had expired, so he had to engage in various pleadings
with Impey to get it back. Hickey gives his impressions of the justices on the
Supreme Court, whom he regards as pompous, egocentric incompetents. Incidentally,
one of Hickey's clients was his near namesake James Hicky, the unfortunate publisher of the *Bengal Gazette* who found himself in jail after crossing Hastings and other
influential people. One of the last things Hastings did before leaving Bengal was to
pardon James Hicky.

On January 16, 1784, Pitt had introduced his own India Bill in Parliament. In a way, he had no choice, for the Company's charter was expiring. Pitt was temporarily sidetracked by an attempt—that actually passed the House—to declare his administration unconstitutional, which he simply ignored. He got away with this because the House needed to consider more urgent matters, such as India. The bill he produced was, if anything, more cumbersome than the Fox bill and certainly, as Hastings understood, less favorable to the Company, though at first glance—which is probably what deceived Scott—it might not seem so. Basically it proposed a double system. The Company would continue to run its affairs in India, but it would be overseen by a Board of Control which would include the chancellor of the exchequer, one of the secretaries of state, and four members of the Privy Council. A secret executive committee would consist of three of the Company's directors, who would be essentially political appointments. The bill had all the defects of Fox's, including the fundamental question of ultimate responsibility for daily governance in India, many months away from directions from London. The bill also deprived the proprietors of their power to save Hastings. It prompted immediate opposition and an ambiguous response from the king, who was scarcely in a position to oppose a bill put forward by his handpicked, newly appointed first minister—even though in many ways it was similar to the bill he had just dramatically helped defeat.

The winter wound on with further attempts to unseat Pitt and even some curious efforts to make a coalition government with Fox or his allies. Finally, at the beginning of March, Pitt's position was sufficiently secure that he could call for a dissolution of Parliament and general elections, which he won handily.

Major Scott, meanwhile, had been as active as usual, and as usual was putting his rosy and misguided spin on matters. On January 11 he wrote to Hastings to say that he had been to see Dundas, who assured him that Hastings's position was secure—the same Dundas, mind you, who had pushed the censure of Hastings in Parliament. "The King," Scott goes on, "speaks of you in the warmest terms, and a prodigious majority through the kingdom espouse your cause and execrate your opponents."[85] After Pitt's bill was passed on August 13 and signed by the king into law, Scott redoubled his attempts to get

Hastings some sort of peerage as a condition of his retirement. There was even talk of making him an Irish peer, as had been done for Clive. Of course, such an honor was at the pleasure of the king, and the route to the king was through Pitt, so Scott tried to go directly to Pitt in order to make the case. Finally he cornered him at a reception given at the court in honor of Marian Hastings.

Scott relates Pitt's remarks: "I am really ashamed, Major Scott," Pitt is reported to have said, "that I have never yet entered upon the business [the peerage] you wrote to me about; but as I have always found you free and open, I will candidly and honestly give you my sentiments. I look upon Mr. Hastings to be a very good man and indeed a wonderful man. [Pitt had never met Hastings.] He has done very essential services to the state, and has a claim upon us for everything he can ask. My only difficulty, and I confess it appears to me to be a material one, is, the resolutions of the House of Commons [those of Dundas], standing upon our journals: for though, I admit that the charges against Mr. Hastings were ridiculous and absurd, and were, as I really think, fully refuted, yet until the sting of those resolutions is done away by a vote of thanks for Mr. Hastings's great service, I do not see how I can with propriety advise his Majesty to confer an honour upon Mr. Hastings. On the other hand, there are many powerful reasons to be assigned for our not waiting till we meet again."

One can only stand in awe at the diabolic deviousness of this statement. And Pitt was only twenty-five! What a future! Read one way—and this is surely how Scott must have read it—it sounds like all that is keeping honors from raining on Hastings like manna from heaven is a mere parliamentary aberration. Needless to say, this aberration could have been resolved if Pitt, who now had a large parliamentary majority, had lifted a finger. Not only did he not lift a finger, but he said nothing while Hastings was being lambasted from all sides in Parliament. True, he never joined the polemic. He didn't have to. He could leave his options open.

Scott tried to press Pitt on making the case for Hastings in Parliament and got nowhere. He then went to Thurlow, the lord chancellor. Thurlow told Scott, ". . . I will ask the King to create Hastings a peer; I am sure he will not refuse me."[86] This extraordinarily optimistic assertion—equally misguided—appears to be the basis of Hastings's reference in his letter to Marian of his "terms" for a resignation. My reading of that letter is that it shows a man with a divided mind. On the one hand, Hastings saw clearly that Pitt was no friend; on the other, he somehow thought the government would give him the honors he felt he deserved anyway. The same divided mind seems to have been at work in his decision as to when to leave India. It would be on a date certain—or after a year if he was asked to stay on to smooth the transition to the new form of administration.

By 1783 Hastings, who was now just past fifty, had begun to think seriously of his financial needs for retirement in England. Although his personal tastes were not extravagant, his wife's were. Typically, Hastings had given the captain of the Indiaman *Atlas*, on which she sailed, five thousand pounds so that she could occupy both the roundhouse and the state cabin. Feiling, who points this out, goes on to say, "Though the thrifty Marian left some jewels to be sold in India, the ship's hold bulged with her treasures; ivory furniture, a silver-plated bedstead, thirteen gallons of rose water, ninety squirrelskins, a tortoise-shell dressings case, and golden cloth trousers, over all of which His Majesty's Customs later on held a serious debate."[87] Hastings had estimated that it would cost him a minimum of seven thousand pounds a year to live in England in the style that he and Marian would need. This did not include the purchase and rehabilitation of Daylesford, his childhood dream. He also realized that he simply did not have the money.

Hastings's financial state was something that Burke and the other managers of the impeachment refused to understand. They saw the example of Clive, whose Indian fortune was hundreds of thousands of pounds, with an annual income of 45,000 pounds, or Barwell, who returned with an estimated fortune of 800,000 pounds, or even Francis, who came back with a minimum of 80,000, and assumed that Hastings must have been rich beyond imagination. The opportunities for lining one's pocket by someone in Hastings's position were so enormous that he, they were sure, could not have failed to take advantage of them. He must have embezzled money; he would have been a fool not to have done so. In fact, a great deal of money trickled through Hastings's fingers. He spent it—all his salary and more. But he stole nothing, and he took no bribes. At the end of his trial, when he was required to give a full accounting of his finances almost to the last penny, he revealed that he returned from India with about 70,000 pounds. In his final days there he had tried to improve his fortune through reasonable and some quite unreasonable tactics, all of which were unsuccessful.

One of Hastings's reasonable initiatives was to ask the Company for reimbursement for expenses he had incurred in sponsoring cultural activities (the very things Burke claimed that the Company had been *deficient* in sponsoring). They included the schools, the translations, the atlas, the two expeditions to Tibet, and the like. The bill came to some 108,827 rupees. In February 1784 Hastings wrote an almost apologetic letter to the directors explaining the circumstances. He says, "I will candidly confess that, when I first engaged in this and the preceeding expense, I had no intention of carrying it to the account of the Company. Improvement for myself, zealous for the honour of my country, and the credit and interests of my employers, I seldom permitted the prospects of my futurity to enter into the view of my private concerns. In the undisturbed exercises of the faculties which appertained to the active season of my life, I confined all my regards to my public character, and reckoned on a fund of years to come for its duration. The infirmities of life have since succeeded, and I have lately received more than one severe warning to retire from the scene to which my bodily strength is no longer equal, and am threatened with a corresponding decay in whatever powers of mind I once possessed to discharge the laborious duties and hard vicissitudes of my station. With this change in my condition, I am compelled to depart from that liberal plan [of financing these activities himself] which I originally adopted and to claim from your justice— for you have forbid me to appeal to your generosity—the discharge of a debt which I can with the most scrupulous integrity aver to be justly my due, and which I cannot sustain."[88]

This curious and somewhat sad letter must be examined in more detail since it involves one of the unreasonable measures Hastings employed to try to repair his fortune. During this period when the Company was going bankrupt, Hastings had to borrow money to pay his own salary. To do this he turned to an Indian moneylender named Naba Krishna, whom the English called Nobkissen. The relationship between Hastings and Nobkissen went way back. He had been Clive's banyan and had testified against Nand Kumar at his trial. He seems to have been a somewhat dubious character; in any event he had become well-to-do. Hastings borrowed three lakhs from him, for which he gave Nobkissen bonds. He intended to deposit the three lakhs on the Company's account, then ask permission of the directors to draw on this both for his salary and to repay himself the lakh he had spent on the cultural activities we have described. The directors would not give permission for this arrangement, which is why, presumably, Hastings was now asking the Company directly for the money.

But the situation was complicated by the fact that Nobkissen had told Hastings he could keep the money as a gift; that is, Nobkissen would return the bonds. Thus Hastings, had he been less scrupulous, could simply have pocketed the money and never informed the Company. Instead he proposed to put this gift onto the Company's books, where it could be recorded, and then to draw from it. The money thus fell into the grey area of "presents," which servants of the Company were not allowed to accept. It became an issue in the impeachment trial. Hastings, who was a notoriously poor financial record keeper, could not clearly establish what had happened to this money. To have involved himself in this way with Nobkissen was clearly a lapse of judgment, and it would cost him dearly.

THE NATURAL PERSON to have been Hastings's immediate successor was Wheler, but he died on October 20, 1784. The most senior remaining member of the Council was a man named John Macpherson, who had come out to India as a purser on an Indiaman in 1767 and carved out a career in the Carnatic. He was recommended to Hastings as someone to appoint to the Council in Bengal. In the late 1770s he had returned to England, where he won election to Parliament. He was then chosen to succeed Barwell on the Council in Calcutta. He seems to have been a slippery character. In the end, Hastings did not like him very much. But upon Hastings's resignation he became governor-general. He lasted only a year, after which he was replaced by Lord Cornwallis, the very man who had surrendered to Washington at Yorktown. One of the conditions he imposed on taking the job was that he would be both the governor-general and commander-in-chief of the army, eliminating the division of powers that had caused Hastings so much trouble. Cornwallis was forty-eight when he became governor-general. He served for the next seven years. None of Hastings's successors matched his twelve years of service.

Hastings sailed from India on February 7, 1775, on the Indiaman *Barrington*. It was, incidentally, his wife's birthday. He had waited until the end of January to make a final decision to leave in case the directors in London asked him to stay on. They didn't, and he resigned. He exported a small menagerie which included goats, cows,[89] and his favorite Arabian horse. He spent the four months of the relatively brief voyage doing a good deal of writing. He finished a preface for Wilkins's translation of the *Bhagavadgita*. He also wrote a *Review of the State of Bengal*, which was really an apologia—if that is the word—for some of what he had tried to do in India and an explanation of the flaws in the divided system that Pitt's bill had introduced. While he was at sea, his possessions in India, down to his china cupboards and card tables, were auctioned off. Much of the staff he had assembled, personal and political, were no longer wanted. The nearly thirty years he had spent in India were disappearing like a dream. He would never return.

Seven

THE DIARIES OF
FANNY BURNEY

Mr. Locke fetched me himself from Twickenham on
Wednesday. I had the pleasure of passing one day while there with
Mr. Hastings, who came to dine with Mr. Cambridge. I was
extremely pleased, indeed, with the extraordinary plainness and
simplicity of his manners, and the obliging openness and
intelligence of his communication. He talked of India, when the
subject was led to, with the most unreserved readiness, yet was
never the hero of his own tale, but simply the narrator of such
anecdotes or descriptions as were called for, or as fell in naturally
with other topics.
            —The Diaries of Fanny Burney (September 24, 1785)[1]

If you look up "Frances Burney" in an encyclopedia, you are likely
to find two listings. One will be under the name "Fanny" Burney,
for that was the nickname many people used. Dr. Johnson, who was
especially fond of her, referred to her as "fannikins." You will also
find her listed as "Madame D'Arblay." That is because, after a brief
courtship, much to the surprise of her family, and probably to her
own surprise, in 1793, at the age of forty-one, she married Alexandre
Gabriel Jean-Baptiste Piochard D'Arblay, adjutant general to Lafayette. It was a first marriage. Fanny Burney was not French. She had
been born June 13, 1752, at Lynn Regis, a Norfolk port town. How

Fanny Burney met and married a French general is, of course, part of the charm of her life story.

Fanny Burney's late marriage was certainly not because she was unattractive. A portrait of her, painted by her cousin Edward Francis Burney, which hangs in the National Portrait Gallery in London, "shows a young woman in half-profile, shyly looking away from the artist (and her audience). She has soft blue eyes, full and shapely lips, rosy cheeks, and lightly powdered fair hair, gently curling on to her shoulders. [She was, incidentally, extremely nearsighted and probably was having a difficult time seeing her cousin.] Her simple gray dress is tightly waisted and has long tapered sleeves; a cream muslin fichu is tucked into the bodice. She wears no jewelry, but a large strawberry-pink bow is pinned to her petite bosom. Black gloves and a black lace shawl would complete the impression that here is a woman of gentle spirit and modest pretensions—except that she is wearing a magnificent hat. This dusky-gold 'Lunardi,' ruffled, trimmed and flounced, was the height of fashion in the autumn of 1784 [about the time the portrait was done; Burney was in her early thirties], named after the daring exploits of the balloonist Vincenzo Lunardi. [To my untutored eye the hat does look something like an inflated, colored balloon.] It dominates the portrait and quite transforms Fanny from an unexceptional society belle into someone who compels our attention."[2] There was also no tradition of unmarried siblings in her family.

Burney was the second daughter of Charles Burney and his first wife Esther. She had three sisters, Hetty [Esther], Susan, and Charlotte, and two brothers, James and Charles. All of them married before Burney did. Indeed, her sister Charlotte, who was nine years younger, in 1786 married Clement Francis. Francis, who was twelve years younger than Hastings, had been his personal physician and secretary in India. It was Dr. Francis whom Hastings sent to tend to the injuries of Philip Francis (no relation) after the duel. He returned to England in 1785 on the same ship with Hastings. It is said that before his return from India, Francis had intended to meet and marry Fanny, but when he met her sister he fell in love and married her instead. The couple went to live in Aylsham, Norfolk, where Francis practiced as a physician until his death in 1792.

Fanny Burney, 1785. (Painting by Edward Francis Burney)

Probably there are as many reasons why people marry late, or not at all, as there are people. In Burney's case one would imagine it might have had something to do with her father. In a famous essay review of her journals[3] published in the *Edinburgh Review* in 1843, a year after they first appeared, Macaulay writes, "Her father appears to have been as bad a father as a very honest, affectionate, and sweet-tempered man can well be. He loved his daughter dearly; but it never seems to have occurred to him that a parent had other duties to perform to children than that of fondling them"[4] As is often the case with Macaulay, there is an element of truth, along with a good deal of hyperbole, in this characterization. The relationship between Burney and her father was quite complex. It is clear from her journals that until she was a mature adult, late in her thirties, it would not have occurred to her to do anything without his permission. It's not that she feared punishment; it was just unthinkable. When she finally decided to marry General D'Arblay, it was the first (perhaps the second) important decision she made about her personal life without her father's approval.

Like Hastings, her father, Charles Burney, had come from an aristocratic family now in decay. Unlike Hastings, he spent his life in England where class distinctions were extremely important. While he was often the guest, even the host, of people in the highest strata of society, he always had the sense that he did not quite belong. When he was a young man he began to demonstrate talent as a musician. He both sang and played the organ. He showed such abilities that it was suggested he go to London from Chester, where he was living, to study. He did, and then found employment playing in theatre orchestras. Actors and musicians were not thought of very highly—certainly not by the upper classes which Charles Burney was always trying to enter—so it is not surprising to find him next engaged as the private music master to an upper-class family. He was meant to go to Europe with them, but he fell in love with a woman named Esther Sleepe. By the time they married in 1749 they had already had their first child, Hetty. This is something you will not find in Burney's journals.

At first Charles supported his family by taking odd musical jobs, such as rehearsing singers for Handel's new oratorios. He was also composing music for the theatre and working as the organist in a London church. He would have happily stayed in London except for his health and that of his family. Hoping to find better air, he moved them all to Lynn Regis, where he became the organist in St. Margaret's Church. (Among his many complaints about the backwardness of Lynn Regis was the mediocrity of the church's organ. A new one was purchased and seems to be in use to the present day.) It was in Lynn Regis where Fanny was born and spent her first eight years. But in 1760, having decided that the family's health was now sound, Burney moved them all back to London. They lived in a variety of places there, but for me the most interesting was a move they made in 1774 to the three-story stone house on St. Martin's Street, number 35—Leicester House, where Isaac Newton lived with his niece Catherine Barton from 1710 to 1725, though he held the tenancy on the house, for which he paid a hundred pounds a year in rent, until his death in 1727. Newton added a special room that he used as an observatory. The house was torn down in 1913, and the site is now occupied by the Central Library of Westminster.

In this house, like the others, the Burneys entertained frequently. Performance, especially musical, was a family tradition, and Fanny's sisters and brothers were cheerful extroverts who were prepared to perform at the drop of a hat. Not her. Perhaps it was her myopia, perhaps it was something deeper, but Fanny Burney was pathologically shy, a trait that remained with her well into adulthood. Performing for her would have been unthinkable. What she was doing was recording. She seems to have had a remarkable memory. If there is such a thing as having a photographic memory for conversation, Fanny Burney had one. But it went beyond this. One has the sense that she created her own imaginary world from the real. When you read her journals with their pages of conversation, often in dialects, you feel not only that these conversations took place, but that their recreation has made them even more real than they must have been. One has the same impression when one sees certain plays that are supposed to be "naturalistic." The dialogue sounds like a conversation, but no conversation sounds like that. No doubt Fanny's sisters, and her mother, understood something of this gift. She must have shared some of her "recordings" with them. But one would imagine that her father was clueless. That may be part of what Macaulay has in mind in characterizing Charles Burney.

In 1762 Fanny's world came crashing down. After a difficult childbirth, her mother died. She had had nine pregnancies in thirteen years—not untypical. (Queen Charlotte, the wife of King George III, who was then on the throne, had given birth to fifteen children.) This might have been another reason for a young woman to hesitate before marrying.

Two years later her father took her two sisters for an extended trip to the Continent, leaving her behind with the two younger children. Fanny was never allowed to go to school, but she began reading extensively within the strict limitations her father had imposed and which she seemed never to have questioned. For example, she was not allowed to learn Latin and Greek, even later, in her twenties, when Dr. Johnson offered to instruct her. Her father considered some of that ancient literature to be unsuitable. She made notes of what she was allowed to read. These were the precursors of the journals that she began in 1768, when she was sixteen.

Much of the journals are in the form of letters; some she received and some she sent. Apart from her family, her most important correspondent was a man named Samuel Crisp, a contemporary and friend of her father. They had a common interest in music and books. Crisp, who was a highly cultivated man, at one point had had a good deal of money. He had retired to a country house in Chesington, which the Burneys often visited. Fanny met him at about the time her father took her two siblings to the Continent. She was immensely taken by him. He became a second father—a father she could confide in and share the world she was reconstructing. Indeed, Crisp encouraged her to write the ten-page letters that one finds in her journals recounting the London life he was no longer experiencing. Without "daddy Crisp," as she called him, the second trauma of Fanny's adolescent life might have been truly unbearable.

In 1767 Charles Burney married a widow named Elizabeth Allen who had three children comparable in age to the Burney children. Perhaps no stepmother would have been welcomed by Fanny, but between her and her stepmother there seems to have been a lifelong hostility. This expressed itself violently when, not long after the marriage, her stepmother caught her in the act of writing. What exactly transpired between them is not clear, but Fanny burned everything she had written and promised herself that she would never write again. One of the things she burned, along with poems, plays, and God knows what else, was part of a novel she was writing, which she had called "The History of Caroline Evelyn." In light of what was about to happen, one would give a good deal to see what was in that novel.

Burney could no more not write than not breathe, and it was the next year that she began her journals, but now more clandestinely than ever. Much was written by candlelight, apparently in the attic bedroom near Newton's old observatory. At some point she began collecting the scraps of what would be her second novel. It is important to understand that for Burney it was not exactly a quantum leap between the sort of thing she was writing in her journals and what she was writing in her novel. To see what I mean, here is a fairly typical entry in the journals, for May 8, 1775. Burney is now twenty-two.

(I apologize for the length of the quotation, but once you begin quoting Burney it is hard to stop.) The italics are in the original.

"This month is called a *tender* one. It has proved so *to* me—but not *in* me. I have not breathed one sigh—felt one sensation—or uttered one folly the more for the softness of the season. However, I have met with a youth whose heart, if he is to be credited, has been less guarded—indeed it has yielded itself so suddenly, that had it been any other month—I should not have known how to have accounted for so easy a conquest.

"The first day of this month I drank tea and spent the evening at Mr. Burney's [a relative—J.B.],* at the request of my sister, to meet a very stupid family, which she told me it would be charity to herself to give my time to. This family consisted of Mrs. O'Connor and her daughter, by a first marriage, Miss Dickenson, who, poor creature, has the misfortune to be deaf and dumb. They are very old acquaintances of my grandmother Burney, to oblige whom my sister invited them. My grandmother and two aunts therefore were of the party:— as was a Mr. Barlow, a young man who has lived and boarded with Mrs. O'Connor for about two years.

"Mr. Barlow is rather short, but handsome. He is very well bred . . . [The ellipses are in the printed journal, perhaps corresponding to things that Burney later inked over—J.B.] good-tempered and sensible young man. . . . He bears an excellent character both for disposition and morals. He has read more than he has conversed, and seems to know but little of the world; his language [therefore] is stiff and uncommon [and seems labored, if not affected]—he has a great desire to please, but no elegance of manners; neither, though he may be very worthy, is he at all agreeable.

"Unfortunately, however, he happened to be prodigiously civil to me, and though I have met with much more gallantry occasionally, yet I could not but observe a *seriousness* of attention much more expressive than complimenting.

"As my sister knew not well how to *wile away the time*, I proposed,

---

*My initials distinguish my editorial explanations from the bracketed information in the printed Journals. The latter seems to represent interpolations between the Journals and the letters, from which some of the entries are taken.

after supper, a round of cross questions. This was agreed to. Mr. Barlow, who sat next to me, took near half an hour to settle upon what he should ask me, and at last his question was—What I thought most necessary in Love? I answered—*Constancy*. I hope for his own sake he will not remember this answer long, though he readily subscribed to it at the time.

"The coach came for me about eleven. I rose to go. He earnestly entreated me to stay one or two minutes. I did not, however, think such compliance at all requisite, and therefore only offered to set my grandmother down in my way. The party then broke up. Mrs. O'Connor began an urgent invitation to all present to return the visit the next week. Mr. Barlow, who followed me, repeated it very pressingly to *me*, hoping I would make one. I promised that I would.

"When we had all taken leave of our host and hostess, my grandmother according to custom, gave me a kiss and her blessing. I would fain have eluded my aunts, as nothing can be so disagreeable as kissing before young men; however they chose that it should go around; and after them Mrs. O'Connor also saluted me, as did her daughter, desiring to be better acquainted with me. This disagreeable ceremony over, Mr. Barlow came up to me, and making an apology, which not suspecting his intention, I did not understand,—he gave me a most ardent salute! I have seldom been more surprised. I had no idea of his taking such a freedom. However, I have told my good friends that for the future I will not chuse [sic—J.B.] to lead, or have led, so contagious an example. [I wonder *so modest a man* could dare be so bold.]

"He came down stairs with us and waited at the door, I believe, till the coach was out of sight.

"Four days after this meeting, my mother and Mrs. Young [a reference to her stepmother and her stepmother's former sister-in-law, "Dolly" Young—J.B.] happened to be in the parlour when I received a letter which from the strong resemblance of the handwriting [in the direction] to that of Mr. Crisp, I immediately opened and thought came from Chesington; but what was my surprise to see 'Madam' at the beginning, and at the conclusion— 'Your sincere admirer and very humble ser' Thos. Barlow.'

"I read it three or four times before I could credit my eyes. An acquaintance so short, and a procedure so hasty astonished me. It is a most tender epistle, and contains a passionate declaration of attachment, hinting at hopes of a *return*, and so forth."[5]

If this were the beginning of a novel and not a journal entry, one would not be at all surprised. It has everything. It creates a little universe waiting to be explored. It is also a work of imagination: Mr. Barlow "waited at the door, I believe, till the coach was out of sight"—something that Burney could only have imagined. There is the beginning of a plot. We can't wait to read Barlow's letter, which is the next entry in the journal, and is as totally besotted as one might expect. Soon the whole family gets into the act. Should the letter be answered? A great debate ensues, and even Mr. Crisp weighs in. "If you don't answer his letter," he advises, "don't avoid seeing him."[6] Eventually she turns down his proposal of marriage.

Not surprisingly, Burney's novel *Evelina*, which she began soon after she burned its predecessor, consists *entirely* of letters, largely to Evelina's substitute father, a Mr. Villars. It could have been one of her journals with the letters addressed to "daddy Crisp." It should have been the sequel to the novel she burned. That novel dealt with Evelina's mother. But two features are surprising. The first is the range of characters. It consists of every level of society, even prostitutes—this from a young woman who was not allowed to study Latin and Greek for fear that the literature might be too risqué. In creating this array of characters she took advantage of her father's wide range of acquaintances. People of the theatre, such as David Garrick, and Omai, a South Sea Islands tribal chief, might show up on the same night at their house, the latter because Burney's brother James had sailed with Captain Cook as second lieutenant on Cook's ship *Adventure*. Actresses and singers as well as duchesses came to visit. Burney was registering all of this and recreating it.

Considering her apparent shyness and the fact that her writing was done in secret—especially in the years 1776–1777 when she was free from her job as her father's amanuensis—with no encouragement from anyone, one would not have been surprised if Burney had kept the novel to herself, perhaps showing it only to her sisters or possibly to "daddy Crisp." But this is not at all what happened. When it was nearly finished in 1776, she decided that it was very good and should be published! I add an exclamation point because there was almost no role model for her. A few women novelists were writing in English, but they were older women with entirely different kinds of reputations. For someone of Burney's class—especially with her father's insecurities and pretensions—and at her age, to wish to publish a novel was unthinkable. It must have ranked somewhere in the neighborhood of wanting to become an actress. This did not daunt Burney. She began to write to publishers, anonymously of course. As Macaulay puts it, "Then came, naturally enough, a wish mingled with many fears, to appear before the public; for timid as Frances was, and bashful, and altogether unaccustomed to hear her own praises, it is clear that she wanted neither a strong passion for distinction, nor a just confidence in her own powers. Her scheme was to become, if possible, a candidate for fame without running any risk of disgrace."[7] Again I think Macaulay has grasped part of the truth. But one should not confuse timidity with lack of conviction. As we shall see in the Hastings trial, Burney was willing to run the "risk of disgrace" for something she believed in strongly, in this case the innocence of Hastings.

The first publisher to show interest in Burney's manuscript was a man named Thomas Lowndes, who was known as a publisher of novels. *Evelina* was far from complete, but Lowndes agreed to read what there was of it and to address his response to a "Mr. King" at the Orange Coffee House. "Mr. King" was Burney's brother Charles, who had been let in on what was going on. It is not clear whether he had actually read the novel. On December 23, 1776, Lowndes wrote to "Mr. King," "Sir, I've read and like the Manuscript and if you'll send me the rest I'll soon run it over."[8] Of the three volumes that eventually made up the novel, Burney had written only two, but what she had finished was duly delivered to Mr. Lowndes. Burney claimed late in life, when she described all of this, that her brother had been heavily disguised. Why he would have bothered is not clear; Lowndes presumably had no idea who he was.

More interesting was the handwriting. Burney was at the time employed by her father. He was then engaged in writing his four-volume *General History of Music*, which is still considered an important source of the study of eighteenth-century music. His daughter was engaged as his amanuensis, transcribing her father's work by hand. That is what she did during the day. The novel was written after hours. She decided that to maintain her anonymity she would have to write *Evelina* in a disguised handwriting. With everything, she was able to write only about half a page a day. Now, feeling the strain of Lowndes's demand, she decided that she had to tell her father something. She explained in a general way what she was doing and that she was trying to get her story published. She begged him not to see it, and fortunately he agreed—fortunately because, as events would show, his disapproval of something she had written was enough to make her drop it. One can be quite sure that if he had read *Evelina*, and criticized it, she would never have tried to get it published. Given the loucheness of some of its characters, he might well have objected to it. But by the time he actually read it, it was too late to do anything.

The third volume was delivered to Lowndes in September. This time the courier was her cousin Edward, who did the painting I described earlier. Her brother Charles had been sent down from Cambridge for stealing and defacing books and was in disgrace. On November 11 Lowndes made an offer—twenty guineas, a bit more than twenty pounds—for all rights to the book. Eventually he raised his offer to thirty pounds. Who is to say if this was a fair offer? In fact, Burney in a letter to Lowndes, written after her identity had been revealed, complained, "I should not have taken the pains to copy & correct it for the press had I imagined that 10 Guineas a volume would have been more than its worth."[9] Where is Burney's vaunted timidity? But who could have predicted that within Burney's lifetime there would appear at least eighteen editions of *Evelina* in English, as well as several foreign translations. From that day to this, it has never been out of print.

Only after the third edition she did manage to collect the additional ten pounds from Lowndes. It took until January for the unbound galleys to be sent to "Mr. Grafton" at the Orange Coffee House. Lowndes asked her to make several corrections and, in the first printing, these were inserted at the beginning of the first volume of the novel, which appeared under the title *Evelina, or, A Young Lady's Entrance into the World*, published with no author given. (Indeed, Burney herself was unaware of its publication until she saw an advertisement for it.) In the next edition she was able to place them in the text. Neither Lowndes nor anyone outside a handful of her confidants knew who the author was, but the general consensus was that it was a man. Only the painter Joshua Reynolds decided it must be a woman. He said he would give fifty pounds to meet and make love to her!

Evelina became an immediate sensation in London. It received good reviews even in newspapers that ordinarily gave short shrift to first novels, especially if the author was unknown. Edmund Burke announced that he had stayed up all night reading it, and Dr. Johnson was full of admiration. Burney herself more or less collapsed under the strain and went to "daddy Crisp" in Chesington to recover. Part of the strain was certainly caused by the fact that, despite the publicity, her father still had not been told. He had read a favorable review and had discussed it with Burney's sister Susan, who confessed that she knew who the author was. The novel was sent for. Preceding a dedication addressed to "Authors of Monthly and Critical Reviews" is a poem which, one assumes, was written by Burney. It begins, "Oh author of my being!—far more dear / To me than light, than nourishment, or rest. . . ."[10] Once the senior Burney understood that he was the object of these rapturous sentiments, he was naturally disposed to like the novel. The fact that nearly all of *le tout* London liked it as well, given his need for this kind of recognition, helped.

Soon the senior Burney began spreading the news. He found the perfect place: the home of Hester Thrale. Hester Thrale was one of those remarkable people who reflect the light of creative geniuses, like planets around the Sun. Although she was only nine years older than Burney, in worldly sophistication she belonged in another universe. In 1763 she had married a wealthy brewer named Henry Thrale, thirteen years her senior. They set up housekeeping in a large manor in London called Streatham. Three years later Dr. Johnson became sort of a permanent fixture there—almost more of a fixture than Thrale himself, who seems to have been more or less eclipsed by the brilliance of his wife. She poured out her trenchant and extraordinarily witty insights about people and events in letters that were ultimately collected and published in various volumes. When you come across a quote from Mrs. Thrale, you are generally in for a treat.

Mrs. Thrale had engaged the senior Burney as a music teacher, but soon he became a regular at their dinners, to which all sorts of people gravitated to listen to Dr. Johnson. At one of these dinners the senior Burney played one of his trump cards; he revealed that it was his daughter who had written *Evelina*. The instant response was a demand that on his next visit he bring Fanny. The visit took place in late March 1777, and Burney's description of it—much quoted—is one of the high points of her early journals. It is from a letter to "daddy Crisp." Here, in part, is what she wrote: ". . . Mrs. Thrale is a very pretty woman still [keep in mind that Thrale was about thirty-five at the time; "still" seems a little pointed—J.B.]; she is extremely lively and chatty; has no supercilious or pedantic airs, and is really gay and agreeable."

Then she turns to Dr. Johnson. "Dr. Johnson was announced. He is, indeed, very ill-favoured; is tall and stout; but stoops terribly; he is almost bent double. His mouth is almost [constantly opening and shutting], as if he was chewing. He has a strange method of frequently twirling his fingers, and twisting his hands. His body is in continual agitation, *see-sawing* up and down; his feet are never a moment quiet; and, in short, his whole person is in *perpetual motion*. His dress, too, considering the times, and that he had meant to put on his *best becomes*, being engaged to dine in a large company, was as much out of the common road as his figure; he had a large wig, snuff-colour coat, and gold buttons, but no ruffles to his shirt [doughty fists, and black worsted stockings]. He is shockingly near-sighted, and did not, till she held out her hand to him, even know Mrs. Thrale." [Spectacles were worn at this time. Burney had them, though she very likely would not have worn them on an occasion like this. Why Dr. Johnson was not wearing them, I do not know.—J.B.][11]

Other observers, such as Joshua Reynolds, who knew him for thirty years, noted that these eccentric gestures seemed to occur only when Johnson was not actually engaged in conversation. He was quite deaf, and when he dropped out of the conversation because he very likely could not hear the words, or was not interested in the subject, he lapsed into these curious body movements. He certainly was never a model of sartorial elegance.

On this occasion Burney's sister Hetty and her father played duets while Dr. Johnson ". . . *poked his nose* over the keys of the harpsichord till the duet was finished. . . ."[12] "His attention, however, was not to be diverted five minutes from the books, as we were in the library; he pored over them [shelf by shelf] almost touching the backs of them with his eye-lashes, as he read their titles. At last, having fixed upon one, he began without further ceremony, to read [to himself] all the time standing at a distance from the company. We were [all] very much provoked, as we perfectly languished to hear him talk; but it seems he is the most silent creature when not particularly drawn out, in the world." Needless to say, Dr. Johnson did begin to talk, and this entry in Burney's journal ends with the first renderings of the conversations that she recorded almost to his dying day in 1784.

Dr. Johnson truly loved Burney, and he loved her book. He considered her as good a novelist as Samuel Richardson or Henry Fielding, two of the most successful novelists of the period, indeed, the veritable founders of the English novel. ". . . There is nothing so delicately finished in all Harry Fielding's work as in *Evelina*," he rhapsodized. "Then shaking his head at me," Burney reports, "he exclaimed, 'Oh, you little character-monger, you!' "[13] To be compared favorably to the author of *Joseph Andrews* and *Tom Jones* by the greatest living literary critic is not something to be forgotten. As one can imagine, this kind of attention changed Burney's life. It also changed her literary style. She began trying to imitate Dr. Johnson. Macaulay comments, "But such imitation was beyond her power. She had her own style. It was a tolerably good one; and might, without any violent change, have been improved to a very good one. She determined to throw it away, and to adopt a style in which she could attain excellence by achieving an almost miraculous victory over nature and over habit. She could cease to be Fanny Burney; it was not so easy to become Samuel Johnson."[14] This severe judgment did not concern the journals, for which Macaulay was full of admiration, but Burney's fiction after *Evelina*.

She was now no longer an appendage to her father but a celebrity in her own right. In our day and age this would have led, one would imagine, to a liberated way of life and a place of one's own. Not so with Burney. She still lived at home and still worked as an amanuensis. What did change was the subject matter of her journals. The bulk of them, written after the publication of *Evelina*, chronicle not only happenings in the family but the great panorama of noted personalities of the day. You will find sketches of Burke and his brother

Richard: "He [Richard—J.B.] is a tall and handsome man, and seems to have much dry drollery," she notes in an entry from June 1782.[15] And of Edmund, whom she met for the first time at the same occasion: "He is tall, his figure is noble, his air commanding, his address graceful; his voice is clear, penetrating, sonorous, and powerful; his language is copious, various, and eloquent; his manners are attractive, his conversation is delightful."[16] (She would have a terrible time reconciling this impression with the Burke she witnessed at the Hastings impeachment trial a few years later.) You will also find sketches of Edward Gibbon and Joshua Reynolds, and both Hastings and his wife: "Mrs. Hastings is lively, obliging, and entertaining, and so adored by her husband, that in her sight and conversation he seems to find a recompense, adequate to all his wishes, for the whole of his toils, and long disturbances and labours. How rare, but how sweet and pleasant, the sight of such unions!"[17] This view of the Hastingses would deepen and moderate in the next few years.

Not everyone was as enchanted with Burney as she perhaps thought. After meeting her with her father, Mrs. Thrale wrote, "... his Daughter is a graceful looking girl, but 'tis the Grace of an Actress not a Woman of Fashion—how should it? her Conversation would be more pleasing if She thought less of herself; but her early Reputation embarrasses her Talk & and clouds her Mind with scruples about Elegancies which either come uncalled for or will not come at all: I love her more for her Father's sake than for her own."[18] Despite Burney's casting Mrs. Thrale in the role of the wiser big sister, there was something about Burney that Mrs. Thrale did not quite trust. In a way, an important way, she was right. Mr. Thrale died in 1781, and three years later Mrs. Thrale married an Italian singer named Gabriele Piozzi, a Roman Catholic. Both Dr. Johnson and Burney dropped her at once, Johnson going as far as to burn her letters. It was not an episode that reflects much credit on either of them.

After the success of *Evelina*, Burney was naturally eager to begin writing something new. She was being encouraged by people like Richard Sheridan, who had taken over the direction of the Drury Lane Theater after Garrick was taken ill in 1776, to write a play. Both men had read the playlike dialogues in *Evelina*. Had they been able to see the journals, they would have been even more convinced of her aptitude for stage work. Thus Burney decided that she would now write a play. She either didn't care, or didn't fully understand, what this might mean for her social reputation. The world of the novel and the world of the theatre were totally different. In the first place, if a reader didn't like one's novel, he or she might, in the most extreme case, burn it, but as a rule readers could not display their distaste directly to its creator. With the theatre, especially the rowdy London theatre, any kind of audience reaction was possible. Even before it got to that, the playwright was expected to be on hand while the play was being prepared, and this meant associating with theatre people in their natural habitat and not in the relative decorum of one's parlor.

"Daddy Crisp," when told about Burney's project, was not very encouraging. Nonetheless she completed part of her play, "The Wiltings," and showed the first act to her father and to "daddy Crisp." She was still seeking parental approval—we are talking about a woman who was now approaching thirty. Both men reacted violently and negatively. What seemed to bother them was not the language of the play but rather that it satirized several socially prominent people. Her father was especially worried that these people might recognize themselves and be terribly insulted. The unspoken subtext, always present with the senior Burney, was that *his* social position might be jeopardized. In any event, Burney immediately stopped writing the play. None of it was ever published, though the first act, and some scraps of suggestions for going further, exist in manuscript form.

But she did manage to salvage the heroine of her play, Cecilia, who became the heroine of her second novel, *Cecilia; or Memoirs of an Heiress*, published in 1782. Considerably longer than *Evelina*, this one was not written in the form of letters. It has the structure of a conventional novel. Toward the end of it one of the characters says, "The whole of this unfortunate business . . . has been the result of PRIDE and PREJUDICE." There is no question that Jane Austen read it and was impressed. (By 1813, when *Pride and Prejudice* was first published, Burney's novels were in the process of being forgotten, something that Macaulay noted in his essay.) In the completion and publication of *Cecilia* her father got heavily into the act. Not only did he press her to finish it rapidly, so that it could be published simultaneously with his own book, but he also chose her publisher, an old friend, a bookseller named Thomas Payne. No doubt with her father's guidance, she sold Payne the full rights to the book for just 250 pounds—a very poor judgment since the book was even more successful than *Evelina*. What it lacks is *Evelina*'s simplicity and sure touch. Whether this was, as Macaulay suggests, because she was now trying to imitate Dr. Johnson, or whether it was because her father stood over her while she was writing it, is not clear. Probably it was a bit of both.

To understand the next phase of Burney's life and how she became both a witness of and a participant in Hastings's trial, it is helpful to know something of the family life of King George III.[19] Born July 31, 1737, George was the first of the Hanoverian kings to have been born in England. Earlier ones had been born in Germany. His father, Frederick, the Prince of Wales, died in 1751 at the age of forty-four, so George inherited the title and became heir to his grandfather's—George II's—throne. Nine years later he became king when George II died. But the young king was not yet married. This was considered to be a sort of crisis, so a search began, especially among the noble houses in Germany, to find a suitable bride. These royal marriages were largely political. The potential brides and grooms were moved around like pieces on a chess board.

The first suitable candidate for George was the Princess Sophie Charlotte of Mecklenburg-Strelitz, who was seventeen. There seemed to be little to recommend her, except for her rectitude. Her little natural beauty had been marred by a bout with smallpox that had scarred her face. She spoke no English, but the king was fluent in German, and throughout their long married life they spoke German to each other. The princess also spoke passable French. When she arrived in England to meet and marry the king—whom, of course, she had never laid eyes on—on September 6, 1761, she was accompanied by a small entourage. Among them were two youngish ladies companions named Johanna Louisa Hagedorn and Juliana Elizabeth Schwellenberg, chosen no doubt because they spoke the future queen's language and thus would help ease the adjustment to her new life and new country.

For a reader with a capacious memory, this last name may ring a bell. This was the "old hag from Germany"—in Macaulay's words[20] who had introduced Baron von Imhoff to Queen Charlotte, beginning the chain of events that led to Hastings's second marriage. In calling Schwellenberg an old hag, Macaulay was just warming up. He went on to describe her as a "hateful old toadeater, as illiterate as a chambermaid, as proud as a whole German Chapter, rude, peevish, unable to bear solitude, unable to conduct herself with common decency in society."[21] Macaulay came to this temperate view by reading Burney's journals where Schwellenberg, who was actually fifty-eight when Burney met her, comes off as one of the most dreadful comic villains in literature, vastly more interesting than any of the fictional characters she created.

ON APRIL 24, 1783, at the age of seventy-eight, "daddy Crisp" died after an extended illness. Burney was with him in Chesington at the end. It was a terrible blow to her, and it was followed by another. On the night of June 16 Dr. Johnson suffered a paralytic stroke. Fortunately he recovered from it, but it was a warning. Burney's descriptions of Dr. Johnson toward the end of his life are particularly moving. When he was younger, Dr. Johnson, who had very strong views on all manner of things from Whigs to Americans, usually managed to keep them under wraps on social occasions. But in his last years he lost this restraint. He seemed to seek confrontations even when it was clear that they would tear the social fabric of the occasion. As much as they loved him, people stopped inviting him to their dinners and soirees. Burney understood this, but she also understood that Dr. Johnson was more in need of her company than ever, and she made a point of seeing him whenever she could. The last time she reports seeing him was on November 28, 1784. He was obviously very sick and, as she was leaving, he said to her, "Remember me in your prayers!"[22] On December 11 Burney's father got to see him. When he was leaving Dr. Johnson said to him, "I think I shall throw the ball at Fanny yet!"[23] On December 12 Burney herself tried to see him, but he was too ill. The next day he died.

The death of "daddy Crisp" and Johnson left Burney with a deep emotional void. When her younger sister married Clement Francis— who had come originally to court *her*—two years later, Burney was left alone in the house with her father and stepmother. She was now thirty-four and in a deep, and understandable, depression. Things would have been much worse except that early in 1783 she had made the acquaintance of a Mrs. Patrick Delany. Mrs. Delany, who was eighty-three when Burney met her, had been born Mary Granville. Her marriage to Reverend Delany, a friend of Jonathan Swift, was her second. He had died in 1768, leaving her with very little money.

Everyone loved Mrs. Delany. She reminded Burney of her maternal grandmother, and the two women developed a wonderful relationship. Mrs. Delany was also close to the royal family, who eventually provided for her. Indeed, it was at Mrs. Delany's house on December 16, 1785, that Burney had her first encounter with the king and queen. It is one of the high points of her journals. Both the king and queen had read and admired *Evelina*. They also knew Burney's father. The king's favorite composer was Handel, one of the specialties of the senior Burney. Their visit to Mrs. Delany was, on this occasion, unexpected.

Burney's first thought was how to escape without being seen. This being impossible, she tried to assume a posture of mute invisibility. But the king would have none of it. As Burney relates, he was looking through a book of prints when he asked Mrs. Delany, " 'Pray, does Miss Burney draw too?'

"The *too* was pronounced very civilly.

" 'I believe not, sir,' answered Mrs. Delany; 'at least she does not tell.'

" 'Oh!' cried he, laughing, 'that's nothing! she is not apt to tell; she never does tell, you know!

" '—Her father told me that himself. He told me the whole history of her *Evelina*. And I shall never forget his face when he spoke of his feelings at first taking up the book!—he looked quite frightened, just as if he was doing it at that moment! I can never forget his face while I live!'

"Then coming up close to me, he said,

" 'But what?—what?—how was it?'

" 'Sir?'— cried I, not well understanding him.

" 'How came you—how happened it—what?—what?'

" 'I—I only wrote, sir, for my own amusement,—only in some odd, idle hours.'

" 'But your publishing—your printing—how was that?'

" 'That was only, sir—only because—'

"I hesitated most abominably, not knowing how to tell him a long story, and growing terribly confused at these questions:—besides—to say the truth, his own, 'what? what?' so reminded me of those vile *Probationary Odes* [These were odes written by alleged candidates for the poet laureateship. One specimen was written by none other than Hastings's representative, Major Scott. It went "What?—what?—what? / Scott!—Scott!—Scott!"—J.B.[24]] that, in the midst of all my flutter, I was really hardly able to keep my countenance.

"The *What!* was then repeated, with so earnest a look, that forced to say something, I stammeringly answered,

"'I thought—sir—it would look very well in print!'"[25]

These deliciously eccentric speech mannerisms of the king were well known, but Burney, with her novelist's ear, has captured them with perfection. It was during the times when the king went truly mad that he stopped using them. Observers could tell that his sanity was returning when the usual "hey—hey" and "what—what?" reappeared in his conversation. Later in this conversation the king asked her about the conjectures people made as to her identity. One of them, she told him, made a bet that *Evelina* was written by a man, "for no woman . . . could have kept her own counsel"[26]

At about the time Burney first met the royal couple, Madame Hagedorn, who had come to England with Schwellenberg, decided to return to Germany. This left open her position of assistant keeper of the robes, assistant to Madame Schwellenberg. For reasons not entirely clear, the job was offered to Fanny Burney. The queen did have some literary interests. She liked having books, or sermons, read to her. But this does not seem reason enough to offer the job of what was essentially that of a lady's dresser to a successful and well-known author. Perhaps it was the cachet. Burney did come from a respectable Tory family, and she did not seem to have any superfluous social attachments, such as a husband or a lover. Keepers of the robes were expected to live at the palace.

Burney had mixed feelings about accepting this offer. On the one hand, she had inherited from her father the notion that being in the royal presence was about the best thing one could aspire to in this life. Furthermore it was a position that came with a salary of two hundred pounds a year, a small apartment in the palace, board, a maid, and a private footman. On the other hand, it meant leaving friends

George III, Queen Charlotte, and their six eldest children, c. 1770. The children are, from left, Prince William, later William IV, holding a cockatoo; the Prince of Wales, later George IV; Prince Frederick, later Duke of York; Prince Edward, later Duke of Kent, with a spaniel; Princess Charlotte; and the infant Princess Augusta, clasping a teething coral. (Painting by Johann Zoffany)

and family for an indefinite period (the job seemed to carry a lifetime tenure) with very little freedom to see them. Later, Burney was to refer to these arrangements as entering a "nunnery." It should also be understood that Burney's life had reached a sort of critical point. She was entering her mid-thirties with no apparent prospects of marriage. She was living at her father's with a stepmother she could not abide. She did not seem to be writing much, apart from her journals. And she had had a bout of undiagnosed illness with symptoms that today we would certainly diagnose as stress and depression related.

Burney explained her misgivings in a letter to a friend. In it she describes a visit, when she was at Mrs. Delany's, from a Mr. Smelt—an emissary from the palace—making her a more formal offer. She says she told him that "no situation of that sort was suited to my own taste, or promising to my own happiness." Then, she goes on, "He seemed equally sorry and surprised; he expatiated warmly upon the sweetness of character of all the royal family, and then begged me to consider the very peculiar distinction shown me, that, unsolicited, unsought, I had been marked out with such personal favour by the Queen herself, as a person with whom she had been so singularly pleased, as to wish to settle me with one of the princesses, in preference to the thousands of offered candidates, of high birth and rank, but small fortunes, who were waiting and supplicating for places in the new-forming establishment. Her Majesty proposed giving me apartments in her palace; making me belong to the table of Mrs. Schwellenberg, with whom all her own visitors—bishops, lords, or commons—always dine; keeping me a footman, and settling on me £200 a year. 'And in such a situation,' he added, 'so respectfully offered, not solicited, you may have opportunities of serving your particular friends—especially your father—such as scarce any other could afford you.' " [27]

That evening she appended a postscript. It wrings your heart. She wrote, "I have now to add, that the zealous Mr. Smelt is just returned from Windsor, whither he went again this morning, purposely to talk the matter over with Her Majesty. What has passed I know not,—but the result is, that she had desired an interview with me herself; it is to take place next Monday, at Windsor. I now see the end—I see it next to inevitable. I can suggest nothing upon earth that I dare say for myself, in an audience so generously meant. I cannot even to my father utter my reluctance—I see him so much delighted at the prospect of an establishment he looks upon as so honourable. But for the Queen's own word *permanent*,—but for her declared desire to attach me entirely to herself and family,—I should share this pleasure; but what can make *me* amends for all I shall forfeit? . . ." [28]

It was surely this heartfelt cry, and the knowledge of what happened, that caused Macaulay to outdo himself in his invective. He writes, "What was demanded of her was that she should consent to be almost as completely separated from her family and friends as if she had gone to Calcutta, and almost as close a prisoner as if she had been sent to jail for a libel; that with talents which had instructed and delighted the highest living minds, she should now be employed in mixing snuff [the queen was addicted to snuff] and sticking pins; that she should be summoned by a woman's bell to a waiting woman's duties; that she should pass her whole life under the restraints of a paltry etiquette, should sometimes stand till her knees gave way with fatigue; that she should not dare to speak or move without considering how her mistress might like her words and gestures. Instead of those distinguished men and women, the flower of all political parties, with whom she had been in the habit of mixing on terms of equal friendship, she was to have for her perpetual companion the chief keeper of the robes, an old hag from Germany, of mean understanding, of insolent manners, and of a temper which, naturally savage, had now been exasperated by disease. Now and then, indeed, poor Frances might console herself for the loss of Burke's and Windham's society [William Windham was a Whig member of Parliament who was to become one of the managers of Hastings's impeachment trial. He and Burney had some remarkable exchanges during the trial.] by joining in the 'celestial colloquy sublime' of his Majesty's Equerries."

"And what was the consideration for which she was to sell herself to this slavery?" Macaulay goes on, "A peerage in her own right? a pension of two thousand a year for life? A seventy four [a seventy-four-gun ship, the largest then in the British navy] for her brother in the navy? A deanery for her brother in the church? Not so. The price at which she was valued was her board, her lodging, the attendance of a manservant, and her two hundred pounds a year."[29]

Macaulay is scathing, with good reason I think, on the subject of Burney's father. He writes, "Dr. Burney [Oxford had awarded him an honorary degree in music] was transported with delight. Not such are the raptures of a Circassian father who has sold his pretty daughter to a Turkish slave-merchant. Yet Dr. Burney was an amiable man, a man of good abilities, a man who had seen much of the world. But he seems to have thought that going to court was like going to heaven; that to see princes and princesses was a kind of beatific vision; that the exquisite felicity enjoyed by royal personages was not confined to themselves, but was communicated by some mysterious efflux or reflection to all who were suffered to stand at their toilettes, or to bear their trains. He overruled all his daughter's objections, and himself escorted her to her prison. The door closed. The key was turned. She, looking back with tender regret on all that she had left, and forward with anxiety and terror to the new life on which she was entering, was unable to speak or stand; and he went his way homeward rejoicing in her marvelous prosperity." He was probably thinking about his as well. There were royal commissions and patronages he might have expected with this new connection. As it happened, none were forthcoming. The only benefit Dr. Burney received was an occasional invitation to the palace to visit his daughter. The benefit that *we* get is that Burney's journals give us an entree into court life that otherwise we might never have had. It also led, as we shall see, to her being an eyewitness to the trial of Warren Hastings.

Burney took up her duties on July 17, 1786. Her journals show that tension with Madame Schwellenberg was apparent almost from the beginning. Schwellenberg attempted to treat her like an ignorant servant who needed instruction in everything, including how to dress, and insisted on calling her "Miss Bernar." But the first explosion she records is in her entry of August 10. Remarkably, the subject of this tantrum was Marian Hastings. Burney was for once not directly in the line of fire. It occurred at an afternoon tea, one of Schwellenberg's daily rituals, at which there appeared a new guest, the Queen's vice chamberlain, a colonel named Stephen Digby.[30] Hastings had been back in England now for a little more than a year. He and Marian had been received at court. It was never clear what the king's real feelings about Hastings were, but Marian had her connection to Schwellenberg. After she had been received by the queen, some newspapers commented about the queen's having had an audience with a divorcée. There was probably more to it than this, but this point had been seized upon. Never anticipating that he was stepping on a land mine, Colonel Digby brought up the subject. Burney described what happened.

"A very unfortunate subject happened to be started during our tea; namely the newspaper attacks upon Mrs. Hastings. The Colonel, very innocently, said he was very sorry that lady was ever mentioned in the same paragraph with Her Majesty. Mrs. Schwellenberg indignantly demanded 'Why?—where?—when? and What?'

"Unconscious of her great friendship for Mrs. Hastings, the Colonel unfortunately repeated his concern, adding, 'Nothing has hurt me so much as the Queen's being ever named in such company.'

"The most angry defence was now made, but in so great a storm of displeasure, and confusion of language that the Colonel looking utterly amazed was unable to understand what was the matter.

". . . The Colonel, whenever he could be heard, still persisted in his assertion, firmly, though gently, explaining the loyalty of his motives.

"This perseverance increased the storm, which now blew with greater violence, less and less distinct as more fierce. Broken sentences were all that could be articulated. 'You might not say such a thing!'—'Upon my vord!'—'I tell you once!'—'Colonel what-you-call,—I am quite warm!'—'Upon my vord!—I tell you the same!'—'You might not tell me such a thing!'—'What for you say all that.'"

Burney goes on, "As I found them now only running farther from general comprehension, I felt so sorry that poor Mrs. Hastings, whom I believed to be a most injured woman, should so ill be defended, even by her most zealous friend, that I compelled myself to the exertion of coming forward now, in her behalf myself; and I therefore said, it was a thousand pities her story should not be more accurately known: as the mode of a second marriage from a divorce was precisely the contrary here of what it was in Germany; since here it could only take place upon misconduct, and there, I had been told, a divorce from misconduct prohibited a second marriage, which could only be permitted where the divorce was the mere effect of disagreement from dissimilar tempers. Mrs. Hastings, therefore, though acquitted of all ill-behaviour by the laws of her own country, seemed by those of England, convicted; and I could not but much regret that her vindication was not publicly made by this explanation."

This explanation seemed to satisfy Colonel Digby. Indeed, he said he regretted that this point had not been made in the newspapers. At the mention of the newspapers, Schwellenberg was set off again.

"Oh, upon my word, I might tell you once, when you name the Queen, it is—what you call—I can't bear it!—when it is nobody else, with all my heart!—I might not care for that—but when it is the Queen—I tell you the same, Colonel [Digby]—it makes me—what you call—perspire."[31]

In all this discussion of Marian Hastings's divorce, it is remarkable that no one mentioned what had happened to her present husband—though this could not have escaped Colonel Digby's attention. On June 13, two months earlier, by a vote of 119 to 79, the House of Commons had voted for the impeachment of Warren Hastings. This action set the stage for the "trial of the century."

Eight
THE TRIAL OF
WARREN HASTINGS

I shuddered, and drew involuntarily back, when as the doors were flung open, I saw Mr. Burke, as Head of the Committee, make his solemn entry. He held a scroll in his hand, and walked alone, his brow knit with corroding care and deep labouring thought—a brow how different to that which when I first met him! so highly as he had been my favourite, so captivating as I had found his manners and conversation in our first acquaintance, and so much as I had owed to his zeal and kindness to me and my affairs in its progress! How did I grieve to behold him now the cruel Prosecutor (such to me he appeared) of an injured and innocent man!

. . . Then began the procession, the Clerks entering first, then the Lawyers, according to their rank, and the Peers, Bishops and Officers, all in their coronation robes; concluding with the Princes of the Blood-Prince William, son to the Duke of Gloucester, coming first, then the Dukes of York, then the Prince of Wales; and the whole ending by the Chancellor, with his train borne.

They then all took their seats.

A Serjeant-at-Arms[1] arose, and commanded silence in the Court, on pain of imprisonment.

Then some other officer, in a loud voice, called out, as well as I can recollect words to this purpose:—"Warren Hastings Esquire, come forth! Answer to the charges brought against you; save your bail, or forfeit your recognizance!"

Indeed I trembled at these words, and hardly could keep my place when I found Mr. Hastings was being brought to the bar. He came forth from some place immediately under the Great Chamberlain's Box, and was preceded by Sir Francis Molyneux, Gentleman-Usher of the Black Rod; and at each side of him walked his bail, Messrs. Sulivan and Sumner.

The moment he came in sight, which was not for full ten minutes after his awful summons, he made a low bow to the Chancellor and Court facing him. I saw not his face, as he was directly under me. He moved on slowly, and, I think, supported between his two bails, to the opening of his own box; there, lower still, he bowed again; and then, advancing to the bar, he leant his hands upon it and dropped to his knees; but a voice in the same moment proclaiming he had leave to rise, he stood up almost instantaneously, and a third time profoundly bowed to the Court.

What an awful moment for such a man!—a man fallen from such height of power to a situation so humiliating—from the almost unlimited command of so large a part of the Eastern World to be cast at the feet of his enemies, of the Great Tribunal of his Country, and of the Nation at large, assembled in this body to try and to judge him! Could even his Prosecutors at that moment look on—and shudder at least, if they did not blush.

—Fanny Burney (February 13, 1788)[2]

I: THE INDICTMENT

On June 13, 1785, Hastings landed at Plymouth. A month later he wrote to his former secretary, George Nesbitt Thompson, who was still in India. The letter is interesting because it describes his voyage, his reception in England, and some thoughts as to his future. It was written at a time when he was still rather optimistic about what was to come. Of his voyage he notes, "I had a pleasant voyage without bad weather; a clean and tight ship; officers of skill and attention, and even of science; and a rapid course [he had left India on February 7]. The worst of the voyage was that my mind was stupid, and that I never passed a night without a slight fever. Thompson, never take the counsel of a physician that shall bid you to go to sea for health."[3]

Marian had no way of knowing when Hastings's ship would arrive, so she had gone to Cheltenham, a health resort not far from Gloucester. Hastings went to London to look for her and finally met her on his way back from London to Cheltenham, where they would take up temporary residence. As he wrote to Thompson, "Having performed all the duties of loyalty, respect and civility, I ran away to this place, where I have been since the 5th. We have been drinking the waters ever since, but without any benefit hitherto, and rather the reverse, which people say is a sign that they will do us good."

In the year that Marian had been in England by herself, she had not been idle. In addition to getting acquainted with Hastings's sister and brother-in-law, she had been received twice by the queen, which, as we have seen, caused some controversy. She had taken a house overlooking South Park with servants and a coach bearing the Hastings arms. Later she rented another house on St. James's Park, where she gave a ball for people Hastings knew. Everywhere she went she cut a striking figure with her Indian dress and abundant jewelry. A few years later she purchased a house on Park Lane.

Once the trial started, questions were raised as to how she had acquired the money to do all this. When Hastings was obliged to divulge his finances he had to divulge hers as well, since there was a suspicion that to conceal his he had transferred them to her. He swore under oath that she had only two sources of money. First was the lakh of rupees he had given to her in 1777 as a marriage settlement. This had been transmitted to England and converted into a pound investment. When she began drawing on it, the sum came to 22,234 pounds. In addition were the jewels she had sold in India, which had netted nearly 18,000 pounds. This was not a vast fortune but was quite consistent with what she was spending. In any event, Hastings was able to report to Thompson "that I found Mrs. Hastings in better health than I have known her to possess for some years. . . ."

By the time he wrote this letter, Hastings himself had been making the rounds. As he wrote to Thompson, ". . . My reception has been as flattering as pride could wish it. I have experienced the distinction of *digito monstrari et dicier* [sic], *hic est* [of being noticed and people saying 'it is he']; but my humility preserved itself by the influence of a monitor within that whispered, All this will expire in less than three months. I think much of it is already gone. But as much of it as I wish to retain will, I am persuaded, remain yet for years,—the esteem of those whom all esteem." Hastings's "reception" had included a visit with the king and queen—in which, needless to say, Madame Schwellenberg had had a hand. He also made a pro forma call on Pitt and informal calls on the lord chancellor, Edward Thurlow, who was and who would remain one of Hastings's greatest admirers. Seeing Thurlow was exceedingly important because of the role of the so-called Law Lords in trials before the House of Lords. Even though the Law Lords—chosen for their judicial abilities—had the same voting franchise as the rest of the Lords, their role gave them a very important influence on the course of a trial. The lord chancellor, the man with the so-called woolsack—the cushion that denoted his rank—was in some sense the chief justice. Again, he had only one vote but could exert great influence. Thurlow was to remain lord chancellor until 1792, but even as an ordinary Law Lord he retained considerable sway.

On June 20, within a week of Hastings's arrival at Plymouth, Burke gave notice in the House of Commons that he "would at a future day make a motion respecting the conduct of a gentleman just returned from India."[4] Hastings did not seem overly concerned, but Burke's notice must have been one of the things that led him to ruminate about how rapidly public esteem might evaporate. Hastings's July letter to Thompson is divided into two parts, since he did not send off the first part right away. To it he appended a second part, dated September 22. By this time, the forces that were assembling against him had become more manifest. He writes:

"We are both well, but neither very well. Mrs. Hastings always remembers you, and speaks of you with an affection kindred to my own. We are at this time in a community [Tunbridge Wells], among which Lord Mansfield's partiality, has made it fashionable to regard us with an uncommon degree of attention and respect. [Mansfield was the great legal scholar and one of the recipients of Halhed's translation of the code of Hindu laws.] Indeed, my dear Thompson, I should wrong your sensibility were I to conceal from you what would afford it the most pleasing gratification, that I find myself everywhere and universally treated with evidences, apparent even to my own observation, that I possess the good opinion of my country. Yet this blessing (for such it is, and I would not forfeit it for lacs [lakhs]), is not without its alloy, since it holds me up as an object of public calumny, which I could well support were I the sole object of it. [This may refer to the fact that his wife was receiving her share of public criticism.] Nor is it malice that assails me. Such is the prolifigacy of the ruling manners, that there are multitudes who get their bread by detraction; but so little of system is there in this vile science, that even the similitude of character is scarce ever preserved in the features which are held forth to the public in such compositions; and for the newspapers, even indifferent anecdotes of persons are often published without a spark of truth to justify them."

He also discusses his future plans. Uppermost, of course, is the repurchase and rehabilitation of his family estate, Daylesford. He notes that ". . . if I get it, I shall pay almost twice its worth, according to the common market price." At Daylesford he envisions the cultivation of Indian plants. This would occupy his attention for the rest of his life. He asks Thompson to send him "seeds of the lichee," "seeds of the cinnamon," and "custard apple seeds." In addition he asks for goats to replace the ones that died during his voyage to England. But he also has plans for a possible role in Indian affairs. In this he seems still to be living an illusion. He notes that he sent a copy of his account of the last three months of his service—which he wrote on his return voyage—to Henry Dundas. Dundas, who was now president of the Board of Control for India, the entity that Pitt's India Bill had created to oversee the affairs of the Company, was one of Hastings's most vigorous detractors. For Hastings to believe, as he writes in his letter, that Dundas and others "profess to have derived much instruction from it," would appear to show that he really did not understand his situation. "I am myself," he adds, "not dissatisfied with it. It will be an antidote against the poison of false '*statements.*' I wish you could see it."

AS I READ this letter and studied Hastings's general behavior both before and during the earlier parts of his trial, I had the strange sensation that some of these elements were already familiar to me, but in a completely different context. I realized finally that I was thinking of the hearing of J. Robert Oppenheimer in April 1954 before the Personnel Security Board of the United States Atomic Energy Commission. At issue was Oppenheimer's security clearance. Like Hastings, Oppenheimer was a man who excited the deepest passions. Many people loved him and some hated him.[5] He could be extremely gracious and extremely arrogant. He did not suffer fools gladly and had no hesitation in making that clear. He was, like Hastings, a great leader, as he had demonstrated at Los Alamos. He was fully convinced of the value of his service and could not comprehend why it was not clear to everyone. He once told me that during the hearing he felt it was happening to someone else. He did not recognize the person being described in the testimony. I am sure that Hastings felt the same way. But the resemblance between these two trials—Oppenheimer's hearing was certainly a trial and, like Hastings's trial, it was conducted under very unclear judicial rules—goes even deeper. In both trials there was a text and a subtext. In both cases it was the subtext, which never emerged overtly in the course of the trial, that really mattered.

Had there been any doubts about Oppenheimer's value as a consultant to the Atomic Energy Commission, the commission could simply have stopped consulting him. There was no need for a hearing in which every dubious act in his life—most of which had been vetted when he was chosen to head Los Alamos—be placed before the public. But to have made this a private, discreet matter would not have dealt with the real problem his enemies confronted. They understood that by publicly destroying Oppenheimer's reputation, they could prevent him from influencing important decisions, even as a private citizen. Hence they set about to destroy his reputation, and in this they succeeded. That was the subtext. The same dynamic was at work with Hastings.

✍

IN HIS LETTER, Hastings writes to Thompson, "I have led a most idle life, but not wholly unprofitable, having been allowed to contribute some little good to the service, which would not have taken place perhaps had I stayed in Bengal. I have not time to detail the particulars, nor am I sure it would be proper. I am sanguine in the hope that I may be instrumental in undoing the mischief's [sic] created by the last Indian Act. I will try at least, and shall think it the best deed of my life if I can effect it. Let my friends, but only special friends, know that I have such hopes and such intentions."

Needless to say, Burke was not a "special friend," but this is just what Burke feared. He made this crystal clear in a letter to Dundas once the pretrial proceedings began to take shape. If people like Hastings were not stopped, Burke foresaw a "body of men," with Hastings as their leader, that would arise and take over Indian politics. Burke writes, "... This body is under Hastings as an Indian leader and will have very soon, if it has not already, an English political leader too. This body if they should now obtain a triumph would be too strong for your Ministry or for any Ministry. . . . The triumph of that faction will not be over us, who are not the keepers of the Parliamentary force [the Whigs were a minority], but over you."[6] One should keep this letter clearly in mind in trying to understand Burke's behavior over the next decade. Otherwise it may appear to make no sense. Burke would certainly have welcomed a conviction of Hastings on specific charges, which would have meant a jail term or worse, but failing that, he wanted to sully Hastings's reputation to such an extent that he would never again have any role in the conduct of Indian affairs. This required innuendo and invective, and there has never been a parliamentary orator who was better at this than Burke.

For the next several months nothing appeared to be happening. Hastings and his wife continued with their social rounds. It was September 1785 when Fanny Burney first reported meeting Hastings. But behind the scenes Francis and Burke were furiously putting together their case and seeking new recruits to the cause. They had two problems. On the one hand, it was unclear what support they had within the Tory government, and whether their own opposition party had much stomach for such an inquest. Indeed, some of his fellow Whigs tried to persuade Burke to back off. Not surprisingly in view of his real agenda, he decided that if necessary he would go it alone.

On January 24, 1786, Parliament reopened after its fall recess. By this time Hastings's agent Major Scott had been elected to the Commons. What he then did has been the subject of controversy ever since. He called the question on Burke's notice, which had been given the previous June. This was done with Hastings's approval.*

One wonders what might have happened if this preemptive step had not been taken. Some commentators believe that by doing nothing, Hastings might have been spared what followed. Perhaps, but it is difficult to believe that Burke and Francis would ever have let the matter drop. In any event, both Fox and Burke rose to the challenge. Fox assured Scott that "the business would not be neglected,"[8] and Burke informed him that a general does not consult his enemy as to the time and place of the battle.

On February 17 Burke moved in a committee of the whole House that the House be furnished with "copies of all correspondence since the month of January 1782, between Warren Hastings, Esq., late Governor-General of Bengal, and the Court of Directors . . . as well before as since the return of said Governor-General relative to presents and other monies privately received by the said Governor-General."[9] This provoked a debate which appears to have had a dual purpose. On its face the debate seemed to be about the propriety of putting these theoretically private documents into the public domain. But in fact the documents were already, in one way or another, available. In one instance the House refused to release the letter of one of Hastings's correspondents. Not only did Burke have access to this letter, but he even introduced it in evidence in one of his impeachment charges. The real purpose of the debate was to allow Burke to assess the government's position. The Whigs were a minority, and without support from the Tory majority there could never be an impeachment. In this maneuver Burke was encouraged by the calculated ambiguity of Pitt. Pitt spoke of Hastings's "almost precedented talents,"[10] and followed this with a discussion of matters such as the Rohilla War, in which he thought that Hastings might be "cen-

---

*A note found among his wife's papers reads, "He (Hastings) desired Major Scott . . . to ask Mr. Burke what he meant by his abuse of Mr. Hastings—he desire(d) to be impeach(d) that he might clear his character of vairious [sic] cal(umnies) which had been throughn [sic] out against him."[7] Her English spelling was always somewhat original. I am again reminded of Oppenheimer, who insisted on hearings so that he could clear "his character."

surable." Indeed, he went on to say that if any of Hastings's alleged crimes were provable, he would not stand in the way of their being prosecuted. One could, as usual, read into Pitt's remarks anything one wanted to.

Burke wanted to begin at once examining witnesses, but here the majority in Parliament insisted that formal charges be brought so that witnesses would appear in a legal context. On April 4 Burke set forth eleven of what soon became twenty-two charges. The rest were introduced within a month. Here are some of them in the language that was reported in the press and with their original numbering.[11] He was charged:

I. With gross injustice, cruelty, and treachery against the faith of nations, in hiring British soldiers for the purpose of extirpating the innocent and helpless people who inhabited the Rohillas.

III. With various instances of extortion, and other deeds of maladministration against the Rajah of Benares [Chait Singh]. This article consisted of three different parts, in each of which Mr. Hastings was charged with a series of the most wanton oppressions and cruelties. He gave in papers concerning the rights of the Rajah his expulsion, and the sundry revolutions which have been effected by the influence of the late Governor-General in the Zemindary. [A zemindar more correctly spelled *zamindar*, can be translated roughly as a landlord. A zamindary was a territory over which the British had landlord status.]

IV. The numerous and insupportable hardships to which the Royal Family of Oude [the begums of Oudh] had been reduced, in consequence of their connection with the Supreme Council.

VI. With impoverishing and depopulating the whole country of Oude, rendering that country, which was once a garden, an uninhabited desert.

VII. With a wanton, and unjust, and pernicious exercise of his powers, and the great situation of trust which he occupied in India, in overturning the ancient establishments of the country, and extending an undue influence by conniving extravagant contracts, and appointing inordinate salaries. [This refers to the bullock contracts and also the way in which the Company's opium monopoly was handled. The "inordinate salaries" are a reference to those of Impey and Eyre Coote.]

VIII. With receiving money against the orders of the Company, the Act of Parliament, and his own sacred engagements; and applying that money to purposes totally improper and unauthorized.

IX. With having resigned by proxy for the obvious purpose of retaining his situation, and denying the deed in person, in direct opposition to all those powers under which he acted. [This refers to the 1776 episode in which Hastings's representatives in London, Graham and MacLeane, tried to broker his resignation against some sort of government honor.]

XI. Charges him with enormous extravagances and bribery in various contracts with a view to enrich his dependents and favorites. [At least in part, this refers to the fact that Laurence Sulivan's son Stephen for a while held the opium contract, which he resold at a great profit. Hastings had to demonstrate that he had no role in this matter and did not himself profit from it.]

These and the rest of the charges dealt both with matters of state that Hastings was responsible for, and his personal behavior. Hastings had to decide how to respond. Here he made what turned out to be a serious mistake. Again, one cannot know what would have happened if he had made a different choice. He instructed Scott to demand that he be given the right to respond in person on the floor of Parliament to all the charges, before any of them was voted on. On April 26 Scott petitioned the House to allow Hastings's appearance. At the same time Burke launched two more charges.

The appearance was scheduled for May 1, giving Hastings less than a week to prepare. To this end, Scott enlisted the aid of several of the men who had returned with Hastings. Nathaniel Halhed wrote the response that Hastings was to give to the charges that involved Chait Singh. Later Scott recalled that this was delivered to Hastings the day before he was to appear. In fact, Scott read aloud to Hastings what Halhed had written, and, as Hastings did not object, a scribe was employed who stayed up all night to transcribe it into a form from which Hastings could read the following day. Later Scott reported that, after the initial reading of Halhed's manuscript, Hastings had said there were parts he did not like. Nonetheless he used them. This was an important element in the fiasco that ensued, since there were factual errors in Halhed's manuscript that were pounced on by Burke and Francis. Hastings was placed in the untenable position of acknowledging these mistakes but claiming he was not responsible since he had not written this part of his defense.

But this was only a sideshow. The real problem was (as Oppenheimer said to me) that Hastings still believed this could not be happening to him. Somehow it was all a misunderstanding which could be readily corrected if the people involved—in this instance the members of the House of Commons—could only be exposed to the truth. Of course this ignored the fact that the Whigs whom Burke had recruited already had their minds made up, and that to have convinced enough Tories to block the impeachment would have required a parliamentary oration that only a Burke could have delivered. Whatever else he was, Hastings was no parliamentary orator. In fact, one of the parliamentarians who heard him reported that he had a slight speech impediment.

An account of the occasion is given by the editor of the Debrett publication I have been quoting. This editor (perhaps there was more than one, since the proceedings extend over nearly a decade) is, in the main, quite sympathetic to Hastings. This gives extra weight to the sense he gives of the impression Hastings made on the House. He begins, "Mr. Hastings proceeded to read his defense. He began by remarking, that the grounds of the crimination were ill-founded, aspersive, and malicious; that the various publications of the times contained the most unwarrantable observations on his conduct, and that the press daily teemed with the most gross libels upon every part of his administration in India. [But Scott, with the aid of Halhed, was churning out his own share of publications and press reports.] That he was obliged to reply to charges containing nothing specific; and that they might be called historical narratives, with voluminous commentaries. That he had been in India from a school-boy; and that, during a period of thirty-six years of servitude, he had always the happiness to maintain a good and respectable character. That by the evil machinations of a few individuals, men of notoriety, he now appeared in an unfortunate situation; but that he chose to come forward on the occasion, and meet his fate, rather than be subjected to the continual threats of Parliamentary prosecution. That to the indulgence now granted, it was a matter of indifference whether it proceeded from the humanity, or the justice of the House; he considered himself as equally indebted to them. That he had acted according to the emergencies of the times; and that he had been frequently reduced to such extremities, as to defy the sanction of any precedent. That no man had been in more perilous situations; and that in those disasters he was entirely left to the resources of his own mind. That he had resigned his government in India amidst the regret of his fellow subjects. That he had repeatedly received the thanks of his employers, the Directors of the East-India Company; and he had the satisfaction of discharging the trust reposed in him with such unanimous approbation, he believed, that no other power on earth had a right to call his conduct in question."[12]

Had Hastings been content to state these general points—especially those involving the exigencies of the situations he often found himself in—succinctly, with a few examples and with less arrogance, he might have helped himself. He began with general remarks about his mandate: "I received the government of Bengal with encumberances," he noted, "which might have intimidated a firmer spirit than mine; and I felt the perilous situation it placed me. I found myself the titular head of a numerous, and not always accordant council, appointed to manage the affairs of a great state, which yet wore the marks of recent acquisition; but had neither determinate form, nor any orders of instructions which could enable them to give it either."[13] But then he chose to continue by giving an excruciatingly detailed and self-serving exposition of his entire career in India. He read for two hours, after which one of his young associates, William Markham, read from the same manuscript, followed by two clerks. The whole performance took two days! Hastings read the last of it the second night. By the end, if not long before, Hastings had worn out his welcome.

While it was apparent to everyone else what a disaster this had been, Hastings apparently regarded it as some sort of triumph. Fanny Burney records in a journal entry dated May 24, some three weeks after his appearance in Parliament, "Mrs. Hastings sent her carriage here before ten o'clock. I made her and Mr. Hastings a visit of about half an hour previously to our journey. I am quite charmed with Mr. Hastings; and, indeed, from all I can gather, and all I can observe—both of which are but little—he appears to me to be one of the greatest men now living, as a public character; while, as a private one, his gentleness, candour, soft manners, and openness of disposition, make him one of the most pleasing."

She goes on, "The little journey was extremely agreeable. He spoke with the utmost frankness of his situation and affairs, and with a noble confidence in his certainty of victory over his enemies, from his consciousness of integrity and honour, that filled me with admiration and esteem for him."[14]

Hastings's extraordinary state of delusion can be seen in a letter he wrote to his former secretary Thompson on May 20. In this long letter he declares (how he got this idea is not clear) that Burke had agreed that the Rohilla charge would be "decisive for the rest." He adds, ". . . In all this long scene, now exceeding three months, I have undergone only twelve or fourteen days of personal labour; and I have no reason to complain of much suffering, as it has never affected either my health or spirits, nor (except a few days of the publication of the charges) my credit with the public; which I believe now stands higher by many degrees than it ever did. I have now, too, a well-grounded hope that a short period will bring the whole to a conclusion. I mean in the House of Commons. This is the summary of the business of the last three months. The detailed history would fill volumes, and much of these as portentous as instructive. They have destroyed the energy of their governments abroad, and are precipitating their own destruction."

But now comes a paragraph that shows clearly how Hastings has been precipitating—by what he has chosen *not* to do—his own destruction: "I have not visited any of the ministers since the prosecution began. I have not been at the levee nor drawing-room. I have not desired the attendance of a single member. I have broken engagements which were officiously, but kindly made to bring me acquainted with members of the House. I have disdained every species of management. [This included seeking legal help.] I have acted against all that the word [sic] calls discretion. Every artifice of a man who has long thrown away the check of shame has been practiced against me. [This probably refers to Francis.] Yet, my friend, I promise you that he will be most foully discomfited, and my name shall shine the brighter for the means which have been taken to distinguish it."[15]

On June 1 the debate opened in the House on the articles of impeachment. After some wrangling, it was decided that the articles should be brought up one after the other, with a vote following the presentation of each article. Pitt's stated intention was to allow a vote on whether to proceed to a trial only after all the articles had been voted on individually. While there was a substantial attendance at these debates by the members, it was not the public spectacle that the actual trial was to become.

The first charge to be debated concerned the Rohillas. The account I have been quoting from notes that "Mr. Burke, at the urgent desire of the House, entered upon his first charge against Mr. Hastings, which was an enquiry into the Rohilla war.

"The debate on this subject was carried out with great warmth till about three in the morning, when a motion of adjournment was put and carried.

"The following day, Mr. Francis resumed the business. It would be impossible to convey even a faint idea of the wonderful displays of oratory, sound reasoning, and sensibility, which were exhibited on the very important transaction—it would require volumes to give but a hasty sketch of these wonderful orations:—this will be more readily conceived by remarking a well known fact, that at seven the next morning, the gallery was cleared. . . ."[16] Remarkably, Dundas spoke against this charge, and Pitt did not speak at all. When the vote came on June 3 it was 119 to 67 against the article, Pitt voting with the majority. For the moment it appeared as if Hastings's troubles might be coming to an end, and that his tactic had paid off.

On June 13 the House took up the Benares charges. This time the debate for the minority was led by Fox, and this time Pitt did speak. Most of his speech was a vindication of Hastings's contention that Chait Singh was a vassal of the Company, hence Hastings had been fully entitled to attempt to extract from him both the extra taxes and the soldiers that were needed to meet the emergency that had been presented in the defense of the Company's territories. Then, suddenly, Pitt reversed his course. In the words of the Debrett account, ". . . After a most elegant and animated speech of several hours, [he] concluded with declaring, 'that upon the whole, Mr. Hastings' conduct in the transaction alluded to had been so cruel, unjust, and oppressive, that it was impossible, he [Pitt], as a man of honor or honesty, or having any regard to faith and conscience, could any longer resist; and therefore he had fully satisfied his conscience, That [sic] Warren Hastings had been guilty of such enormities and misdemeanors, as constituted a crime sufficient to call upon the justice of the House to impeach him."[17] In short, while Hastings had been fully justified in fining Chait Singh, setting the fine at fifty lakhs was a high crime and misdemeanor.

Macaulay describes what ensued, with, as usual, his own take on the matter. He writes, "The House was thunderstruck; and it well might be so. For the wrong done to Cheyte Sing [sic], even had it been as flagitious as Fox and Francis contended, was a trifle when compared with the horrors which had been inflicted on Rohilcund [sic]. [This was the Rohilla War, for which Pitt had exonerated Hastings two weeks earlier.] But if Mr. Pitt's view of the case of Cheyte Sing were correct, there was no ground for an impeachment, or even for a vote of censure. If the offense of Hastings was really no more than this, that having a right to impose a mulct [a penalty], the amount which mulct was not defined, but was left to be settled by his discretion, he had, not for his own advantage, but for that of the state, demanded too much, was this an offence which required the highest solemnity,—a criminal proceeding to which, during sixty years, no public functionary had been subjected?"[18] Nevertheless the damage was done. The vote for impeachment on this charge was 165 ayes, 54 noes. Among the abstentions was North, who, though infirm and half blind, and who had had years of difficult relations with Hastings that became the subject of his speech on this occasion, simply could not bring himself to vote for Hastings's impeachment.

The great question was, and is, why?—why had Pitt acted in this way? Since he never apologized and never explained, no one can be certain. Some commentators—these include Macaulay and Hastings himself—believe there was collusion between Dundas and Pitt. Macaulay found an entry in Hastings's diary asserting that, on the morning of the debate, Pitt and Dundas met for several hours during which, it is claimed, Dundas talked Pitt out of his resolution to support Hastings. This is at least theoretically possible. Dundas certainly had the motive. But Pitt did not need Dundas to instill feelings of doubt about Hastings. Furthermore Pitt and Dundas were in constant communication. Pitt was in deep financial straits and had no house of his own, so he often stayed with Dundas. It is quite unclear why a special meeting would have been necessary.

As I have been trying to make clear, Pitt was dubious about Hastings from the time he became first minister. On no occasion did he lend himself to an unambiguous endorsement of Hastings—quite the contrary. The puzzle is why he chose such a bizarre issue for impeachment and why he suddenly changed direction in the middle of his speech. One wonders if this was not some impulse that came over him as he was speaking. If not, did he consult the king, whose minister he was, before making such an important decision? Perhaps he felt that his speech constituted only a censure, since proceeding to an actual trial required a second vote after all the articles had been voted on individually. He might have reasoned that if this article failed, the whole attempt to impeach Hastings would fail, and there would never be debate on the serious issues that demanded discussion. Another intriguing possibility is that this was a masterful political maneuver by Pitt.[19] The Whigs were still smarting from the machinations of the king that had removed them from power and installed Pitt. To make matters worse, Pitt then went on to win a general election in which money and support from returning colonials from India—the nabobs—played a significant role. He was vulnerable to the charge of having accepted corrupt Indian influence. Voting against impeachment would have made him even more vulnerable. Hence Burke and the Whigs had placed Pitt in a position where he would either have to double-cross his old Indian allies by voting for impeachment or lay himself open to charges of corruption by voting against it. On this view, Pitt chose to vote for impeachment since he was sure that Hastings would never be convicted and that the Whigs would be saddled with a losing cause. This sounds pretty Machiavellian, but Pitt was pretty Machiavellian.

Hastings still was not persuaded of the seriousness of the matter. He seemed to think that this vote was an aberration which would be undone by the rest of the debate. With this in mind, his supporters in Parliament hoped to continue the session into the summer in order to get the impeachment hearings over and done with. But the majority decided to adjourn, and Parliament did not reconvene until the following January. Long parliamentary recesses were common during this period.

When the body reconvened, the charge dealing with the begums of Oudh became the issue. After an examination of witnesses, including Impey, it was concluded that Hastings's account of the affair before Parliament had contained serious errors. Hastings had to concede these, arguing that he had not written that portion of his testimony and that, in any event, the disputed facts were not central to his defense. On February 7 came one of the most decisive episodes in the entire impeachment process and, indeed, one of the great moments of eighteenth-century parliamentary debate. This was the speech of Richard Sheridan on the begums of Oudh.[20]

Sheridan had become one of the most successful playwrights in England. In 1774 he had written *The Rivals*, and two years later *The School for Scandal*. He had also written pro-American pamphlets and had developed a close friendship with Fox. In 1780, by which time he had the controlling interest in what had been Garrick's Drury Lane Theater, Sheridan became a member of a committee, chaired by Fox, to study parliamentary reforms. That year he had won election to Parliament from Stafford. By 1783, the year of Fox's India Bill, Sheridan began turning his attention to India. By this time Francis had been in England for two years, and he and Burke had begun to orchestrate their attempt to destroy Hastings. By the early winter of 1787, Sheridan was taking an active part in the impeachment attempt. Then came the speech. This time the visitors' galleries were full. A star performance was anticipated.

Sheridan began by arguing that it was not a waste of Parliament's time to investigate incidents that had taken place six years earlier. He then proceeded to ridicule Hastings's attempts at a defense: "In his mind all is shuffling, ambiguous, dark insidious, and little; all affected plainness, and actual dissimulation;—a heterogeneous mass of contradictory qualities; with nothing great but his crimes, and even those contrasted by the littleness of his motives, which at once denote both his baseness and his meanness, and mark him for a traitor and a trickster. Nay, in his stile [sic] and writing there is the same mixture of vicious contrarities;—the most grovelling ideas are conveyed in the most inflated language, giving mock consequence to low cavils, and uttering quibbles in heroics; so that his compositions disgust the mind's taste, as much as his actions excite the soul's abhorrence."[21] After five more hours of this, Sheridan concluded by saying, "You cannot behold the workings of the heart, the quivering lips, the trickling tears, the loud and yet tremulous joys of the millions whom your vote this night will forever save from the cruelty of corrupted power. But though you cannot directly see the effect, is not the true enjoyment of your benevolence increased by the blessing being conferred unseen? Would not the omnipotence of Britain be demonstrated to the wonder of nations by stretching its mighty arm across the deep, and saving by its *fiat* distant millions from destruction? And would the blessings of the people thus saved dissipate in empty air? No! if I may dare to use the figure,—we shall constitute Heaven itself our proxy, to receive for us the blessings of their pious gratitude, and the prayers of their thanksgiving.—It is with confidence, therefore, that I move you on this charge, 'that Warren Hastings be impeached.'"[22]

The effect on the House was electrifying. Hastings's defenders on the floor were hooted down. It would seem that Pitt had intended to oppose the begums charge, but after Sheridan's speech he decided that the tide was too strong to stand against it. The motion to impeach on this article was carried by a vote of 175 to 68. This did not entirely settle the business. Pitt was still insisting that all the charges be voted on before the vote to proceed to a trial. Meanwhile a rumor had been planted in the press that Hastings had 300,000 pounds in Company stock which he was planning to sell, after which he would flee to the Continent. This was false, but it gave urgency to Burke's contention that the trial must be voted on and Hastings arrested. By the end of March, after additional charges had been voted on favorably, Pitt relented. But he insisted that the charges be rewritten and clarified, because as they stood they resembled generalized moral indictments rather than precise legal documents. This rewriting never happened, however, and the failure to do so hung over the actual trial from beginning to end. Burke wanted the charges ill-defined so that he could paint Hastings with a broad brush—the real agenda. He was less concerned with legalities. On April 3 the House voted to proceed to trial on the charges at hand and any future ones that might be brought to bear.

Richard Brinsley Sheridan

The House now had to appoint managers—a managing committee—for the conduct of the trial, and Hastings had to be arrested.
The majority decided that it would have no representative on the
committee; Pitt was still keeping his options open. Burke and Fox
were immediately nominated and appointed. The third nomination
was that of Francis. During the impeachment process Francis had
been omnipresent, constantly popping up to add some fresh bit of
venom. He did not realize that this had alienated many of the members, even those who wanted to see Hastings impeached. Pitt had already criticized Francis during his controversial speech. Thus when
it came time to vote Francis in as a manager, the House rejected him
by a large majority. This was a blow that Francis never really got over.
He was bitter about it for the rest of his life. He had spent more than
a decade trying to bring Hastings down, and now he was being denied the satisfaction of personally being in on the kill. He would have

to play his role in the shadows. On May 21 Hastings was arrested by the serjeant-at-arms and brought to the House of Lords to be arraigned. He was released on a bail of four thousand pounds. He was about to go on trial for his life.

II: THE TRIAL

Parliament adjourned until early in 1787. By the time it reconvened, Hastings had at last begun to take his situation seriously. This was no longer happening to someone else, it was happening to *him*. He decided to retain legal counsel, something he should have done a year earlier. The men he obtained were Edward Law, who later became attorney-general, lord chief justice, and the first Lord Ellenborough; Thomas Plumer, who later became solicitor-general and attorney-general; and Robert Dallas, who was later chief justice of the Court of Common Pleas. This formidable team made its impact felt from the beginning.

At the same time Hastings sought testimonials from people in India, such as the residents of Murshidabad. In soliciting these he first asked the permission, which was willingly granted, of Lord Cornwallis, who was by then the governor-general. These testimonials are moving and seem sincere, but they were easily ridiculed by Burke as being fraudulent. They do not seem to have played any important role in the final outcome of the trial, though they are fascinating to read. They certainly meant a great deal to Hastings personally.*

*While this was gong on, Impey was facing his own inquest, one of the charges being his role in the execution of Nand Kumar. This was rejected by the House in May 1788, and other charges were eventually dropped.

A view of the trial of Warren Hastings, Westminster Hall, February 13, 1787. (Aquatint by E. Dayes)

The trial began at ten o'clock on the morning of February 13, 1787, when the House adjourned to Westminster Hall where the actual proceedings were to take place. At about eleven, just before the Lords arrived, the queen and other attending members of the royal family took their places. The editor of the Debrett chronicle remarks, "Previous to their lordships approach to the Hall, about eleven o'clock, her Majesty, with the Princesses Elizabeth, Augusta and Mary, made their appearance in the Duke of Newcastle's gallery. Her Majesty was dressed in a fawn-coloured satin, her head-dress plain, with a very slender sprinkling of diamonds. The Royal box was graced with the Duchess of Gloucester and the young Prince. The ladies were all in morning dresses; a few with feathers and variegated flowers in their head-dress, but nothing so remarkable as to attract public attention." As it happened, that morning Madame Schwellenberg had dressed the queen alone, since the queen had given Fanny Burney two of the coveted tickets for the opening day of the trial. The second ticket was for her father, but since he declined to come, Burney received permission from the queen to be escorted by her brother Charles.

By the time the actual proceedings began, it was noon. Hastings was read his rights by Lord Thurlow, who was then the lord chancellor. Thurlow declared, "You are called upon, after every expedient allowance for your defence. You have had bail; you have Counsel. Much time has also been granted you—becoming well the circumstances of your case."[23] When this was done, Hastings responded, "My Lords, I am come to this high tribunal equally impressed with a confidence in my own integrity, and in the justice of the Court before which I stand."[24] Now the reading of the charges began, followed by Hastings's answers, which this time had been prepared by counsel. Burney describes the scene:

"A general silence again ensued, and then one of the lawyers opened the cause. He began by reading from an immense roll of parchment the general charges against Mr. Hastings, but he read in so monotonous a chant that nothing more could I hear or understand than now and then the name of Warren Hastings." In the trial transcript, presented in Burke's collected works, these charges consume more than a hundred pages![25] She goes on, "During the readings, to which I vainly lent all my attention, Mr. Hastings, finding it, I presume, equally impossible to hear a word, began to cast his eyes around the House, and having taken a survey of all in front and at the sides, he turned about and looked up; pale looked his face—pale, ill, and altered. I was much affected by the sight of that dreadful harass which was written on his countenance. Had I looked at him without restraint, it could not have been without tears. I felt shocked, too, shocked and ashamed to be seen by him in that place. I had wished to be present from an earnest interest in the business, joined to a firm confidence in his powers of defence; but *his* eyes were not those I wished to meet in Westminster Hall."[26]

Despite the solemnity of the occasion, select members of the gallery could converse with the managers and their entourage. Burney reports exchanging signals with Joshua Reynolds and having a brief but pleasant conversation with Burke's brother Richard. She laments the fact that these otherwise amiable people had joined in the prosecution—"Why will any man of principle join any party? Why not be open to all, yet belong to none?"[27] Then she reports on a conversation with just such a man of principle, a Whig politician named William Windham, one of the managers.

Burney did not know Windham well, which made this conversation all the more remarkable. He was a representative from Norwich and a neighbor of her sister Charlotte, who it may be remembered had married Clement Francis, Hastings's last doctor in India. Everyone admired Windham's integrity. Burney writes that he was "a man of family and fortune, with a very pleasing though not handsome face, a very elegant figure, and an air of fashion and vivacity." He was also a good friend of Samuel Johnson, despite their political differences. He helped to see to it, among other things, that Dr. Johnson had a carriage to get about in when, in his last years, he felt up to it. Windham inspired trust, which was very important here. Burney's conversation, had it been reported maliciously, could have gotten her in very deep trouble indeed. She was, as she was well aware, a representative of the royal family, and she had to be cautious that her own strong views were not attributed to the palace, where they were not necessarily shared.

Windham had come to the box where Burney was seated. Looking at the gathering, he began, "What an assembly is this! How striking a *spectacle*! [He may have noticed that people in the boxes were eating and drinking. The clatter could be heard during the trial.] I had not seen half its splendour down there. You have it here to great advantage; you lose some of the Lords, but you gain all the Ladies. You have a very good place here." Windham then commented on Thurlow, the lord chancellor: "He looks very well from hence . . . and how well he acquits himself on these solemn occasions! What dignity, what loftiness, what high propriety, he comports himself!" After commenting on various of the dignitaries, Burney reports that, "his eye dropped down upon poor Mr. Hastings: the expression of his face instantly lost the gaiety and ease with which it had addressed me; he stopped short in his remarks; he fixed his eyes steadfastly on this new, and but too interesting object, and after viewing him some time in a sort of earnest silence, he suddenly exclaimed, as if speaking to himself, and from an impulse irresistible,—'What a sight is that! to see that man, that small portion of human clay, that poor feeble machine of earth, enclosed now in that little space, brought to that Bar, a prisoner in a spot six foot square—and to reflect his late power! Nations at his command! Princes prostrate at his feet!—What a change! how he must feel it!'"

Burney goes on, "He stopped, and I said not a word. I was glad to see him thus impressed; I hoped it might soften his enmity. I found by his manner, that he had never from the Committee Box looked at him.

"He broke forth again, after a pause of some length—'Wonderful indeed! almost past credibility, is such a reverse! He that, so lately, had the Eastern World nearly at his beck; he, under whose tyrant power princes and potentates sunk and trembled; he whose authority was without the reach of responsibility!—'

"Again he stopped, seeming struck, almost beyond the power of speech, with meditative commiseration; but then, suddenly arousing himself, as if recollecting his 'almost blunted purpose,' he exclaimed, 'O could those—the thousands, the millions who have groaned and languished under the iron rod of his oppressions—could they but—whatever region they inhabit—be permitted one dawn of light, and see him *there!—There*—where he now stands—it might prove, perhaps, some recompense for their sufferings!'"

This was too much for Burney. She addresses her sister Susan, to whom this is written: "I can hardly tell you, my dearest Susan, how shocked I felt at these words! words so hard, and following sensations so much more pitying and philosophic! I cannot believe Mr. Hastings guilty; I feel in myself a strong internal evidence of his innocence; I can regard the prosecution as a party affair; but yet, since his adversaries now openly stake their names, fame, and character against him, I did not think it decent to intrude such an opinion. I could only be sorry and silent."*

She goes on, "Still he [Windham—J.B.] looked him [Hastings—J.B.], earnest in rumination, and as if unable to turn away his eyes; and presently he again exclaimed, 'How wonderful an instance of the instability of mortal power is presented in that object! From posses-

*The physicist I. I. Rabi, who had been a close friend of Oppenheimer's for many years, was asked to testify at his hearing. He was told that there might be damaging evidence against Oppenheimer that Rabi did not know about, that might have significance. Rabi replied that *his* "evidence" was his knowledge of the man. He went on to say, "That is what novels are about. There is a dramatic moment and the history of the man, what made him act and what he did, and what sort of person he was. That is what you are doing here. You are writing a man's life."[28] What Rabi had was "strong internal evidence," which was more important to him than anything else. Burney did not know much about India, but she knew about people.[29]

sions so extensive, from a despotism so uncontrolled, to see him now there in that small circumference! In the history of human nature how memorable will be the records of this day! a day that brings to the great tribunal of the nation a man whose power, so short a time since was of equal magnitude with his crimes!'

"Good Heaven! thought I, and do you really believe all this? Can Mr. Hastings appear to you such a monster? and are you not merely swayed by party? I could not hear him without shuddering, nor see him thus in earnest without alarm. I thought myself no longer bound to silence, since I saw, by the continuance as well as by the freedom of his exclamations, he conceived me of the same sentiments with himself; and therefore I hardly resolved to make known to him that mistake, which, indeed, was a liberty that seemed no longer imperti-nent, but a mere act of justice and honesty."

Here Burney was about to step over the line. Nothing in her posi-tion—quite the contrary—gave her the right to express this sort of opinion publicly, above all to one of the managers. One can only stand in awe of her courage and the depth of her convictions. She continues, "His very expressive pause, his eyes still steadily fixed on Mr. Hastings, gave me ample opportunity for speaking; though I had some little difficulty how to get out what I wished to say. However, in the midst of his reverie, I broke forth, but not without great hesita-tion and, very humbly, I said, 'Could you pardon me, Mr. Wyndham [sic], if I should forget, for a moment, that you are a Committee-man and speak to you frankly?'

"He looked surprised, but laughed at the question and very ea-gerly called out, 'Oh yes, yes, pray speak out, I beg it!'

" 'Well, then, I may venture to say to you, that I believe it utterly impossible for any one, not particularly engaged on the contrary side, ever to enter a court of justice, and not instantly, and involuntarily, wish well to the prisoner!'

"His surprise subsided by the general speech, which I had not courage to put in a more pointed way, and he very readily answered, ' 'Tis natural, certainly, and what must almost unavoidably be the first impulse; yet where justice—'

"I stopped him; I saw I was not comprehended, and thought else he might say something to stop me.

" 'May I,' I said, 'go yet a little farther?'

"'Yes,' cried he, with a very civil smile, 'and I feel an assent beforehand.'

"'Supposing then, that even you, if that may be supposed, could be divested of all knowledge of the particulars of this affair, and in the same state of general ignorance that I confess myself to be, and could then, like me, have seen Mr. Hastings make his entrance into this Court, and looked at him when he was brought to that bar; not even you, Mr. Wyndham, could then have reflected on such a vicissitude for him, on all he has left, and all he has lost, and not given him, like me, all your best wishes the moment you beheld him.'

"The promised assent came not, though he was too civil to contradict me; but still I saw he understood me only in a general sense. I feared going farther; a weak advocate is apt to be a mischievous one; and, as I knew nothing, it was not to a professed enemy I could talk of what I only believed."

Windham chose, at least for the moment, to change the subject. He began to discuss personalities, both present and absent. The most stunning absence was that of Pitt. "A trial is brought on by the whole House of Commons in a body," Windham said, "and he is absent at the very opening. . . . I am glad of it. for 'tis to his eternal disgrace." Pitt was quite content to leave the conduct of the trial to the opposition. Then Windham pointed out Major Scott. Burney had strong feelings about him. She writes, "What a pity that Mr. Hastings should have trusted his case to so frivolous an agent! I believe, and indeed it is the general belief, both of foes and friends, that to his officious and injudicious zeal the present prosecution is wholly owing." Then she is shown Francis and muses on the strange coincidence that one of Hastings's greatest admirers—her brother-in-law—and one of his greatest enemies should have the same last name. The subject of Francis brings Windham back to Hastings. "A prouder heart" cried he, "an ambition more profound, were never, I suppose lodged in any mortal mould than in that man! With what a port he entered! did you observe him? his air! I saw not his face, but his air! his port!"

"'Surely there,' cried I, 'he could not be to blame! He comes upon his defence; ought he to look as if he gave himself up?'

"'Why no; 'tis true he must look what vindication to himself he can; we must not blame him there.'

"Encouraged by this little concession, I resolved to venture further, and once more said, 'May I again, Mr. Wyndham, forget that you are a *Committee-man*, and say something not fit for a *Committee-man* to hear?'

"'Oh yes!,' cried he, laughing very much, and looking extremely curious.

"'I must fairly, then, own myself utterly ignorant upon this subject, and—and—may I go on?'

"'I beg you will!'

"'Well then,—and originally prepossessed in favour of the object!'

"He quite startled, and with a look of surprise from which all pleasure was separated, exclaimed—'Indeed!'

"'Yes!' cried I, ''tis really true, and really out now!'

"'For Mr. Hastings, prepossessed!' he repeated, in a tone that seemed to say—do you not mean Mr. Burke?

"'Yes,' I said, 'for Mr. Hastings! But I should not, to you, have presumed to own it just at this time,—so little as I am able to do honour to my prepossessions by any materials to defend it,—but that you have given me courage, by appearing so free from all malignity in the business. 'Tis, therefore, your own fault!'

"'But can you speak seriously,' cried he, 'when you say you know nothing of this business?'

"'Very seriously: I never entered into it at all; it was always too intricate to tempt me.'

"'But, surely you must have read the charges?'

"'No; they are so long, I never had the courage to begin.'

"The conscious look which he heard this, brought—all too late—to my remembrance, that one of them, was drawn up and delivered in the House by himself! I was really very sorry to have been so unfortunate; but I had no way to call back the words, so was quiet perforce.

"'Come then,' cried he emphatically, 'to hear Burke! come and listen to him, and you will be mistress of the whole! Hear Burke, and read the charges of the Begums, and then you will form your judgment without difficulty.'

"I would rather (thought I) hear him upon any other subject: but I made no answer; I only said, 'Certainly, I can gain nothing by what is going forward to-day. I meant to come to the opening now, but it seems rather like the shutting up!'

"He was not to be put off. 'You will come, however, to hear Burke? To hear truth, reason, justice eloquence! You will then see, in other colours, "That Man!" There is more cruelty, more oppression, more tyranny, in that little machine, with an arrogance, a self-confidence, unexampled, unheard of.'"

At this point one might imagine that anyone else would have backed off. But not Burney! Once launched, *nothing* was about to stop her.

"'Indeed sir!' cried I; 'that does not appear to those who know him; and—I—know him a little.'

"'Do you?' cried he earnestly; 'personally, do you know him?'

"'Yes; and from that knowledge arose this prepossession I have confessed.'

"'Indeed! what you have seen of him have you then so much approved?'

"'Yes, very much! I must own the truth!'

"'But you have not seen much of him?'

"'No, not lately. [Recall that Burney had been in service to the queen during much of this period, and her social life was at the pleasure of the queen—J.B.] My first knowledge of him was almost immediately upon his coming from India: I had heard nothing of these accusations; I had never been in the way of hearing them, and knew not even that there were any to be heard. I saw him, therefore, quite without prejudice, for or against him; and, indeed, I must own, he soon gave me a strong interest in his favour.'

"The surprise with which he heard me, must have silenced me on the subject, had it not been accompanied with an attention so earnest as to encourage me still to proceed. It is evident to me that this Committee live so much shut up with one another, that they conclude all the world of the same opinions with themselves, and universally imagine that the tyrant they think themselves pursuing is a monster in every part of his life, and held in contempt and abhorrence by all mankind. Could I then be sorry, seeing this, to contribute my small mite towards clearing, at least, so very wide a mistake? On the contrary, when I saw he listened, I was most eager to give him all I could to hear.

"'I found him,' I continued, 'so mild, so gentle, so extremely pleasing in his manners—'

"'Gentle?' cried he, with quickness.

"'Yes, indeed; gentle even to humility!'

"'Humility? Mr. Hastings and humility!'

"'Indeed, it is true; he is perfectly diffident in the whole of his manner, when engaged in conversation; and so much struck was I, at that very time, by seeing him so simple, so unassuming, when just returned from a government that had accustomed him to a power superior to our monarchs here, that it produced an effect upon my mind in his favour which nothing can erase!'

"'Oh yes, yes!' cried he, with great energy, 'you will give it up! you must lose it, must give it up! it will be plucked away, rooted wholly out of your mind!'

"'Indeed, sir,' cried I, steadily, 'I believe not!'

"'You believe not?' repeated he, with added animation; 'then there will be the more glory in making you a convert!'

"If 'conversion' is the word, thought I, I would rather make than be made.

"'But, Mr. Wyndham,' cried I, 'all my amazement now is at your condescension in speaking to me upon this business at all, when I have confessed to you my total ignorance of the subject, and my original prepossession in favour of the object. Why do you not ask me when I was at the play? and how I liked the last opera?'"

Windham persisted—and so did she, never giving ground. "And then," she writes, "he very civilly bowed, and went down to his box, leaving me much persuaded that I had never yet been engaged in a conversation so curious, from its circumstances, in my life. The warm well-wisher myself of the prisoner, though formerly the warmest admirer of his accuser [this certainly refers to Burke—J.B.], engaged, even at his trial, and in his presence, in so open a discussion with one of his principal prosecutors; and the Queen herself in full view unavoidably beholding me in close and eager conference with an avowed member of the opposition."

She continues, "These circumstances made me at first enter into discourse with Mr. Wyndham with the utmost reluctance; but though I wished to shun him, I could not, when once attacked, decline to converse with him. It would not but injure the cause of Mr. Hastings to seem to fear hearing the voice of his accusers; and it could be attributed to undue Court influence had I avoided any intercourse with an acquaintance so long ago established as a member of the opposition."

Then, she concludes, "Long since, indeed, when I considered with myself the accidents by which I might occasionally be thrown in the way of the Court adversaries, I formed this resolution:—To let them see no difference whatsoever in my behaviour, but to conduct myself uniformly among them, just as I had done formerly when I resided in St. Martin's Street"—her father's house.[30]

But she was not residing in St. Martin's Street, and, as the following quotation shows, her conversation had not gone unremarked. It is Lord Bulkeley who remarks, "I have made every inquiry whether the King ever expresses himself to his people about him in favour of Hastings, and I am told he is very guarded and reserved on this subject, but that some *females* in his house talk loud and warmly in his [Hastings's] favour, which occasions the attributing the same opinions to him [the king]."[31] In fact, Burney recounts in her journal that she went to the queen herself to give a full account of her conversation with Windham. She claims that the queen was "herself touched even to tears by the relation."[32] One wonders.

THE SECOND DAY of the trial, which Burney did not attend, was a continuation of the first, with the rest of the charges being read. On the third day, which Burney did attend, Burke began his opening. It lasted four days, which was not untypical for Burke's orations. He began in a judicious tone, one suitable for the tribunal he was addressing. His first important point was that under the circumstances of an impeachment trial—above all in *this* impeachment trial—the usual laws of evidence in jury trials should not apply. He declared, "It is by this tribunal that statesmen who abuse their power are accused by statesmen and tried by statesmen, not upon the niceties of a narrow jurisprudence, but upon enlarged and solid principles of state morality. It is here that those who by the abuse of power have violated the spirit of the law can never hope for protection from any of its forms; it is here that those who have refused to conform themselves to its perfections can never hope to escape through any of its defects."[33] Days, if not weeks, which added up to

Edmund Burke, 1771. (Painting by an artist in the studio of Sir Joshua Reynolds)

months, were spent in the subsequent years of the trial in which this principle was attacked and defended in innumerable specific instances, followed by lengthy deliberations by the sitting Lords. In the end, the Lords decided in essentially all these instances that this *was* a judicial process and that the usual laws governing a trial by jury applied. Every impeachment process has had to confront this question.

By the second day of his opening, Burke had turned his attention to Hastings directly. Making a point that became central to the prosecution, he rejected any contention that one morality applied to the affairs of England and another to India—what he called "geographical morality." As he put it, "This geographical morality we do protest against; Mr. Hastings shall not screen himself under it; and on this point I hope and trust many words will not be necessary to satisfy your Lordships. But we think it necessary, in justification of ourselves, to declare that the laws of morality are the same everywhere, and that there is no action which would pass for an act of extortion, of peculation, of bribery, and oppression in England, that is not an act of extortion, of peculation, of bribery, and oppression in Europe, Asia, Africa, and the world over. . . . I trust and hope your Lordships will not judge by laws and institutions which you do not know, against those laws and institutions which you do know, and under whose power and authority Mr. Hastings went out to India. . . ."[34]

But which laws to choose if the laws conflict? Burke seemed to be saying there was only one set of laws and one standard of behavior—those of England. Those laws, he argued, were a gift of God. But which God? While one may agree or disagree with these contentions in Burke's opening remarks, they were certainly appropriate and were stated in a language appropriate to the occasion. It was on the third day when things took a dramatic turn. Indeed, one wonders whether Burke had now abandoned the aim of seeking a verdict favorable to his case in this court and had turned his full attention to the wider court of public opinion. In a letter to Francis, he made it clear that he had now decided to "work upon the popular sense."[35]

He did so by dealing with the allegation that in 1783 there had been widespread use of torture in a district in northern Bengal, employed in the collection of taxes. Even if these allegations had been all or partially true, what this had to do with Hastings was entirely unclear. Burke evidently thought that if he could make this charge sufficiently graphic, it would somehow spill over onto Hastings anyway. "Those who could not raise the money, were most cruelly tortured," he declaimed, "cords were drawn tight round their fingers, till the flesh of the four on each hand was actually incorporated, and became one solid mass: the fingers were then separated again by wedges of iron and wood driven in between them.—Others were tied two and two by the feet, and thrown across a wooden bar, upon which they hung, with their feet uppermost; they were then beat on the soles of the feet, till their toe-nails dropped off." And the women! They were dragged from their homes and some of them had "the nipples of their breasts put in a cleft bamboo, and torn off."[36] During this account, it was reported, Mrs. Sheridan fainted and had to be removed from the chamber. Since there was no cross-examination—Burke was after all not a witness—the materiality of this charge to the impeachment of

Hastings, to say nothing of its factual basis, was never debated. It simply stood on the record.

Burney missed the first day of what she referred to as Burke's "harangue,"[37] but she was there for the second. She writes (note the nuances), "All I heard of his eloquence, and all I had conceived of his great abilities, was more than answered by his performance. Nervous, clear, and striking was almost all he uttered: the main business, indeed, of his coming forth was frequently neglected, and not seldom, wholly lost; but his excursions were so fanciful, so entertaining, and so ingenious, that no miscellaneous hearer like myself, could blame them. It is true that he was unequal, but his inequality produced an effect which in so long a speech, was perhaps preferable to greater consistency, since, though it lost attention in its falling off, recovered it with additional energy by some ascent unexpected and wonderful. When he narrated, he was easy, flowing, and natural; when he declaimed, energetic, warm, and brilliant. The sentiments he interspersed were as nobly conceived as they were highly coloured; his satire had a poignancy of wit that made it as entertaining as it was penetrating; his allusions and quotations, as far as they were English and within my reach [Burke often used Latin quotations—J.B.], were apt and ingenious; and the wild and sudden flights of his fancy, bursting forth from his creative imagination in language fluent, forcible, and varied, had a charm for my ear and my attention wholly new and perfectly irresistible."

But to what end? Burney goes on, "Were talents such as these exercised in the service of truth, unbiased by party and prejudice, how could we sufficiently applaud their exhalted possessor? But though frequently he made me tremble by his strong and horrible representations, his own violence recovered me, by stigmatising his assertions with personal ill-will and designing illiberality. Yet at times, I confess, with all I felt, wished, and thought concerning Mr. Hastings, the whirlwind of his eloquence nearly drew me into its vortex." In this paragraph, with her uncanny insight, Burney has foreseen the entire arc of the trial.

On the sixth day of the trial, Fox introduced a motion which could have been decisive to the outcome. There were now twenty-one charges, which included only eight of the original ones. Of these, the managers ultimately limited their case to the four they thought were the strongest. Fox proposed that each of these four charges be heard and then voted on separately, just as had been done in the House. Thurlow asked Hastings's counsel Edward Law if this procedure was acceptable. Law responded most emphatically that it was not, and a debate ensued. According to the Debrett account, "Mr. Fox rose, and stated to their Lordships, that the mode proposed in such a complicated case was adopted to avoid obscurity—to place the various questions in such a clear point of view, that their Lordships might with the greater case determine *seriatim* upon the respective merits of each article of impeachment."[38] After further statements by the managers, "Mr. Law entered into a most elaborate argument to prove it would be inconsistent with the rules of justice to suffer the prosecution to proceed in the mode proposed by Mr. Fox. He cited the case of Archbishop Laud [Archbishop William Laud had been impeached in the seventeenth century, just before the civil war. The impeachment was abandoned, but Parliament, in a special act, declared him guilty anyway, and had him executed.] and was very urgent to prove that all the cases in which impeachments had been determined article by article were by consent of the party under prosecution. In the warmth of his zeal, he dropped a few words which reflected on Mr. Burke, for the harsh and cruel manner in which he had opened the prosecution." What neither side said explicitly—which was the real point—was what might happen if, in the presentation of one of the charges, the managers should have another day like the one they had when Sheridan spoke in the House. Hastings might never get another chance.

The Lords adjourned for three days to consider the matter. When they reconvened, Thurlow addressed the managers: "Gentlemen of the House of Commons, the House of Lords have ordered me to acquaint you, that they have made the following order:—'To hear the WHOLE Evidence in support of ALL the Charges of impeachment and THEN to let the Defendant enter on his defence."[39] The vote had been 88 to 33, which indicated that the managers might have their work cut out for them.

Fox then opened the managers' case with a presentation of the Benares charges—the episode involving Chait Singh which had moved Pitt to vote in favor of impeachment. As it happened, Burney was in the audience on that day as well. She notes, "Mr. Fox spoke

Charles James Fox, 1793. (Painting by Karl Anton
Hickel)

five hours, and with a violence that did not make me forget what I
had heard of his being in such a fury. . . . I shall only say a word of the
speakers as far as relates to my own feelings about them, and that
briefly to say that I adhere to Mr. Burke, whose oratorical powers appeared to me far more gentleman-like, scholar-like, and fraught with
true genius than those of Mr. Fox. It may be I am prejudiced by old
kindnesses of Mr. Burke, and it may be that the countenance of Mr.
Fox may have turned me against him, for it struck me to have a bold-
ness in it quite hard and callous."

Fox was a curious mixture of a man who had had a somewhat disreputable private life but who had become one of the most successful
politicians of his age. His was not a "countenance" that Burney
would have admired. On her next visit to Westminster Hall, on a day
when no speeches were scheduled, only the hearing of witnesses,

Burney ran into Burke himself. She reports that upon seeing her "he immediately made up [the stairs] to me, and with an air of such frank kindness that, could I have forgot his errand in that Hall, would have made me receive him as formerly, when I was almost fascinated with him." Burke was a great admirer of her novels. She goes on, "But far other were my sensations. I trembled as he approached me, with conscious change of sentiments, and with a dread of his pressing from me a disapprobation he might resent, but which I knew not how to disguise.

"'Near-sighted as I am,' cried he, 'I knew you immediately. I knew you from our box the moment I looked up; yet how long it is except for an instant here, since I have seen you!'

"'Yes,' I hesitatingly answered, 'I—live in a monastery now.'

"He said nothing to this. He felt, perhaps, it was meant to express my inaccessibility.

"I inquired after Mrs. Burke. He recounted to me the particulars of his sudden seizure when he spoke last, from the cramp in his stomach, owing to a draught of cold water which he drank in the midst of the heat of his oration. [On February 18, in the course of his speech, Burke suffered some sort of spasm and was momentarily unable to continue.—J.B.]

"I could not even wear a semblance of being sorry for him on this occasion. . . ."

Burney's cold answer caused Burke to turn away. But a little later when she said something, Windham, who was standing next to her, called out, "Mr. Burke, Miss Burney speaks to you!" She notes that "He gave me his immediate attention with an air so full of respect that it quite shamed me. 'Indeed,' I cried, 'I had never meant to speak to Mr. Burke again, after hearing him in Westminster Hall. I had meant to keep at least that *geographical timidity*.' I alluded to an expression in his great speech of 'geographical morality' which had struck me very much. He laughed heartily, instantly comprehending me, and assured me that it was an idea that had occurred to him on the moment he had uttered it, wholly without study."[40]

Sometime later, after more exposure to Burke's oratory, Burney had another discussion with Windham. She comments, "How finely he has spoken! with what fullness of intelligence and what fervour!" Windham completely agreed, but then Burney adds, "'Yet—so much!—so long!' 'True!,' cried he, ingenuously, yet concerned. 'What a pity he can never stop!' And then I enumerated some of the diffuse and unnecessary paragraphs which had weakened his cause, as well as his speech. He [Windham—J.B.] was perfectly candid, though always with some reluctance. 'But a man who speaks in public,' he said, 'should never forget what will do for his auditors: for himself alone, it is not enough to think; but for what is fitted and likely to be interesting to them.'" Then Burney adds, "He wants nothing but a flapper." ("Flappers" were functionaries invented by Jonathan Swift in *Gulliver's Travels*. These useful individuals had bladders which they used to strike gently the mouth of the speaker and the right ear of the listener if there was a company of two or more.) Windham replied, "He [Burke—J.B.] takes flapping inimitably." "You then," Burney suggests, "should be his flapper." "And," Windham responded, "sometimes I am." As great an orator as Burke was, he was also at times his own worst enemy.

On April 11 the managers completed their case on the mistreatment of Chait Singh with an oration by Burke in which he justified the rebellion, and slaughter of the sepoys, that ensued after Chait Singh's arrest. This was, said Burke, an act of citizens doing their duty to preserve their government, just as he hoped any British citizen would do his or her duty in comparable circumstances. The defense would get its chance to respond only after all the charges were heard, so the court next turned its attention to the matter of the begums of Oudh, the second charge. Its management was turned over to Sheridan in light of his brilliant performance in the House. The hearing on this charge began on April 15 and involved, for several weeks, the examination of witnesses, including Impey, who attempted to explain to the court that the begums had sponsored a rebellion against the Company that justified the actions taken against them. This caused Burke to declaim of the East India Company, "O miserable state! O abandoned fortunes of Mr. Hastings! O fallen lot of England! when no assistance could be found but what was given by Sir Elijah Impey!—a man who was to act extrajudicially, and in a district where even his judicial capacity had no force."[41]

With the taking of evidence, and the odd adjournments, Sheridan did not begin his summary speech until June 3. This too was a gala occasion. The Debrett account notes that "Since the commencement of this memorable trial, Westminster Hall has not seen so numerous or so brilliant an assemblage of persons as crowded every part of it this day. By eight o'clock in the morning the avenues leading to the Hall, through New and Old Palace Yards, were filled with ladies and gentlemen of the most respectable appearance, many of them Peeresses in full dress for upwards of an hour before the gates were opened. The exertions made to push forward, with a view to get convenient seats, had like to have proved fatal to many."[42] To this it may be added that some of them had paid as much as fifty guineas for a ticket.

Sheridan spoke for four days, much of it a reprise of what he had said in the House. On the fourth day he reached a kind of oratorical climax. In particular he delivered a homily on filial piety which has often been quoted. He said, "FILIAL PIETY: It is the primal bond of society—It is that instinctive principle, which, panting for its proper good, soothes, unbidden, each sense and sensitivity of man!—It now quivers on every lip!—It now beams from every eye!—It is that gratitude, which softens under the sense of recollected good, is eager to own the vast countless debt it ne'er, alas!, can pay—for so many long years of unceasing solicitude, honourable self-denials, life preserving cares!—It is that part of our practice, where duty drops its awe!—where reverence refines into love!—It asks no aid of memory!—it needs not the deductions of reason!—Pre-existing, paramount over all, whether law or human rule—few arguments can increase and none can diminish it!—It is the sacrament of our nature—not only the duty but the indulgence of man—It is his first great privilege—It is amongst his last and most endearing delights! when the bosom glows with the idea of reverberated love—when to requite on the visitations of nature, and return the blessings that have been received! when—what was emotion fixed into vital principle—what was instinct habituated into a matter—passion—always all the sweetest energies of man—hangs over each vicissitude of all that must pass away—aids the melancholy virtues in their last sad tasks of life—to chear [sic] langours of decrepitude and age—explore the thought—explain the aching eye!"[43]

One marvels that the inspiration for this afflatus was none other than Asaf-ud-Daula, the nawab of Oudh, who it may be recalled had fifty barbers and four thousand gardeners. The junior of the two begums was his mother, and the senior his grandmother, and both women despised him. The notion that his mother had lavished "long years of unceasing solicitude" on her son borders on the ludicrous. It was probably more like long years in which she wished to see his throat slit. Of course, Sheridan's audience did not know this. They were overcome with grief at the idea that Hastings had encouraged the nawab, after much hesitation, to recover by force the money that was probably stolen from him in the first place and which he owed the Company anyway. Sheridan was overcome as well. At the end of his speech he fainted in the arms of the fortunately stationed Burke. The historian Edward Gibbon, who witnessed this performance, noted that "Sheridan, on the close of his speech, sunk into Burke's arms, but I called this morning, he is perfectly well. A good actor."[44]

After Sheridan's speech, Parliament adjourned. The next convening of the court was scheduled for the first Tuesday of the next session of Parliament in November. But, before it met, the king went mad. The modern diagnosis of George III's illness seems to be that he suffered from an hereditary disorder called porphyria. Among the symptoms are discolored urine and rambling speech, accompanied by hallucinations and symptoms of paranoia, all of which the king exhibited in full measure. Burney was, of course, a witness to this. Her first reference to the king's illness is dated October 17, 1788. It is quite brief and reads, "Our return to Windsor is postponed till tomorrow. The King is not well; he has not been quite well some time, yet nothing I hope alarming, though there is uncertainty as to his complaint not very satisfactory; so precious too his health."[45] But on the 26th she reports, "The King was prevailed upon not to go to chapel this morning. I met him in the passage from the Queen's room; he stopped me, and conversed upon his health near half-an-hour, still with that extreme quickness of speech and manner that belongs to fever; and he hardly sleeps, he tells me, one minute all night; indeed, if he recovers not his rest, a most delirious fever seems to threaten him. He is all agitation, all emotion, yet all benevolence and goodness, even to a degree that makes it touching to hear him speak. He assures everybody of his health; he seems only fearful to give uneasiness to others, yet certainly he is better than last night. Nobody speaks of his illness, nor what they think of it."[46] Curiously, during this period the king stopped his incessant and characteristic use of the "what, what's" and "heh, heh's" that Burney remarked on the first time she met him.

Despite efforts of the palace to curtail information about the king's illness, the news soon spread to Parliament, and on November 20 the new session was postponed indefinitely. Immediately it became clear that there might be need of a regency act by which George, Prince of Wales, would become king or regent. The Prince of Wales had an exceedingly tempestuous relationship with his rather puritanical father, who saw his eldest son as a free-spending, womanizing rake. The notion of a regency with George as the regent would have been an abomination to the king. Likewise it was an abomination to Pitt, who understood that because of the prince's Whig sympathies, were he to become king or regent it would mean a new government with the Whigs taking power. Sheridan was one of the prince's closest friends and advisers, and could expect an important cabinet role in such a government. Had this happened, Hastings probably would have been doomed. For example, the regent might have been able to create peers inimical to Hastings. Pitt managed to put off the enactment of a regency act as long as possible in the hope that the king would recover.

During the period of the king's most intense illness, the queen was not allowed to see him. Neither was Burney, but she was directed by the queen to stand outside the king's bedroom at dawn each day to receive from the doctors a report of how he seemed. She was then to convey this information to the queen in all its detail. Thus she was in as good a position as anyone to know the king's true state. But nothing prepared her for the events of the morning of February 2, 1789.

After her usual briefing from the king's doctor, Burney asked him where the king might be walking that day so that she could choose someplace else. There were strict instructions that unless authorized by his doctors, no one should have contact with the king. She was told that Kew Gardens would be safe since, if the king went out, he would walk elsewhere. As she was finishing her stroll there later, she was horrified to see the king with two of his doctors. She writes, "Alarmed past all possible expression, I waited not to know more, but turning back, ran off with all my might. But what was my terror to hear myself pursued!—to hear the voice of the King himself loudly and hoarsely calling after me, 'Miss Burney! Miss Burney!'

"I protest I was ready to die. I knew not in what state he might be at the time; I only knew the orders to keep out of his way were universal; that the Queen would highly disapprove any unauthorised meeting, and that the very action of my running away might deeply, in his present state, offend him. Nevertheless, on I ran, too terrified to stop, and in search of some short passage, for the garden is full of little labyrinths, by which I might escape."

Finally the king's doctors caught up to her and begged her to stop, since it hurt the king to run after her. When the king was a few yards from her he asked, "Why did you run away?" She writes, "Shocked at a question impossible to answer, yet a little assured by the mild tone of his voice, I instantly forced myself forward to meet him, through the internal sensation which satisfied me, this was a step the most proper to appease his suspicions and displeasure, was so violently combated by the tremor of my nerves, that I fairly think I may reckon it the greatest effort of personal courage I have ever made.

"The effort answered: I looked up, and met all his wonted benignity of countenance, though something still of wildness in his eyes. Think, however, of my surprise, to feel him put both his hands round my two shoulders and then kiss my cheek!"

She then had a remarkable private conversation with the king, away from his doctors and attendants. He was concerned, he said, about her relations with Madame Schwellenberg. These had grown so bad that it was making Burney physically ill. Indeed, people who saw her at the later stages of the trial feared for her life. The king said, "Never mind her!—don't be oppressed!—I am your friend! don't let her cast you down!—I know you have a hard time of it—but don't mind her." She was, as she writes, "thunderstruck with astonishment." The king also talked about her father and his *History of Music*, which discussed at great length his favorite composer, Handel. He said he was planning to form a new government: "I shall be much better served; and when once I get away, I shall rule with a rod of iron!"[47] Clearly the king was on the road to recovery. There would be no regency act.

On April 21, 1789, the trial resumed. Because of the interruptions, the Lords had sat as judges for only thirty-five days during the preceding year. Remarkably, in terms of the number of days in which they convened as a court in any given year of the trial, this turned out to be the high-water mark. The year 1788 also saw the peak of public interest. Except for the odd session, in which people such as Lord Cornwallis testified, the public spectacle of that opening year was never repeated.

Burke began this new session by mocking a complaint of Hastings (it would become a recurrent theme) that the costs of his defense were bankrupting him. He had spent to this point, he said, some 30,000 pounds on legal fees and the rest. Burke had no sympathy. He was sure, he said, that this was a trivial sum compared to what Hastings must have accepted in bribes, the charge now on the docket. Perhaps Burke knew that in August of the previous year, Hastings had finally completed the purchase of his beloved Daylesford, which he was now restoring. Burke would probably not have known the final cost of both the purchase and the restoration. It was 54,400 pounds—a fortune.

By this time, many, even in Burke's own party, were beginning to weary of the whole exercise. To compound matters, in his opening statement Burke made a charge against Hastings that almost brought the entire proceedings to a close. During his general discussion of what he felt were Hastings's illegal money dealings, and without warning, he suddenly claimed that Hastings had murdered Nand Kumar "by the hands of Elijah Impey."[48] Whether this was a spontaneous flourish, like his "geographical morality," or whether it was something that Burke had planned beforehand, one does not know, but the reaction was instantly hostile. In the first place, Impey had undergone his own impeachment trial and had been acquitted on all counts, to say nothing of murder. Now Burke had offhandedly introduced this charge with no presumption of innocence and no opportunity for Impey to defend himself. In the second place, the trial and execution of Nand Kumar is nowhere to be found among the charges the managers had made against Hastings. Nand Kumar had entered the charges at all because Francis had resurrected the accusations of bribery that Nand Kumar had invented and presented to the Council, of which Francis had been a member. The managers, in preparing their case against Hastings, had been careful to stay away from Nand Kumar's own trial and execution. After all, Francis had been part of the Council majority that had let Nand Kumar go to his death with no attempt on their part to save his life, or even to demand a judicial review. This was not a place that the managers wished to go.

Hastings's defense team immediately objected. Major Scott introduced a petition that stated that "all those extraneous facts, which had been advanced by the Hon. Manager [Burke] were false and unfounded, and that the Hon. Manager had coolly and deliberately misrepresented facts, knowingly and wittingly."[49] The trial was postponed while the matter was debated. Burke, according to the Debrett account, said "he believed he must look at some distance for a character and approbation—to cool and dispassionate posterity. He had trusted to the goodness of the cause, and to the approbation of his own mind. The House had appointed him the prosecutor of Mr. Hastings, and he had executed that important trust in such a manner as appeared most agreeable to his own best judgment, and was most consistent with the honour and dignity of the House; and if after he had gone through such a world of labour and fatigue, they thought it proper to remove him, he should not be sorry for it: it was what he wanted—he would then enjoy ease and quiet, and be happy."[50]

Needless to say, Burke was not removed, but he was censured by the House. This time Pitt sided with Hastings. But that did not stop Burke and the other managers from finding ways to introduce this accusation anyway. In the very speech in which Burke accepted the censure, he noted, according to the Debrett account, that "as the Commons had been pleased to censure him for having mentioned the death of Nundcomar [sic] as a charge against Mr. Hastings, he [Burke] would not attempt in the course of the trial to shew [sic] that Mr. Hastings had any hand in that death. He would leave it to be supposed that an execution, which at least for that time put an end to a charge pending against Mr. Hastings, and which was consequently a most useful event to him, had been effected by a fortuitous coincidence of circumstance, in which Mr. Hastings had no concern, but from which, happening so very opportunely, he derived the greatest advantage."[51] Clearly this kind of subterfuge was not lost on the Lords who were judging the case. It could only prejudice them against the prosecution. But by this time Burke may well have re-

signed himself to the likelihood of losing his case. He may have decided to work almost entirely on the "popular sense." Certainly his
language was becoming increasingly reckless—*vulgar* may not be too
strong a word.

During the same speech Burke brought up the matter of
Nobkissen, the wealthy Bengali who had advanced Hastings money
and eventually gave it to him as a present, a present that Hastings
placed on the Company's account. Of Nobkissen, Burke said, "This
Nobekissen [sic] was a Banyan; and if there was anything more flinty,
more gripy, more thrifty, or more careful to improve the value of
money than a Jew, it was a *Gentoo Banyan,* or Money Broker."[52] Burke
was by no means a notorious anti-Semite. Indeed he had written ad-
miringly of the Jews. But here one senses he was playing to the
gallery. There is no question that Hastings had been sloppy with his
accounts. Burke was not far from wrong when he said that Hastings
had "exhibited accounts in all colors—black, white and mezzotinto,
in all languages—Gentoo, Persian and English;—yet by simple rules
of comprehension, they could not be understood. . . ."[53] But this did
not mean that he had taken bribes or concealed money. The managers then tried to introduce as evidence the bribery testimony that
Nand Kumar had given to the Council, but this request was also denied. On July 8 Parliament adjourned. The trial did not reconvene
until February 16, 1790. In 1789 there had been seventeen days of
actual trial.

✍

ON JULY 14, 1789, the Bastille fell. The French Revolution was
under way. Burke had a growing distrust of it, which by early 1790
had developed into an active opposition. On February 9, a week before the trial reconvened, he addressed Parliament and declared that
"The French had shown themselves the ablest architects of ruin that
had hitherto existed in the world. In that very short space of time
they had completely pulled down to the ground, their monarchy,
their navy, their commerce, their arts and their manufactures. Our
friendship and our intercourse with that nation had once been, and
might again become, more dangerous to us than their worst hostility."[54] There are echoes here of Burke's attitude toward the behavior

of the East India Company in India—now repeated, he felt, in the behavior of the French toward their own institutions. In both cases he saw traditional institutions of immense value being torn asunder by forces that had no appreciation of what they were destroying. Someone like Chait Singh was for Burke a representative of an ancient nobility; Hastings had acted toward him the way the French middle class was acting toward its own nobility.

These views put Burke in opposition to essentially all of the Whig hierarchy. As his outlook hardened, he fell out with Fox, Sheridan, and even Francis. That they did not replace him as the lead manager in the Hastings trial is remarkable. One senses that, in light of everything else that was happening, they now had only a marginal interest in the trial and had decided to let Burke ride his hobbyhorse with their cooperation, but with less and less enthusiasm.

In the 1790 session the Lords heard more testimony on Hastings's alleged financial misdeeds. This was summarized in a final address by Fox. The court session ended on June 9. But there had been an important development. During the session of 1789 the managers had decided to seek permission of the House to bring their case to a close with only one additional article, this having to do with contracts. The remaining articles would be abandoned. Now, on May 11, the House gave the managers formal permission to choose any selection of articles they saw fit. This action may have reflected a growing impatience with the proceedings.

On June 11 the king dissolved Parliament. This was different from an adjournment. It meant that a new Parliament, the first in more than six years, would have to be elected and then seated. That did not occur until November. Meanwhile one of the members of the House had become a Lord, so that he had gone from being a prosecutor to becoming a member of the jury. Of much greater importance was the question of whether the new Parliament should simply continue the trial from where it was, or whether the whole impeachment process had to start over again. This question had far-reaching consequences for the whole notion of impeachment. If impeachment was a method of checking the power of royal appointees, and if the process were discontinued when Parliament was dissolved, then the king might stop an impeachment he did not favor by dissolving Parliament. This would render impeachment impotent. A lengthy debate ensued, and by the time the matter was resolved, it was December 23. The House voted to continue the impeachment from where it had left off the previous June. Parliament then recessed for the year. In the year 1790 only fourteen days had been devoted to the trial.

On February 17, now 1791, the Lords received a formal announcement from the House of Commons that it had been resolved to continue the impeachment. The Lords were asked to set a date for recommencing the trial. But the Lords decided that this was a matter of such importance that they would independently study the question. A committee was formed and, among other things, produced a report describing the circumstances of all preceding impeachments, dating back to King Edward III in the fourteenth century. The last relevant case had occurred in 1678, when five Lords were impeached and Parliament had decided to continue with their trial after a dissolution. It took until May before the Lords voted, by a substantial majority, to support the Commons and continue the impeachment. The court reopened on May 23 to consider the fourth article of impeachment, which involved allegations that Hastings's contractual dealings with such items as bullocks and opium had been corrupt. Hastings asked permission to address the court. Here is what he said:

"My lords, I shall take up but a very few minutes of your time; but what I have to say, I hope will be of sufficient importance to justify me in requesting that you will give me so much attention. A charge of having wasted 584,000 [pounds] is easily made where no means are allowed for answering it. [It should be recalled, however, that it was Hastings's counsel who insisted on this method of trial, in which all the charges were offered before any defense was made.] It is not pleasant for me, from week to week, from month to month, from year to year, to hear myself accused of crimes, many of them of the most atrocious die, and all represented in the most shocking colours, and to feel that I never shall be allowed to answer them. In my time of life—in the life of a man already approaching very near to its close, four years of which his reputation is to be traduced, and branded to the world is too much. I never expect to be allowed to come to my defence, nor to hear your Lordships' judgment on my trial. I have long been convinced of it, nor has the late Resolution of the House of Commons [to continue the trial], which I expected to have heard announced to your Lordships here, afforded me the least glimpse of

hope, that the termination of my trial is at all nearer. My Lords, it is now four years complete since I first appeared at your Lordships' bar; nor is this all, I came to your bar with a mind sore from another inquisition in another place [the House of Commons], which commenced, if I may be allowed to date it, on the day I arrived in this capital, on my return to England after thirteen years of service [as governor-general]. On that day was announced the determination of the House of Commons, for arraigning me for the whole of my conduct; I have been now accused for six years; I approach very near (I do not know whether my recollection fails me)[55] to sixty years of age, and can I waste my life in sitting here from time to time arraigned, not only arraigned, but tortured with invectives of the most virulent kind? I appeal to every man's feelings, whether I have not borne many things, that many even of your Lordships could not have borne, and with a patience that nothing but my own innocence could have enabled me to shew [sic]. As the House of Commons have declared their resolution that for the sake of speedy justice (I think that was the term) they had ordered their Managers to close their proceedings on the Article which has now been opened to your Lordships, and to abandon the rest, I now see a prospect which I never saw before, but which it is in your Lordships' power alone to realize, of closing this disagreeable situation in which I have been so long placed; and however I may be charged with the error of imprudence, I am sure that I shall not be deemed guilty of disrespect to your Lordships in the request which I make; that request is, that your Lordships will be pleased to grant me that justice which every man in every country in the world, free or otherwise, has a right to; that where he is accused he may defend himself, and may have the judgment of the Court on the accusations that are brought against him. . . . My Lords, the request I have to make to your Lordships is, that you will be pleased to continue the session of this court till the proceedings shall be all closed, I shall be heard in my defence, and your Lordships shall have proceeded to judgment. . . ."[56] In other words, it would be over, one way or the other, once and for all.

Burke, as might be anticipated, objected. Once again he managed to state that Hastings had been charged with murder. His main point was that much of the court's time had been spent in dealing with objections by Hastings's counsel and the problem caused by the dissolution of Parliament, neither of which was the fault of the managers. With this, the evidence on the contracts was presented, including the alleged overpayments to Eyre Coote. These accusations were not the manager's strongest suit. After the first day the Debrett editor commented laconically, "This was the dullest of all dull days. Mr. Burke appeared for half an hour, made two or three speeches in support of certain questions proposed by himself; but not convincing the Court, he went away and did not return again." On May 30 the managers closed the evidentiary portion of their case.

To this point the Lords had not acted on Hastings's petition to continue the session until a judgment was reached. Since this appeal seemed to be lost, against the advice of his own counsel Hastings made another request. He asked that the Lords remain in session one more day so that he could make a statement in his defense. It is not clear what he thought he could accomplish by this maneuver, and it is not clear why the Lords agreed, but they did on June 2. This time Hastings produced a much more compact and coherent document. He made several important points. He noted that many of the witnesses he had hoped to call had not been able to remain in Britain because of the length of the trial. Some had died and some had returned to India. He also noted that "Every year has taken from me some of my Judges. New have succeeded, some by creation, some by inheritance, and others by election."[57] During the course of the trial, some 230 peers had attended at least once, but only 40 had attended more than half the time. Hastings spoke with some bitterness about the atmosphere surrounding the trial and the effect on the auditors of the excesses in presentation by the managers. "They [the auditors] are pleased and deluded by the talents of the orator; and whatever prejudices he wishes to create in their minds, they of necessity receive, and, after the entertainment of the day, depart with their passions inflamed to communicate their effects to the circle of their acquaintance." He then dealt with the specific charges in terms that are now familiar to us. Chait Singh was a disobedient vassal, and the begums of Oudh had taken money that properly did not belong to them.

On the matter of the contracts, his defense of giving the opium contract to Laurence Sulivan's son Stephen is interesting. In explaining why the contract was not put up for auction, as the Company had ordered, he said, "To this, my Lords, I answer, that opium was of that nature, and so liable to frauds and adulteration, that it was detrimental to the interest of the Company to give a contract upon such low terms as to drive the contractor to the necessity of debasing its quality, to preserve himself from loss. It was absolutely necessary in such a case, as it was in many others, to have a man of credit, honour, and property, upon whom we could rely for a just and faithful performance of his engagement." In this case the man just happened to be the son of his old protector in the Company. On the matter of the alleged overpayments to Eyre Coote, he said simply, "My Lords, I so well knew the value of Sir Eyre Coote's presence on the coast [Madras], at the time when the army was defeated, that there is hardly anything he could have asked which I should not have given him."

As it happened, Burney was in attendance for this speech. She notes that the hall was almost as crowded as on the opening day of the trial. She witnessed an angry exchange between Hastings and Burke and Fox. It came about because Hastings had expressed anger at being accused of things that the ministry itself appeared to have approved. Burke and Fox then entered the fray. She writes, "Mr. Hastings then lost his patience and his temper: he would not suffer the interruption; he had never, he said, interrupted their long speeches; and when Mr. Burke again attempted to speak, Mr. Hastings, in an impassioned but affecting manner, extended his arms, and called out loudly, 'I throw myself upon the protection of your Lordships!—I am not used to public speaking, and cannot answer them; what I wish to submit to your Lordships I have committed on paper; but if I am punished for what I say, I must insist on being heard!—I call upon you, my Lords, to protect me from this violence!'"[58] Interestingly, the Debrett account reproduces this exchange with a slightly different language. It has Hastings saying, "My Lords, I really lay under a great disadvantage. If what I have said is wrong, punish me for it; but I beseech you do not let me be interrupted. I cannot speak from the sudden impulse of my own mind—I am not accustomed to it. I have written down what I wish to read; and I call God to witness that I did it with a due regard to the reverence due this honourable Court."[59] In either case, it is clear that Hastings was no match for the rough and tumble of parliamentary debate.

After his long speech, Parliament adjourned. The trial did not recommence until February 14, 1792. In 1791 the court had been in session only five days.

On June 29, three weeks after the trial had adjourned, the Hastingses moved into their house in Daylesford. He must have had mixed feelings—joy mingled with despair. The trial had not yet finished. At the end of his speech on June 2 he had told the court that he had "enlarged, and gave shape and consistency to the dominion you hold there [in India]. . . . I maintained the wars which were of your formation, or that of others, *not of mine*. . . . I gave *you all*, and you have rewarded me with *confiscation, disgrace, and a life of impeachment*."[60]*

While this rhetoric may have affected some of his judges, Burke and Francis were more determined than ever to go on. So the trial continued. Burney was there on the opening day in February 1792, which was given over to Hastings's defense counsel, Edward Law. She reports, "All the managers attended the opening, but the attendance of all others was cruelly slack. To hear the attack, the people came in crowds; to hear the defense, they scarcely came in *tête-à-têtes*! 'Tis barbarous there should be so much more pleasure given by the recital of guilt than by the vindication of innocence!

"Mr. Law spoke the whole time; he made a general harangue in answer to the opening harangue of Mr. Burke [Burney must have come in late, because, according to the Debrett account, Burke actually interrupted Law in midstream—J.B.], and he spoke many things that brought forward conviction in favour of Mr. Hastings; but he was terrified exceedingly, and his timidity induced him to so frequently beg quarter from his antagonists, both for any blunders and any deficiencies, that I felt angry with even modest egotism, when I considered that it was rather his place to come forward with the shield and armour of truth, undaunted, and to have defied, rather than deprecated the force of talents when without such support."

She was also thoroughly angry with the managers, Windham being the exception. She writes, "Mr. Sheridan I have no longer any ambition to be noticed by; and Mr. Burke, at this place, I am afraid I

---

*One could imagine Oppenheimer saying to his accusers almost the same thing about the atomic bomb.

have already displeased, so unavoidably cold and frigid did I feel my-self when he came to me formerly."[61] Curiously, some of Burney's an-noyance now extended to Marian Hastings, of whom she used to have nothing but good things to say. Some days later she met her at a reception and noted, "I have always been very sorry that Mrs. Has-tings, who is a pleasing, lively, and well-bred woman, with attractive manners and attentions to those she wishes to oblige, should have an indiscretion so peculiarly unsuited to her situation, as to aim always at being the most conspicuous figure wherever she appears. Her dress was like that of an Indian princess, according to our ideas of such ladies, and so much the most splendid, from its ornaments, and style, and fashion, though chiefly of muslin, that everybody else looked under-dressed in her presence. [Apparently she did not pow-der her hair, something that was common to the upper class of both sexes at the time.—J.B.] It is for Mr. Hastings I am sorry when I see this inconsiderate vanity, in a woman who would so much better manifest her sensibility of his present hard disgrace, by a modest and quiet appearance and demeanour." Burney does not seem to appreci-ate the fact that Marian had also been humiliated—indeed, at least as much as Hastings—by the events of the impeachment, and that she was not manifesting "inconsiderate vanity" but attempting to pre-serve her pride.

During the rest of the session, which lasted until June 12, various witnesses for the defense were introduced and then cross-examined. One of the most interesting was William Markham, son of the Arch-bishop of York. He had been, for a time, Hastings's private secretary. Indeed, it was to Markham that Hastings had dictated the letter that in essence challenged Francis to the duel. Markham had been brought in by the defense to testify as to the status of Chait Singh. He was subjected to a withering cross-examination by Burke. The Debrett account reports, "The close of his examination was singular and striking, and appeared to affect the Court and the auditors as much as it did Mr. Markham himself. He was asked if there was any part of Mr. Hastings's conduct to Cheyt Sing [sic] that appeared to him as resulting from vindictive, malicious, or interested motives? He replied that he had known Mr. Hastings for many years most inti-mately, and was convinced, that in no part of his public conduct was he biased by vindictive, malicious, or interested motives; that he was convinced he had ever made the public good, and the honour and advantage of his country, his first object; that on himself or his own interest he never bestowed a thought: and with a voice scarcely audible (probably from the reflection that such a man should have been so treated by a combination of parties against him), laying his hand upon his heart at the time he added, 'I am convinced, my Lords, he is the most virtuous man of the age in which he lives.'"

The session of 1792 ended on June 12, and the next one began on February 15, 1793. The trial had consumed twenty-two days in 1792. Between the two sessions there had been a development with possibly important consequences for the outcome. The lord chancellor, Edward Thurlow, always a difficult character, had crossed Pitt. Pitt went to the king and said that if Thurlow were not removed he would resign. With some reluctance the king acquiesced, replacing Thurlow as lord chancellor with Alexander Wedderburn, Lord Loughborough. Loughborough had sided with the managers on every issue. He had proposed in the beginning that the trial be conducted extrajudicially, which had been resoundingly voted down. He was firmly persuaded of Hastings's guilt on all counts. And now he would be, in effect, the chief justice of the Supreme Court. For Hastings this was not a favorable development. Nonetheless Mr. Law, who had grown more confident with time, continued with the defense.

The subjects were the begums of Oudh and the contracts. Witnesses were examined and cross-examined. Some days fewer peers were present than were needed to constitute a court. Hastings was not the only one to have had more than enough. In order to expedite matters, on May 24 Hastings offered to truncate his defense on the contracts to one day only so that the managers might finish their reply within the session and thus the case could go to the Lords for decision.

Burke ridiculed the idea. "With respect to the defence made by the Gentleman at your bar, he has had all the support that the learning of the bar, the affection of a Host of Friends, or his great fortune could procure—If, from whatever cause, he may now to wish to narrow the bounds of his vindication, it is for him to do so, and for your Lordships to consider, whether in so doing supposing he should be found *Guilty*, it is not meant to be insinuated that, but from voluntary

William Pitt, 1805. (Painting by John Hoppner)

design, he might have availed himself of testimony, which would have cleared his character."[62] This reference to Hastings's "great fortune" inspired a final set of remarks by Hastings, which he delivered on May 28. He swore that on his return to England his fortune had been between eighty thousand and ninety thousand pounds, and that nothing had been added to it. With this the session of 1793 ended. The court had been seated for twenty-two days. One might think that with both the prosecution and the defense having stated their cases, matters now would move toward a rapid resolution. In fact, it required another two years.

The tenor of the 1794 session was set the first day, February 21. The managers attempted to reopen their case by calling *Francis* to give supposedly new evidence on Chait Singh. It is not clear what they hoped to accomplish by this maneuver, which was clearly extra-judicial. Perhaps they thought that with a new lord chancellor who was sympathetic to their views, they had a chance to prevail. Or perhaps they were simply trying to extend Hastings's ordeal. In any case the Lords turned them down, including the lord chancellor, who declared that the rules of evidence had been decided at the beginning of the trial.

On April 9 Lord Cornwallis testified. By this time he was no longer governor-general and had returned from India. His appearance brought out a full attendance of peers and spectators. What he had to say generally supported Hastings. He was asked, "Were the Begums [of Oudh] reduced, or are they now reduced to a state of great pecuniary distress?"[63] No, he answered. He was also asked, "Did the inhabitants of the countries under the conduct of Mr. Hastings complain of his government on his Lordship's arrival in India?" Cornwallis answered, "They did not." Conducting the cross-examination, Burke tried to put the reliability of Cornwallis's information in some doubt. One of the questions and answers is interesting because it shows how, in the post-Hastings era, the British and the Indians had drifted even further apart. Burke asked "Whether your Lordship has not, in stating the dispositions of the Natives of the Provinces towards Mr. Hastings, received your account chiefly from the English?" To this Cornwallis answered, "I must have received all accounts ultimately from the English, as I did not speak the country languages; but I certainly have, through interpreters, conversed with the Natives on the subject. I learned such accounts from them. I speak from their authority as well as the authority of the English." Here was a man who had been governor-general of India for seven years and had never bothered to learn the "country languages."

The managers succeeded in prolonging the session until May 28 with new attempts to reopen their case. At last Burke began his closing address. To understand what he said one must appreciate the circumstances Burke now found himself in. First off, he had succeeded in alienating his former colleagues largely because of his views on the French Revolution. Second, Burke was planning to retire from Parliament after this session. So not only was this speech his last chance to excoriate Hastings, it was his last opportunity to speak in Parliament. He had arranged things so that his beloved and only surviving son Richard would have a safe seat in Malton and thus be, in some sense, his successor. (Burke retired on June 20, and his son was elected on July 18.) During his campaign Richard was already beginning to show the signs of the illness that was to kill him—tuberculosis. Whether Burke understood the gravity of his son's state of health at the time of his speech is not clear, but he must have known that something was not right. In any event, Richard died on August 2 in the presence of his father and mother. He was thirty-six. Added to all of this, Burke's brother Richard had died suddenly on February 5, 1794. The grief was almost more than Burke could bear. This is the context of his closing speech.

Burke's speech lasted *nine* days! This was clearly not a "performance." It came from the depths of his soul. Nonetheless, by any standards it reached a level of excess that is difficult to excuse. It is not even clear to whom the speech is addressed. Could Burke have believed that a passage like the following would influence the judges? "But the Counsel [Hastings's] have fancied that we compare Mr. Hastings to Tamerlane and others, and they have told you of the thousands of men slaughtered by the ambitions of those Princes. Good God! have they lost their senses? Can they suppose that we mean to compare a maker of Bullock-contracts with an illustrious Conquerer? We never compared Mr. Hastings to a Lion or a Tyger [sic]; we have compared him to a Rat or a Weasel. When we assimilate him to such contemptible animals, we do not mean to convey an idea of their incapability of doing injuries. When Pharaoh was to be punished, it was by Locusts, by Lice, which though small and contemptible are capable of the greatest mischiefs."[64]

Burke seemed beyond caring. Day after day he went on, piling invective upon invective: "He is a captain general of iniquity—thief—tyrant—robber—cheat—sharper—swindler. We call him all these names, and are sorry that the English language does not afford terms adequate to the enormity of his offenses."[65] Perhaps most revealingly, he said, "Revenge is a sort of wild justice—it is the test of heroic virtue—we will continue to the end to persecute. I vow, that we bear immortal hatred against this scum, filth, and pollution of Indian guilt; if the Commons do not, I take it all to myself."[66] On June 14 Burke concluded with a final plea: "My Lords, it is not the criminality of the prisoner—it is not the claims of the Commons to be passed upon him—it is not the honour and dignity of this Court, and the welfare of millions of the human race that alone call upon you—When the devouring flames have destroyed this perishable globe, and [it] sinks into the abyss of Nature, from whence it was commanded into existence by the great Author of it—then, my Lords, when all Nature, Kings, and Judges themselves must answer for their actions, there will be found what supercedes creation itself, namely, ETERNAL JUSTICE. It was the attribute of the Great God of Nature before worlds were; it will reside with him when they perish; and the earthly portion of it committed to your care, is now solemnly deposited in your hands by the Commons of England—I have done."[67]

III: THE VERDICT

B ecause of an indisposition of Thurlow which prevented his attendance, the Lords did not begin to consider the case until February 26, 1795, almost exactly seven years after it had begun. During this period, 87 peers had died, 44 had been newly created, and 49 had taken their seats by means of inheritance. In other words, over this time there had occurred 180 changes in the composition of the House of Lords. It was pointed out that some of the members who were now seated as peers had been at Eton as schoolboys when the trial began. The number of Lords who felt qualified—it was left up to each Lord to decide for himself—to take part in actual votes on the various charges was fewer than thirty.

In reading the transcripts of their debates, two features are striking. In the first place, the level of the rhetoric had moderated. Strong differences of views remained, but they were expressed in the temporate language of mutual respect that one would associate with a judicial process. Second is the role of Edward Thurlow. Bear in mind that Thurlow was no longer the lord chancellor. That was, as we have

Edward Thurlow, 1806. (Painting by Thomas Phillips)

noted, now Lord Loughborough. Nonetheless Thurlow totally dominated the process. For reasons not clear, there seemed to be no objection to this. Whether this had to do with the enormous force of Thurlow's personality, or his total mastery of the details of the case, I am not sure. One shudders to think of what might have happened to Hastings if Thurlow's views had been different. Thurlow had been, from beginning to end, one of Hastings's staunchest supporters.

Now, as the trial came to a vote, Thurlow first fixed the rules of the game. He remarked that on many of the charges the Commons had offered no evidence at all, therefore on these Hastings should be acquitted at once. He went on to say, the Debrett editor reports, "As to the articles on which the Commons had given evidence, he thought it impossible, either in justice to the Commons or the defendant, to put one question only on each, as had been the general practice; because each article comprised so many criminal facts, that if any difference of opinion should arise amongst their Lordships, it would be necessary to put a separate question on each allegation."[68] He proposed that the House of Lords resolve itself into a committee of the whole in which all these matters might be discussed. The lord chancellor agreed to this and asked Thurlow when he wished to begin. Thurlow said he was ready any time, so the date was fixed for the following Monday, March 2.

That day Thurlow announced that he would open the proceedings with a discussion of the Benares charge—Chait Singh. From the outset he orchestrated the procedure. As the Debrett account notes, "Lord Thurlow rose to open the mode of proceeding, and explained at considerable length his idea of the nature of the present trial. His Lordship complained much of the looseness and inaccuracy with which the Articles were drawn, containing many assertions either palpably false or grossly absurd, and which a very moderate application to the documents in the possession of those who supported the prosecution, would have convinced them could not be substantiated." Of course Burke and the other managers must have known this. But it was not relevant to their real agenda, which was to "work on the popular sense."

Thurlow goes on, as described by the Debrett editor, "He [Thurlow] was far from wishing to throw an imputation on the Managers for these inaccuracies, and still less on the House of Commons, who could not be supposed to look at the minutiae of such extensive Articles, comprehending the important transactions of a large empire for thirteen years. The zeal of the parties who drew the Articles had certainly exceeded their discretion. The Impeachment, however, might now be said to rest upon four points—Breach of Faith, Oppression and Injustice, as in the two Articles of Cheyt Sing [sic] and the Begum [sic]; Corruption, as in the Article of the Presents; and a wanton Waste of the Public Money for Private purposes, as in the Contracts. In considering the first two points, in his opinion, it would become their Lordships to reflect on the situation in which Mr. Hastings was placed. Possessed of absolute power, the question would be, Had he exerted that power for the public good, or had he, on any occasion been actuated by base or malicious motives. If in the case of Cheyt Sing and the Begums they should be of the opinion that he was neither malicious nor corrupt, the Charges naturally fell to the ground. It was the duty of Mr. Hastings to preserve the empire committed to his care, and in pursuit of that object to adopt measures best adapted to attain his end."[69]

Thurlow noted that each article contained so many different charges that the only sensible procedure was to proceed point by point. After further discussion, which spilled over to the following day, on March 5 the Lords came to grips with the first issue. To cut the Gordian knot, and presumably to test the waters, Francis Lord Rawdon (Earl of Moira in Ireland) introduced a motion which he said that he himself would vote against. It was, "The government of Bengal had no right to exact a tribute from Cheyt Sing." If this was voted down, it would follow "That the government of Bengal had regularly exercised their right of sovereignty in exacting tribute from Cheyt Sing."[70] After some discussion and amendment, Lord Rawdon's motion was voted down, and Hastings was on his way to being acquitted of the Benares charge. The actual vote on guilt or innocence of the various charges would not occur until this point-by-point discussion was completed for all the charges. The vote on the charges themselves would take place in full view of the public in Westminster Hall.

The following day the Lords turned their attention to the question of whether Hastings had taken a "present" for his own personal use from Chait Singh, and whether the fine of fifty lakhs had been imposed on the basis of personal malice. Thurlow proposed a motion which in the affirmative would have made good the House of Commons assertions about the abusive and unjust acts of Hastings toward Chait Singh. (It was just this presumption that had resulted in Pitt's voting with the Whig opposition, which became the catalyst for the impeachment process in the first place.) The Lords again voted in the negative. It was becoming clearer and clearer where these deliberations were heading. It took until Friday, March 13, for all the points in the Benares article to be debated. Thurlow then moved that "the Commons had made good on the ten remaining allegations in the First Article."[71] This too was voted in the negative. On Monday the 16th the Lords turned their attention to the begums of Oudh, the second article.

Without mentioning him by name, Thurlow proceeded to cut through Sheridan's rhetorical accusations like a knife slicing soft butter. On the matter of the eunuchs who were attempting to guard the begums' treasure, Thurlow noted that no proof had been offered that they had been treated as alleged. Furthermore, if such treatment had occurred, it would have been without Hastings's knowledge and contrary to his orders. Thurlow then reviewed the history of the murky relations between the nawab and his mother and grandmother, the begums. As sordid and repellant as he found it, Thurlow could find no evidence presented by the managers that Hastings had engaged in criminal acts. There was not even evidence that the begums had suffered much materially. This elicited a strong response from the lord chancellor, which continued to the following day. Here Thurlow showed his mastery of the details. He seems to have read and memorized every exchange between Hastings and the rest of the principals. Nonetheless, there was sufficient doubt so that when Thurlow put the motion that the "Commons had made good the charges in their Second Article respecting the Begums,"[72] it failed by only one vote. The Lords then turned to the matter of "presents."

The debate on this article began on Friday, March 20, which gives some idea of how rapidly this process could move once it adhered to a true judicial forum. Thurlow cautioned that the Lords would have to separate the suggestions and innuendos about bribes and presents, which had been a theme that reappeared throughout the trial, from those instances where actual evidence was presented. It was decided to try to divide charges chronologically, separating the years 1772 through 1774 from the years 1780 through 1783 (no allegations had been made concerning the intervening six years). Thurlow reviewed the evidence. At one point he said, "It is nearly nineteen years ago since I was called upon in another situation to consider and to give my opinion on one of the material points in the Charge now under your Lordships' consideration. I did not therefore conceive that facts which at that period were not deemed worthy of public inquiry, would, after a lapse of many years, have been thought matter for Impeachment, unless, which I supposed to be the case, some strong and decisive evidence on the points alluded to had been discovered."[73]

He then proceeded to give his fellow Lords a history lesson. He reviewed every transaction for every year, including the charges brought by Nand Kumar and the actions of the majority of the Council. He was detailed and scathing. For example, of the Munni Begum he said, "Your Lordships heard, and with much pain, I am sure, a great deal of coarse invective uttered against this lady. She was described as a dancing girl—a common prostitute—a dealer in spirits; and many other epithets were applied to her, which I shall not enumerate; but I certainly have taken some pains to trace, as far as I could, both from the evidence and the history of the times, the real situation of this lady. I find that the only authority on which she has been called a dancing girl by the Manager, is a letter written from a man of the name of Nuned Roy to General Clavering, in which he tells the General, 'Every day's news is transmitted to you'—and then he encloses a paper, which contains the history of Munny [sic] Begum; stating that her mother being poor, she sold her to a mistress of dancing girls: that she came to Moorshedebad [sic], danced before Meer Jaffier [sic], who took her to his house, where she became the mother of the Nabob Nudjum ul Dowlah [sic]—Here the story ends." The evidence runs out. We are in a court of law. At the end of the day, Thurlow put the motion "That the Commons had made good the Sixth Article, as far as it related to a corrupt receipt of Presents in the years 1772, 1773 and 1774." It was defeated.

This left the second half of the charges. Here the most contested matter was the undeniable fact that Hastings had taken money from Nobkissen, which he hoped the Company would allow him to keep. On this question, Thurlow insisted that whatever Hastings may have hoped, the money went on the Company's books with none going to him. (As we shall see, this was not exactly true.) The full debate on these charges took two days, after which the Lords voted that the Commons had not made good this case either. That left the contracts and the matter of Eyre Coote's compensation. Debate on these finished on Monday, April 13, with another vote to the same effect. In a little more than a month the Lords had gone through seven years of testimony and evidence and had decided by majority vote that none of it supported the charges that had been made. There was one final step: the vote of guilty or not guilty on each charge, which would take place in the public forum at Westminster.

On Thursday, April 23, the Lords met for the last time as a committee of the whole dealing with the impeachment. Before they adjourned to Westminster they had a bit of remaining business—a residue of charges which they had not bothered to consider carefully. They decided to lump all of them together in a sixteenth charge, "High Crimes and Misdemeanours, charged upon him by the residue of the Impeachment of the Commons."[74] If Hastings were found guilty of whatever this was, they agreed to examine the details more fully. It was 12:30 before the Lords finally arrived in Westminster. Hastings, still a prisoner, was called into the hall with his bail and, after kneeling, was asked to withdraw. The galleries were full, and so were the seats of Parliament. The sixteen charges were voted on one after the other. Lord Loughburough, the lord chancellor, found Hastings guilty of fourteen of the sixteen charges. He was in the small minority. Two charges, including that of the begums, received as many as six guilty votes out of twenty-nine. The Debrett editor described what happened next.

"Having thus collected the Judgement of their Lordships on each of the sixteen Charges, the Lord Chancellor declared that a large majority of the Lords present had answered the said questions in the negative;—and then declared 'That WARREN HASTINGS, Esq. is ACQUITTED of the Articles of Impeachment exhibited against him for High Crimes and Misdemeanours, and all things contained therein.'

"Then the Defendant was ordered to be called to the bar, and kneeling was bid to rise.

"Then the Lord Chancellor said, 'Warren Hastings, Esq. I am to acquaint you that you are ACQUITTED of the ARTICLES of IMPEACHMENT, &c. exhibited against you in the House of Commons for High Crimes and Misdemeanours, and all things contained therein, and you are discharged, paying your fees.'"

Then, the account goes on, "Mr. Hastings bowed respectfully and retired.

"The Lord Chancellor then put the question, 'Is it your Lordships' pleasure to adjourn to your Chamber of Parliament?' Ordered: and their Lordships adjourned accordingly to their Chamber of Parliament."[75]

The trial had ended.

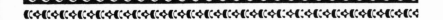

Nine
EPILOGUE: FINAL YEARS

The East India Company Today. The East India Company is now a United Kingdom based public company which brings its unrivalled heritage to bear on the modern commercial world. Such was the power, authority and diversity of the East India Company in the past that the name gives credibility to virtually any product or service, in virtually any major consumer market. It allies the great strengths of British brand associations— tradition, old-fashioned luxury, impeccable class—with the general appeal of exotic countries, seafaring, travel and adventure. The Company trades in a wide range of goods, including those historic staples, tea and coffee. It has also developed products for consumer markets. It is forging partnerships in many parts of the world where the Company is a household name, and provides a familiar authoritative port of call for many businesses looking to expand into new markets.

—The British East India Company Website (June 16, 1999)

On May 7, 1795, Dr. Charles Burney wrote to his daughter Fanny with the latest gossip. "And so dear Mr. Hastings is honourably acquitted!" he noted, "and I visited him the next morning, and we cordially shook hands. I had luckily left my name at his door as soon as I was able to go out, and before it was generally accepted that he would be acquitted."[1] The letter was written from London to Great Bookham in Surrey, where Burney was now living. Much had happened to Burney since 1792 when she had last been to the trial. People who had seen her there could see that she was seriously ill. The strain of her position at the palace, with Schwellenberg and all the rest, had taken its toll. Windham, for example, was so alarmed that he told her father—presumably as a joke—that he was prepared to introduce an act of Parliament to obtain her release. Dr. Burney was surprised and no doubt disappointed—he had hoped to gain some sort of recognition from the king, perhaps even a royal pension. But when Burney told him in May 1790 that she wished to leave the palace, he did not try to stand in her way. In October she made a formal request to the queen to leave her post, but it was not granted until the following July. Schwellenberg was beside herself. The queen was correct but not overly generous. She granted Burney an annual pension of one hundred pounds—half her salary—stating that it was "solely from me to you."[2]

On July 7, nearly five years to the day of her arrival there, her father met her at the palace and took her to where he was now living with his wife and her daughter. There was not really space for Burney; she had to share a room with her stepsister. So it was with some relief that she allowed herself to be taken off on a tour of the spas with an older widowed friend named Anna Ord. One of their first stops was Winchester, where a small colony of French aristocrats had taken refuge from the Revolution. This was Burney's first encounter with this group who would come to dominate her life. They included people such as the Comte de Mirabeau, Talleyrand,[3] Madame de Staël, and Burney's future husband, General Alexandre Gabriel Jean-Baptiste Piochard D'Arblay, who had been an adjutant general to Lafayette. Burney's sister Susan met him first, and her letters to Burney are full of admiring references. In January 1793 Burney met him herself. It is soon clear from her letters to her father that she has fallen in love. On February 4 she writes that M. D'Arblay "is one of the most delightful characters I have ever met, for openness, probity, intellectual knowledge, and unhackneyed manners."[4]

Burney's French was self-taught and limited, while the general's English was not much better. But the general had an idea. They would write essays to each other in their respective languages and then correct them. Soon the essays turned into love letters, and by the spring of 1793 they had decided to marry. Given Burney's life history, it was clear that a sanction from her father was very important. It was not forthcoming. Apart from the fact that D'Arblay had no prospects for earning a living in England, so that he and his wife would be living on her pension from the queen, which could also be withdrawn, Dr. Burney objected to D'Arblay's being both a foreigner and a Catholic. But this time Dr. Burney did not get his way. Burney and D'Arblay were married on July 28, 1793, in a Protestant church and two days later in a Catholic ceremony so that Burney might be able to inherit D'Arblay's property in France, if ever he could reclaim it. Her father did not attend the weddings. By August the newlyweds had moved into a rented cottage in Great Bookham. She was still living there when, on December 18, 1794, at the age of forty-two, she gave birth to her son, Alexander Charles Louis Piochard. She was there in April 1795 when Hastings was acquitted, so she missed the celebrations.

The Debrett account describes two of them. The first was sponsored by the Bengal Club and took place on May 22, with some five hundred people present at a banquet presided over by Marian. But the real celebration took place on July 21 at the country home of Sir John and Lady D'Oyley. D'Oyley had been one of Hastings's loyal associates in India. The Debrett account gives a vivid idea of what such a festival in the country—a *fête champêtre*—was like. "The day was ushered in," it reports, "with the ringing of bells, and other demonstrations of joy. The company assembled at twelve o'clock in a large open Pavilion, surrounded with wood, except in front, which opened to a lovely lake, the banks of which were fringed with weeping willows, laburnums, roses, &c. The eight pillars which supported the roof of the Pavilion, were ornamented with wreaths of natural flowers, winding to the top. In the centre of the roof, in front, Mr. Hastings's arms, placed like a medallion, in a wreath of flowers, made a very handsome appearance. Wreaths of flowers and laurels hung from the roof in light festoons: the inside of the Pavilion was hung with pictures applicable to the occasion; Mr. Hastings's occupied the centre, elegantly decorated with a wreath of white lillies and lilacs: on one side was that of Lord Thurlow; on the other the late venerable Lord Mansfield: the remainder consisted of the arms of the East-India Company and the City of London; the print of the 'Judgment of Britannia'; and the admirable caricature of 'The Last Scene of the Managers' Farce' by Sayer. A curtain of white silk, with gold fringe and taffeta, hung in festoons above the pictures. On a small wooded Island up the lake was placed a martial band, over whose heads waved a silk banner. Besides the Pavilion there were many tents erected on the lawn for the entertainment of the company."

The account goes on, "An elegant breakfast, with fruits, ices, &c. was laid out in the Pavilion; in the centre of the table was a very beautiful temple, in which was a figure of Justice holding in her hand a pair of golden scales. In one scale were the Charges that had been exhibited against Mr. Hastings; in the other, on a small scroll of white silk, in letters of gold, the names of all those Noble Peers who so honourably acquitted him." One wonders if this included the lord chancellor who voted Hastings guilty on almost every charge, to say nothing of the five other peers who had found Hastings guilty of at least one charge. To continue, "The Ladies and Gentlemen were presented with bouquets tied with white ribbons, on each side of which was the motto 'Virtue Triumphant,' in letters of gold. These bouquets were presented by children dressed alike in white.

"Dancing, music, and various other amusements, filled up the hours till dinner was served in the Pavilion.

"After dinner the following toasts were drunk:

"'King and Constitution.'

"'Mr. and Mrs. Hastings; and may they live long to enjoy the triumph of their merits!'

"'Lord Thurlow and Peerage of England, for their firm and constitutional support of the honour and justice of the Country.'

"'The East-India Company, for their uniform and liberal patronage of oppressed merit.'

"These were followed by the usual public toasts."[5]

༄

THE SOMEWHAT CURIOUS TOAST to the East India Company may well have had its origins in a sequence of events that had occurred the previous month. Soon after his acquittal, Hastings drew up a petition to the House of Commons for compensation for his legal expenses during the trial. His solicitor had been a man named Richard Shawe, whose bill had come to 66,080 pounds. With other incidental legal expenses, Hastings faced a total bill of 71,080 pounds.

At the end of the trial he had been able to pay only 19,080 pounds of Shawe's fee.*

The remaining 47,000 he owed Shawe was in a bond that carried 5 percent interest. He had been lent money by friends, and some of his Indian colleagues, including his former banyan Cantoo, who was now quite wealthy, had sent money to help. But this money was rapidly spent, leaving him in serious financial straits—hence the petition to Parliament. Pitt responded with a formal note that he would not be able to lay Hastings's case before the king.

Hastings was extremely reluctant to turn to the Company for help. "My claim lies, not against the Company, but against the British nation," he wrote.[6] But on May 29 the chairman of the proprietors, Sir Stephen Lushington, joined by eight others, made a formal motion in a meeting of the directors that the Company indemnify Hastings for his legal expenses and, starting from January 1, 1795, award him an annuity of five thousand pounds a year. This was the amount that had been awarded the retiring Cornwallis. A lively debate ensued. Those who were opposed believed, like Hastings himself, that this was not the responsibility of the Company but of the government under whose auspices the trial had taken place. On the positive side, in addition to Hastings's general merits and service to the Company, the important point was made that his victory had saved the Company a fortune. The money that Hastings was alleged to have taken went on the Company's books and was, in general, used to defray Company expenses. Hence if Hastings had lost, the Company would have been responsible for returning that money with possible fines and interest. Major Scott estimated that this might have come to eight million pounds! Against this, the amounts that were being proposed for Hastings were negligible.

On June 2 and 3, respectively, the directors voted on the indemnification of legal expenses and the pension. Both passed by wide margins. This may account for the toast to the Company at the *fête champêtre* the following month. But the champagne flowed a little too quickly. Since the passage of Pitt's India Bill in 1784, the Company had not been free to dispense money as it saw fit. A Board of Control

*Shawe used the money he earned from the Hastings trial to build a mansion in Dulwich. He called it Casino.

chaired by Henry Dundas, no friend of Hastings, in principle super-
vised how money was to be spent. Indeed, on June 3, the very
evening of the final vote on Hastings's compensation, a member of
Parliament asked Dundas if the Company had any right to propose to
pay Hastings's legal expenses. Dundas said the proprietors had no
such right and that the directors had better be cautious since they
were legally responsible. On June 30 the matter was put to Pitt, who
referred it to the legal authorities. In September, in a lengthy statement, the lawyers concluded that if any money was to be paid to Hastings, it must come from the territorial revenues in India and not
from the stockholders' equity. They argued that the legal expenses
could be considered only as a cost that Hastings had incurred in the
course of his service in India. Furthermore the directors were not free
to spend these revenues in this way without the approval of the
Board of Control.

Anticipating trouble, on September 17 Lushington wrote an
apologetic letter to Hastings: "The late Resolutions of the General
Court [of Directors] in your favour, with respect to the Charges incurred by you in consequence of the Impeachment; and the Annuity,
as a reward for your services to the East India Company; are sufficient proofs of the high estimation in which you stand with the Proprietors at large." But: "These Resolutions have not been carried into
immediate effect, because doubts have arisen as to the legality of the
measure under the provisions of the Act of Parliament, as to the application of the profits of the Company, after certain defined payments are made; and with regard to the Annuity, the approbation and
confirmation thereof being expressly, under the provisions of the Act,
with the Commissioners for the Affairs of India.

"Whilst these questions have been agitated, and remain undecided, the Public and every individual Proprietor have, in the exercise of their judgment upon the propriety of the measures (to which
they most undoubtedly have a right) canvassed with precision your
character and conduct whilst exercising the high office of Governor-
General of all their affairs in India, and particularly the fortune you
acquired in their service. Upon the first two points, I trust, there is no
doubt; but as to the latter, [a] variety of opinions are entertained by
men of the first character and honour in the country, from some hasty
and perhaps unnecessary declarations made some time ago and from

appearances since. [One wonders if the "appearances" here refer to the seemingly affluent life, including the purchase of Daylesford, that the Hastingses appeared to be enjoying.] Gentlemen of this description have entertained doubts of the truth of the assertions; and though a printed paper has been in circulation as to the state of your fortune, yet your immediate constituents, the East-India Company and the Public, whose interests I consider as inseparable, remain without any declaration or avowal from you personally as to the true state of your affairs."[7]

In short, Hastings was being asked for a sworn statement as to his finances with special emphasis, as the letter goes on to say, on the finances of his wife. On December 22 Hastings delivered it. In his statement he noted that his total debts to his solicitors and others amounted to 97,000 pounds. The "others" included his former fellow councilor Barwell and Major Scott, to whom he owed 5,000 pounds. On the credit side there was, of course, Daylesford. Since he had been publicly accused of spending more than a hundred thousand pounds on his estate, with continuing expenditures of sixteen thousand pounds a year, he felt constrained to write, "In 1789, I purchased the principal part of Daylesford, and about two years since the remainder; it was an object that I had long wished to possess; it was the spot in which I had passed much of my infancy; and I feel for it an affection of which an alien could not be susceptible, because I see in it attractions which that stage of my life imprinted on my mind, and my memory still retains. It had been the property of my family during many centuries, and had not been more than seventy-five years out of their possession. I should not notice these trivial circumstances, but that detailing the process of my expenses, I feel that this part of them which relates to this place, I have to defend myself, if I can, against the charge of extravagance, and I fear I have no better excuse to make for it."[8] He lists among his disbursements 54,400 pounds spent on the purchase and rehabilitation of Daylesford. Adding up all the money in his possession since his arrival in England, exclusive of the 17,000 pounds he received as donations from India, he reckoned a total of 125,313, pounds, to be balanced against 127,385 in money spent, including an estimated 3,500 pounds a year in personal expenses. Of this he notes that "My style of living . . . has borne no marks of extravagance or splendour. To those who have witnessed it, I think I may say, that it was rather below than exceeding the rank in life which my former station might have entitled me to assume."[9] Included in these numbers were any assets in Marian's name.

This estimate of Hastings's financial situation in the year 1795 has not been seriously challenged. But it does not present the whole story. Hastings was not asked to tell the rest, and he didn't. The fact was that a great deal of money had passed through Hastings's hands during the time he was in India.[10] From 1772 to 1775 he sent back to England some 122,000 pounds, presumably from private trade in commodities such as diamonds.

There was also the matter of the three lakhs of rupees offered to him by Nobkissen—an important charge in the impeachment trial, where it was claimed to be a bribe. No persuasive evidence was presented by the managers that it *was* a bribe. But what happened to the money? Here things become murky. In the trial, Hastings testified that he had accepted the money for the Company's use. In fact this "use" was to reimburse himself for expenses he claimed the Company owed him. That the Company owed him this money was a defensible claim, but his method of obtaining it was not. Furthermore, in 1792 Nobkissen had presented a bill for this sum plus interest, claiming it was a loan that Hastings had never paid back. A lawsuit followed and was not decided until 1804, seven years after Nobkissen's death, in favor of Hastings's contention that the money had been a gift. What stands out is that this seems to be the only case during Hastings's entire tenure where he navigated this close to the edge. Compared to the money that was available, Nobkissen's thirty thousand pounds seem rather minor.

In any event, by the time his administration ended, Hastings had been able to remit some 218,000 pounds to England, which had shrunk to about 75,000 once he returned there. The rest was spent. His agents in England, including Scott, received a small fortune, and he gave much away to relatives and the like. Had he been wiser about his money, he would not have found himself in the trouble he was now facing.

It took until early March 1796 before the proprietors could reach an agreement with Dundas and the Board of Control. In the end it was decided that Hastings should receive an annual pension of four thousand pounds over a period of twenty-eight and a half years retroactive to June 24, 1785. This peculiar arrangement reflected the fact that the Company's charter was to expire in 1813. Hastings was also given an interest-free loan of fifty thousand pounds, which was to be paid off by deducting two thousand pounds a year from his pension. This money was to be invested in Company bonds, and the principal and interest would cover the loan. This enabled Hastings to meet his immediate debts but required financial discipline in the long run. In fact, by 1804 he was again in financial difficulties and was bailed out when the Company agreed to give him the remainder of his annuity in a lump sum which he could presumably invest with interest. With this he should have been able to live out the rest of his life comfortably, if relatively modestly.

News of the acquittal and the subsequent pension was of course soon widely known. Francis reacted with characteristic pith. "Hastings has been impeached, and I have been condemned," he noted.[11] For Burke, the injury went much deeper. He was furious. It was not only that Hastings had been acquitted, but that now, with the approval of the Board of Control, he was to be awarded a substantial pension for life. When Burke retired from Parliament he was offered a peerage and a pension of twelve hundred pounds a year, which his wife could continue to collect in the event of his death. He refused the former and accepted the latter. Now Hastings was being given a pension three and a half times his own, with the approval of the same government. But was it the money that was at issue? One suspects that any pension awarded to Hastings would have driven Burke to do what he did, which was to seek to have the pension withdrawn.

He began with a letter to Dundas, written on March 6, 1796, before the ink on the documents confirming Hastings's pension had had a chance to dry. The letter reads, "It is with pain inexpressible, I am driven to the Step I *must* take. Costs and damages, to an immense amount are given by you, on the publick Estate administered by the East India Company, to Mr. Hastings against the House of Commons. [Here, it would seem, Burke's anger has gotten in the way of a careful understanding of the facts, a not uncommon circumstance in Burke's polemic rhetoric. "Costs and damages" had *not* been given to Hastings; the Company never paid his legal costs. There is also the tricky notion of the East India Company's administering a "publick

Estate." Was India a "publick Estate"? What exactly was the "publick Estate" to which Burke referred? The Company was a public company with stockholders, of which Burke had been one. But these stockholders had voted to give Hastings his pension. Then there is also the phrase "against the House of Commons," which Burke is about to adumbrate in the letter. Does he mean that the Lords had no right to acquit Hastings once the House of Commons had impeached him?] The House has charged him with robbing that fund; and the people from whose labours the fund arises; and we reward that Robbery, by a new Robbery. [Even a common criminal, one would think, would have been entitled to a presumption of innocence once acquitted.] I cordially wished well to your India administration; and except in one Instance in the beginning, I never even whilst I was otherwise in warm opposition, opposed it; hoping, that redress would be given to India; and that Gang of Thieves called the Court of Directors and proprietors would be kept in some order. But there am I, acting under your own *individual* authority, as well as *publick* authority attempted to be disgraced with the present Age or by Posterity. But it shall never be said, either by the present Age or by Posterity, that the blood of India has been compromised by a Pension to the accuser and another to the party accused. I shall therefore, I hope before the End of next week to present a Petition to the House of Commons; and know whether they will confess themselves false accusers—whether they will deliberately betray those whom they have employed in their accusation, and whether the only satisfaction they will give to undone nations as the result of their twenty four years Enquiry into their Grievances, is an enormous sum of Money, from their Substance, to reward the person they have charged as the author of their Grievances."[12]

This letter is so extreme that one is led to wonder if Burke was beginning to lose his reason. In any event, he was persuaded not to petition the House as this would lead only to another humiliating defeat. He would now have to rest his case with posterity.

He did not have long to wait. On July 9, 1797, Burke died. Six months before his death he wrote to his friend Dr. French Laurence a letter that can serve as Burke's last testament on Hastings. He wrote, "But you remember likewise, that when I came hither in the beginning of last summer [Burke was in Bath on the orders of his doctors in the hope that his declining health would improve], I repeated to you that dying request which I now reiterate . . . you will erect a cenotaph most grateful to my shade, and will clear my memory from that load, which the East India Company, King, Lords, and Commons, and in a manner the whole British Nation (God forgive them) have been pleased to lay as a monument upon my ashes. I am as conscious as any person can be of the little value of the good or evil opinion of mankind to the part of me that shall remain, but I believe it is of some moment not to leave the fame of an evil example, of the expenditure of fourteen years labour, and of not less (taking the expense of the suit, and the costs paid to Mr. Hastings, and the parliamentary charges) than near £.300,000. This is a terrible example, and it is not acquittance at all to a public man, who, with all the means of undeceiving himself if he was wrong, has thus with such incredible pains both of himself and others, persevered in the persecution of innocence and merit. It is, I say, no excuse at all to urge in his apology, that he had had enthusiastic good intentions. In reality, you know that I am no enthusiast, but [according] to the powers that God has given me, a sober and reflecting man. I have not even the other very bad excuse, of acting from personal resentment, or from the sense of private injury—never having received any; nor can I plead ignorance, no man ever having taken more pains to be informed. Therefore I say, *Remember.*"[13] In a letter written about the same time, he referred to Marian as Hastings's "paramour."

The last mention of Hastings in Burney's journals is in a letter she wrote to her father from Bookham on July 27, 1797, not long after Burke's death. She writes, "I was surprised, and almost frightened, though at the same time gratified, to find you assisted in paying the last honours to Mr. Burke. How sincerely I sympathise in all you say of that truly great man! That his enemies say he was not perfect is nothing compared with his immense superiority over almost all who are merely exempted from his peculiar defects. That he was upright in heart, even when he acted wrong, I do truly believe . . . and that he asserted nothing he had not persuaded himself to be true, from Mr. Hastings's being the most rapacious of villains to the King's being incurably insane. He was as generous as kind, and as liberal in his sentiments as he was luminous in intellect and extraordinary in abilities and eloquence. Though free from all little vanity, high above envy, and glowing with zeal to exalt talents and merit in others, he had, I believe, a consciousness of his own greatness that shut out those occasional and useful self-doubts which keep our judgment in order, by calling our motives and passions to account."[14] With her uncanny insight, and in a very few words, Burney has again captured the essence of a human soul.

We must now confront one of the most difficult matters that anyone choosing to deal with this subject must confront: what was Burke's legacy when it came to the governance of India? How much influence did the many years he spent trying to reform what he thought were the perversities in this governance have on later events? To make any sense of this, we must first drastically limit the scope of the inquiry. If we try to find Burkean echoes in everything that occurred in India from Hastings to the partition in 1947, we may dilute the subject to where it becomes meaningless. It would be like looking for the influence of Thomas Jefferson on the events that led to the New Deal. People may now proclaim that they are Jeffersonians or Burkeans, but that is quite different from asking the question how did Jefferson, or Burke for that matter, influence events that were nearly contemporaneous? In the case of Burke and India, the answer falls between two extremes. One school of thought argues that Burke had no influence,[15] the other that Burke's influence was decisive.[16] Even if one takes a middle ground, the problem is whether a specific reform was due to Burke's influence or whether it would have been adopted even if Burke had never existed. To try to assess Burke's influence, I will confine my observations to the administration of Lord Charles Cornwallis, which began in 1786 and ended in 1793, a period in which Burke was alive and the trial of Hastings was in full swing.

Cornwallis surrendered at Yorktown on October 19, 1781. When he was repatriated to Britain the next year it was as a prisoner of war who had been liberated by parole, which could be lifted only if there were a formal peace agreement with the Americans or if a suitable British prisoner could be exchanged. As long as this parole was in force, Cornwallis was not free to accept a position such as the governor-generalship of India. But by the end of 1783 the parole had been lifted, and Pitt's new government was giving serious consideration to appointing Cornwallis.

Cornwallis had never been blamed for the fiasco with the American colonies. The king had a high regard for him, and everyone respected his high standard of personal morality. But Cornwallis had serious doubts as to whether he really wanted the job in India.[17] He was widowed and was anxious to spend time with his children in England. Moreover he had apparently gone to school on some of the difficulties of Hastings's regime. In view of his conclusions, one might argue that if Burke had an influence here, it was not one that he would necessarily have acknowledged. Cornwallis saw that many of Hastings's problems stemmed from the fact that his authority as governor-general had been seriously restricted. He was not commander-in-chief of the army, and he had to contend with a fractious Council—of which Burke's friend Francis had been a member—that could, and did, outvote him. Cornwallis made it a condition of considering the position that both these restrictions be removed. He would be governor-general *and* command the armed forces. Moreover he, not the Council, would make all final decisions. In April 1786 the government met all his terms by passing an amendment to Pitt's India Act, giving Cornwallis the powers he had asked for. It is worth noting that Burke vehemently opposed this extension of the powers of the governor-general but was unable to influence the outcome of the vote. It was typical of Cornwallis that when he was offered additional compensation for being commander-in-chief as well as governor-general, he refused to accept it—and Cornwallis was not a wealthy man.

When he went to India, Cornwallis had an agenda for reform. Again it is difficult—perhaps impossible—to say whether Burke's influences were at work. To take a specific example, Hastings had always lamented the fact that he was unable to raise the salaries of the Company's more junior employees. They were paid very little in the expectation that they would engage in private trade, which was not considered illegal. This applied even to the tax collectors the Company employed who, as one might imagine, had splendid opportunities to line their pockets. Cornwallis was determined to use his prestige to get these salaries raised and to put a stop to this kind of corruption. He was more successful than Hastings had been, but he still could not overcome the Company's reluctance to pay all its junior functionaries a living wage. Once Cornwallis did succeed in raising someone's wages, he was absolutely intolerant of any activity by that individual to continue to feather his nest. He set the example by refusing presents of any kind, except those that protocol absolutely demanded, and returning any that had been sent without his foreknowledge. William Hickey noted in his journals that Cornwallis even modified the celebration of Christmas. He writes, "It having always been the custom for the members of Government and the principal persons of the settlement to dine together at the Court-house on Christmas day, followed by a ball and supper for the ladies at night, the same took place on the 25th of December this year [1786, Cornwallis's first year], although somewhat against the inclination of Lord Cornwallis, who expressed his disapprobation, as according to his idea the day ought to be celebrated rather as purely religious than in feasting and mirth. The dancing he particularly objected to, and from that year no public dinner or entertainment has ever been given on Christmas Day in Calcutta."[18]

Cornwallis's noted rectitude and the government's eagerness to appoint him might have been an echo of Burke's campaign, but as far as I know, Cornwallis never acknowledged it. It is also possible to read traces of Burke's influence in some of the other reforms. For example, a persistent problem for Company officials—and above all the governor-general—was the use of political and personal pressure to influence appointments in India. These appointments were increasingly difficult to obtain as the cadre of writers and cadets filled up. Hastings was certainly subject to these pressures, and some of his appointments were open to the charge of nepotism (the appointment of Stephen Sulivan, for example). Cornwallis was determined to put a stop to this. Appointments were to be made on the basis of merit and competence alone whenever possible. He was willing to give preferences to people who had connections, personal or political, but only if they were competent to do the job.

Like many reforms, the introduction of a meritocracy had unintended consequences—or at least consequences that in the long run made the governing of India even more oppressive. Indians were now formally excluded, as inferiors irrespective of merit, from the higher echelons of both the government and the army. Cornwallis's reform, with its high standards, was the first intimation of what ultimately became the Indian Civil Service. This was a great institution which by the mid-nineteenth century was accessible only to those who passed an examination that had been set by Macaulay himself. But there was never any doubt that these civil servants were meant to rule *over* Indians and not beside them. One wonders if this is what Burke had in mind.

Another reform with unintended consequences had to do with taxation, a constant problem since the days of Clive. Now the Company and Cornwallis were determined to fix it once and for all. Cornwallis found a collaborator who was at least as zealous a reformer as he was. This was a man named John Shore, one of the cadre of civil servants left over from the Hastings era. He had come to India as a writer in the 1770s. Ironically, one of his complaints at the time was that Hastings's own program of reform had made a lucrative career impossible. But later he became one of the most dedicated of all the civil servants, both to the welfare of the Indians and to the strict probity of the Company's officials. Shore had returned to England with Hastings and was a strong witness on his behalf at the trial. (Burke never forgot this, and when Shore was nominated to succeed Cornwallis in 1792 as governor-general, Burke did whatever he could, unsuccessfully, to block the appointment.)

When Cornwallis went to India he persuaded a somewhat reluctant Shore to accompany him. Shore took on the task of drawing up a new tax code, with a vengeance. It was a monumental job which produced a ninety-page document. In essence the zamindars—the landlords—would now become hereditary landowners. This reduced the peasants who worked the land to the status of tenants. As landowners, the zamindars would pay a tax that would be fixed for a substantial period of time. Shore suggested ten years, but Cornwallis and the Company fixed the rates in perpetuity. The system bore a vague family resemblance to something that Francis had tried to introduce decades earlier. The problems with it became evident over time. In good years the Company would gain no additional revenue, and in bad years the zamindars could not pay the fixed tax. As a result, many of them were forced to sell their land, which accumulated in the huge landholdings of a few families. Again, Burke's influence here is unclear.

∽

THE CORNWALLIS REGIME in India ended before the conclusion of Hastings's trial. His successor Shore's lasted until 1798. By this time Hastings had assumed the life of a country squire. He created a park, mansion, and museum at Daylesford.[19] He had a wonderful collection of paintings, including a portrait of Thurlow and a number of Moghul miniatures, which he would later have to sell. The house staff included as many as seven men servants and at least a half-dozen maids as well as gardeners and grooms. As usual, Hastings spent more money than he had. At one point he built a church where he and his neighbors could worship. He was also generous with gifts and donations. It was typical that when, in 1808, he realized that his old friend and protégé Halhed was destitute, not only did he and Marian send the customary Christmas goose but she enclosed a check from both of them, representing money they could ill afford to give away. Hastings had spent a lifetime watching money disappear in his hands like melting ice. Now that he was passing through his seventies, this was not about to change.

The year 1806 was a memorable one. Both Pitt and Fox died within a short time of each other, and Thurlow in September. Pitt was only forty-seven. Contemporary accounts[20] say he died celibate. There was something inhuman about him. He was admired greatly but not especially well-liked—the mirror image of Fox.* The king, who was if anything even more puritanical than Pitt, found this side of him appealing. The king loathed Fox. But more extraordinary was the impeachment of Henry Dundas, who was by now the first Viscount Melville. He was accused of financial improprieties that had occurred some twenty years earlier when he had been secretary of the navy. His impeachment trial, which took place in Westminster Hall with much spectacle, must have brought the trial of Hastings back to mind. All the more so since the lawyer who successfully defended him was none other than Thomas Plumer, now Sir Thomas Plumer, who had been one of Hastings's lawyers. Although acquitted, Dundas never again held public office. He died in 1811. His was the last impeachment ever prosecuted in Britain.

Emboldened by these dramatic changes, Hastings attempted

---

*One of the last things that Fox attempted to do before his death was to promote Francis as the next governor-general of India. He did not succeed.

once again to seek public recognition. To this end he obtained an audience with the Prince of Wales in March 1806. He seems to have prepared a short speech for the occasion, which he copied into his diary. It begins, "Since the great changes which have taken place in the administration of this country [the death of Pitt and the subsequent breakdown of the Tory government] I have purposely forborne to obtrude myself on your Royal Highness's notice, fearing to appear importunate and mistrustful of your Royal Highness's remembrance of me. But it has been suggested to me, that this caution, if extended too far, would render me liable to the imputation of disrespect, by marking a seeming indifference to your Royal Highness's intentions towards me. Under this influence, but not quite satisfied that I have done right in yielding to it, I have ventured to solicit the honour of presenting myself to your Royal Highness, but claiming nothing, and expecting nothing, till your Royal Highness, in your own time, shall do me the honour to make me the subject of your direct and effectual consideration."

The prince, in response, asked quite sensibly what exactly Hastings wanted. "I answered," the diary goes on, "my first object has been employment . . . either the Board of Control or the Government of India, but of this I now relinquished all thoughts, perhaps I ought not to have entertained them. My next view was to obtain a reparation from the House of Commons for the injuries which I had sustained from their impeachment of me. Though acquitted, I yet stand branded on their records as a traitor to my country and false to my trust. . . . The third point principally regards the expectations which your Royal Highness has yourself excited in the breast of the person in the world, whose wishes I have ever preferred to my own [Marian]. Though the best, the most amiable of women (the Prince said courteously, 'she is so'), she is still a woman, and would prefer her participation in a title that could be bestowed upon me (these last were not the words, I have forgotten them). [Nonetheless the message was clear.] The Prince cordially assenting, but (I thought) not as a thing to be done, but to be tried. . . ."[21]

Whatever Hastings's expectations may have been, nothing came of this meeting. Indeed the prince, later George IV, was a rather fragile reed on which to hang one's expectations. He was on very bad terms with his father and had a general, and largely deserved, reputation as a profligate womanizer. By 1808 Hastings could write to his former secretary George Thompson, "There is certainly some mysterious spell put upon me, for I can not otherwise account for the utter neglect of me even by those who proclaim their belief of my past services and subsequent retention of what talents I formerly possessed. My opinions upon matters that come more within the cognizance of my experience than that of any other man have never been asked, but on personal occasions in which it was hazardous to give them. It is now too late to look for a change. . . ."[22]

By this time he had found solace with his friends and family— with Marian above all, but also with her children and their children. She had two sons from her previous marriage. The younger one, Julius, found a career in India, where he died in 1799. While there he had set up a ménage—shades of Bogle—with an Indian woman. They had three children, one of whom was sent to England to be educated. He was accepted as part of the Hastingses' household. (This probably would not have happened a decade or so later. By this time the "memsahibs"—British women who were, or became, married to the colonials in India—were transforming the social order. They very likely had vastly more to do with the reform of the mores of British India than all the Burkes and Francises put together.[23] Interracial liaison became unacceptable.) Marian's older son, Charles, became almost a son to Hastings. He had a career as an army officer and was later knighted. When, just as the trial was ending, he married Charlotte Blunt, the daughter of another old India hand, Hastings was able to give the young couple ten thousand pounds which he had raised by selling his London house on Park Lane, the house in which he had lived before the purchase of Daylesford was completed. Marian had remained on good terms with her previous husband and even became godmother to one of his children when he remarried. Hastings had affectionate relationships with the children of his former associates such as Impey, who often visited Daylesford.

In 1813 the Company's charter was up for renewal and Hastings's pension was due to end. He was now eighty-one. But to his surprise and great satisfaction, he was asked to come to London to testify before both the House of Commons and the House of Lords. There were concerns about the continuation of the Company's trading monopoly and the scope of activity to be allowed to Christian missionar-

Warren Hastings, 1795. (Painting by Lemuel Francis
Abbott)

ies. Licensed missionaries and private traders were subsequently allowed in India. This was Hastings's first official connection with Indian affairs since the trial. He wrote a letter to Charles D'Oyley, the
son of his old Indian associate John D'Oyley, just afterward, describing the occasion:

"I have lately received two most convincing and affecting proofs
of my having outlived all the prejudices which have, during so many
past years prevailed against me. I have been called before both
Houses of Parliament, and questioned at large concerning the points
that bore a principal relation to the conditions proposed by the administration for the new charter of the East India Company. By the
Commons I was under examination between three and four hours,
and when I was ordered to withdraw, and was retiring, all the members, by one simultaneous impulse, rose with their heads uncovered,

and stood in silence, till I passed the door of their chamber. The House was unusually crowded. The same honour was paid to me, though, of course, with a more direct intention, by the Lords. [This may refer to the fact that it was the Lords who had acquitted him.] I consider it, in both instances, as bestowed on character, not on the worth of any information which they had drawn from me; for your father knows that I am in a singular degree deficient in the powers of utterance. To the same predilection I attribute it, that what I said on both occasions gave unanimous satisfaction. The Duke of Gloucester, with his accustomed goodness, took me with him in his carriage, calling upon me for the purpose, to the House of Lords, sat with me in the outer room till I was called in, conducted me to the chamber, where the Lords sat in full committee, afterwards reconducted me to his carriage, which reconveyed me home by his orders; and when the House broke up, he himself came to make his report of what had passed to Mrs. Hastings, with the same kind of glee that you, or your dear father, would have expressed upon the same occasion. And I bless him for it."[24] The Company agreed to renew Hastings's pension for life but refused to continue it for his wife in the event she outlived him.

The India ruled over by the Company in 1813 would have been quite unrecognizable to both Burke and Hastings. One wonders if much remained that reflected their concerns. The transformation began relatively modestly during the administration of Cornwallis. Tipu, Hyder Ali's son, was once again on the warpath. In 1792 Cornwallis took command of some forty thousand troops and delivered a firm beating to Tipu's army. The Company then enlarged its domain somewhat in the south. But this is nothing compared to what happened under Shore's successor as governor-general, Richard Wellesley, the Earl of Mornington. By the time he left India in 1805, along with his two brothers (Henry was his private secretary and Arthur, later the Duke of Wellington, his military commander), the British controlled great tracts of India from Madras to the Himalayas. Tipu was dead and the Marathas neutralized. Against Company orders, the Wellesleys had gone on a colonial rampage the like of which had not been envisioned since the days of Clive. To all intents and purposes, the governor-general had been turned into a viceroy. Not only were Indians not invited to be part of the government, there were now strict orders that they should never appear at social occasions that included British guests. Cornwallis, who was unwell, was sent back to India briefly—he died there in October 1805—to try to undo some of what Wellesley had left behind.

What Cornwallis and his successors did not do—it was not done until 1947—was to return India to the Indians. In 1833 the Company's trading monopoly was ended, and on August 2, 1858, Parliament passed the Government of India Act, transferring all the Company's rights to the crown. The East India House in Leadenhall Street, from which the Company ran its affairs, was demolished in 1862. The site where it stood is now occupied by the Lloyd's of London building. After 1858 the East India Company returned to its roots as a trading company. As such it still exists. It sells, among other things, coffee grown on that old Indiaman stopover, the island of St. Helena. It costs twenty-three dollars a pound.

As the first decades of the nineteenth century unfolded, most of the remaining actors in our drama departed the scene. Elijah Impey, Hastings's old schoolmate, died in 1809, and Richard Sheridan in 1816. In 1805 he and Hastings met for the first and last time. It was the Prince of Wales, a close friend of Sheridan's, who introduced them. The scene, which took place in the prince's residence, the Pavilion in Brighton, was described in his journals by a man named Thomas Creevey, a member of Parliament and a friend of Sheridan's, who witnessed it. Creevey reports that "Among the other persons who came to pay their respects to the Prince during the Autumn of 1805 was Mr. Hastings, whom I had never seen before excepting at his trial in Westminster Hall. He and Mrs. Hastings came to the Pavilion, and I was present when the Prince introduced Sheridan to him, which was curious, considering that Sheridan's parliamentary fame had been built upon his celebrated speech against Hastings. However, he lost no time in attempting to cajole old Hastings, begging him to believe that any part he had ever taken against him was purely political and that no one had a greater respect for him than himself, etc. etc., upon which old Hastings said, with great gravity, that 'it would be a great consolation to him in his declining days if Mr. Sheridan would make that sentence more publick': but Sheridan was obliged to mutter and get out of such an engagement as well as he could."[25]

Francis, who had protested vigorously against Wellesley's imperial policy, had lost his parliamentary seat in 1806. He spent the rest
of his life as a private man writing about various matters unrelated to
India, such as British policy toward Norway. His first wife died in
1806, and in 1811 he married his second wife, Emma Watkins. On
their marriage he gave her as a first present a copy of the letters of Junius. Considering that these had been written some four decades earlier, this was a remarkable gift, unless it was his way of telling her that
he had written them. (Of the various arguments I have read concerning the authorship of these letters, this is to me the most convincing.[26]) One can only wonder whether their relationship would have
been affected if Hastings had known that Francis was Junius. It will
be recalled that Hastings had charged his brother-in-law with the task
of sending him the letters as they appeared because he admired them
so. What would he have made of their author? Francis died on December 23, 1818. By this time the king, who was nearly blind and in
the final stages of dementia, had been replaced by the Prince of
Wales, who in 1811 had become regent. The king died in January
1820. He was unaware of the fact that the queen, whom Burney had
helped to dress for those five years, had died two years earlier.

Fanny Burney, who died on January 6, 1840, outlived all the other
actors in our drama. She outlived her husband by twenty-two years
and her son, and only child, by three. Her father died in 1814, and
the last of her siblings, her sister Charlotte, the one who had married
Clement Francis, Hastings's doctor, in 1838. Many of the later years
of Burney's life were as full as those that had preceded. In 1796 she
wrote her third novel, *Camilla*, which even she thought was too long.
She dedicated it to the queen. It gave the financially strapped D'Ar-
blays some needed income. Once Napoleon took power, General
D'Arblay was determined to return to France to resume his military
career. With much trepidation—more for him than for herself—she
followed him to France in 1802, which was the first time she had ever
been abroad. Miraculously D'Arblay survived the war and, even more
miraculously, she survived a mastectomy, without benefit of anesthe-
sia, performed in 1811 in France. At first Burney admired Napoleon,
and then she came to loathe him. From Brussels, where she had
taken refuge in 1815, she witnessed the preparations for the Battle of
Waterloo which took place some ten miles from the city. Soon after

she returned to England, where she remained for the rest of her life. The last entry in her journals is dated March 5, 1839. It is a letter to her niece, Charlotte Barrett, who would be the first person to edit the journals. The letter ends, "My spirits have been dreadfully saddened of late by whole days—nay weeks—of helplessness for *any* employment. They have but just revived. How merciful a reprieve! Now merciful is ALL we know! *The ways of Heaven* are not *dark* and intricate, but *unknown* and unimagined till the great teacher Death, developes them."[27]

In 1802 another of Hastings's disciples, a man named John Osborne, who had returned to Britain from India with Hastings on the *Berrington*, decided to build a testimonial to Hastings on his grounds in Melchet Park in Wiltshire. It was hardly a memorial since Hastings was still very much alive. Nevertheless Osborne commissioned the artist Thomas Daniell to design it. Daniell and his uncle William had spent two years in India in the 1790s. They were both superb artists and had done beautiful paintings and drawings of what they had seen. These must have come to Osborne's attention, and he asked Daniell to design a miniature Indian temple. Inside it he placed a bust of Hastings that the sculptor John Rossi had made. Hastings is depicted as arising from a lotus leaf. Nothing remains of this curious construction, though fortunately William Daniell made an engraving both of the temple and the bust.

Considering Hastings's fame during his lifetime, it is remarkable how few monuments were made in his memory after his death. Neither Parliament nor the Company tried to have something erected in either Westminster Abbey or St. Paul's Cathedral. It was Marian herself, who outlived Hastings by some two decades, who commissioned a bust and a tablet for the Abbey. Hastings died on August 22, 1818, but it was 1823 before the Company erected a statue of him in India House. Soon after word of his death reached Bengal, a public meeting took place in which a resolution was passed to have a statue of Hastings erected in Calcutta. Interestingly, the governor-general who approved was the Marquess of Hastings—no relation. The fact that a peerage had been created with his own name while he got no recognition from his government was also deeply hurtful to Hastings. One additional form of recognition was made by the Company while Hastings was still alive. One of its Indiamen was named the *Warren Has-*

Daylesford House.

tings, from all reports a stout ship though she was later captured by the French.

In his final years Hastings wrote some of his most personal letters to a man called David Anderson. Anderson had been another of Hastings's disciples in India and had returned to England when Hastings did and helped in the preparation of his defense. The two men had kept in touch. While none of Hastings's letters, even those to Marian, seem very intimate, one has the feeling that his letters to Anderson are about as intimate as he was capable of being. On December 9, 1816, he wrote to Anderson about the parish church he just had rebuilt in Daylesford:

"You will have known how much I have interested myself in the rebuilding of our parish church, and will be pleased to hear that we had divine service performed in it for the first time yesterday, to as full a congregation as it would hold. I was unexpectedly gratified by an appropriate sermon, with a prefatory prayer, both in my judgment of the first merit. [Hastings was always loyal to the Church of England, though he seemed to have more interest in Eastern religions than his own.] This work [the rebuilding of the church] undertaken

from necessity, but attributed by my neighbors to a much more laud-
able motive, has afforded me five months of constant recreation, both
of body and mind; and I verily believe that it has been the means for
suspending the decay of both. What has given me most cause for regret is my inability to walk to the distance of the village; and the difference which it has more strongly impressed upon my mind than I
ever felt it before, between executing a purpose from the instant of
its impulse, and giving orders for many consecutive operations, and
waiting for their tardy execution, with an equal chance of its being
defeated at last by the coming (I love my neighbours too well to call
it intrusion) of a long seated country visit. It just occurs to me to observe that the kind of amusement to which I have been alluding is
the most conformable of any to the last stage of mental infirmity, by
engaging the attention upon corporeal objects (like those of idola-
trous worship), which my day-labourers and I alike comprehend
without effort, and like the better for that poor facility."

Hastings was buried behind the chancel of this church under a
stone urn with an inscription that reads simply, "Warren Hastings
Died August 22, 1818." The church itself did not survive much past
mid-century, when Daylesford passed into other hands. Marian Hastings lived there until her death in 1837 at the age of ninety. Then
her son Charles and his wife occupied it until his death in 1853, when
the house was sold and the contents dispersed. The gravesite remains. After the house passed through several owners, in 1946 the
second Viscount Rothermere, the press baron, bought it and returned
to it much of Hastings's memorabilia, including many of the original
artworks. In 1977 the estate was once again sold and the contents of
the house once again dispersed. It is now owned by Sir Anthony
Bamford, who has restored it.[28] If one looks up walking tours in the
Cotswolds, in what is now Gloucestershire (Worcestershire in Hastings's day), one will find references to Daylesford. One wonders if
the people who walk by it realize what it once meant.

Hastings's health remained reasonably good until close to the end
of his life. He was much more worried about Marian's welfare than
his own. One of the truly moving features of Hastings's correspondence during these final years are his references to Marian's beauty.
He loved her as much then as he had when he first met her on the
voyage to India a half-century earlier. She, and her son Charles and

his wife, were at Hastings's bedside when he died. The final days in 1818 had been an agony of pain, which he had accepted stoically. At seven in the evening of August 22, he placed a handkerchief over his face and died, a last private act.

NOTES

PREFACE

1. For a discussion of the comparison of British and American impeachment processes, see, for example, A. W. Bradley, "Personal Responsibility and Government: A Role for Impeachment," in G. Carnall and C. Nicholson, eds., *The Impeachment of Warren Hastings* (Edinburgh, 1989), p. 164. Hereafter *Impeachment*.

Chapter 1. PROLOGUE: GEORGE BOGLE

1. Clements R. Markham, *The Mission of George Bogle to Tibet and the Journey of Thomas Manning to Lhasa* (facsimile edition, New Delhi, 1971). Hereafter *Bogle*.

2. *Bogle*, pp. 64–65.

3. *Bogle*, p. cxxxix.

4. For this and many other fascinating insights into the history of the Company, see John Keay, *The Honourable Company* (New York, 1994). The observation on the origin of the term "writer" will be found on p. 141.

5. John Riddy, *Warren Hastings: Scotland's Benefactor* (1989), pp. 30–57. *Impeachment* describes this aspect of the Company's politics.

6. Eyer Wilbur and Richard R. Smith, *The East India Company* (New York, 1945), p. 462.

7. A. Mervyn Davies, *Strange Destiny* (New York, 1935), pp. 14–15. Hereafter *Destiny*.

8. *Bogle*, p. cxxxix.

9. *Bogle*, pp. 1–3. Markham offers alternate possibilities in footnotes, and one may also consult Peter Collister, *Bhutan and the British* (London, 1987), pp. 11–12, both for this history and for another translation of part of this letter.

10. *Bogle*, p. 6.

11. See, for example, Peter Fleming, *Bayonets to Lhasa* (Oxford, 1985) for a description of Francis Younghusband's 1904 invasion of Tibet.

12. *Bogle*, pp. 8–9.

13. *Bogle*, p. 12.

14. *Bogle*, p. 71.

15. *Bogle*, p. 107.

16. *Bogle*, pp. 122–123.

17. *Bogle*, p. cxiv.

18. Markham quotes a portion of this letter. The entire letter is given in the second volume of G. R. Gleig's biography of Hastings, *Memoirs of the Life of the Right Hon. Warren Hastings* (London, 1841), pp. 17–20. See the following section for a full discussion of this reference.

19. *Bogle*, p. cliv.

20. Hugh M. Richardson, *Tibet and Its History* (Shambala, 1984). See also Richardson, *High Peaks, Pure Earth: Collected Writings on Tibetan History and Culture* (Serindia, 1998). In a recent correspondence, Richardson informed me that he has not been able to unearth further details about these children and their descendants.

Chapter 2. A BIBLIO-BIOGRAPHICAL INTERLUDE

1. In three volumes (London, 1841). Hereafter *Gleig*.

2. *Gleig*, I, 163–164.

3. "Warren Hastings" in Macaulay, *Critical and Historical Essays* (Boston, 1900), III, 114–242. Hereafter *Machast*.

4. *Machast*, p. 114.

5. Sir Alfred Lyall, *Warren Hastings* (London, 1889; reprinted Freeport, N.Y., 1970). Hereafter *Lyall*. Of the less interesting genre, see Captain L. J. Trotter, *Warren Hastings* (London, 1890; reprinted Freeport, N.Y., 1972).

6. *Lyall*, p. 234.

7. The quotation can be found on p. 107 of a remarkable collection of historical sketches by H. E. Busteed, entitled *Echoes from Old Calcutta* (London, 1888). Busteed had been assay-master at the Calcutta mint. He combed correspondence and contemporary newspapers and gazettes to produce his "echoes." While the book is not meant as a systematic history, it is filled with small jewels. Hereafter *Echoes*.

8. *Destiny*, pp. 364–365.

9. Keith Feiling, *Warren Hastings* (London, 1954). Hereafter *Feiling*. A nice biography, on the scale of the present one, was published in 1947 by Pendrel Moon, *Warren Hastings and British India* (London), as part of the "Teach Yourself History Library." Sir Pendrel Moon had served in the Indian Civil Service, and he notes that his book about the first governor-general of India coincided with the end of the reign of the last. Moon is less interested than I am in Hastings as a person, so that many of the details I find fascinating are either mentioned in a sentence or not mentioned at all. He is generally sympathetic to Hastings.

10. It is not surprising that the Tollygunge Club in Calcutta, an upscale plantation cum hotel run by an Englishman, has a wing of rooms called "Hastings."

Fort William still survives, as does the Maidan, the large green that was, and is, a park.

Chapter 3. HASTINGS, 1732–1769

1. *Destiny*, p. 165.

2. Quoted in *Destiny*, p. 398.

3. These are taken from a remarkable contemporary account of the trial published in 1796 by the London firm of J. Debrett, entitled *The History of the Trial of Warren Hastings*. It is unclear who the author of this history is. He describes himself only as the "Editor." Nor is it clear how the book was compiled. Perhaps newspaper accounts were used, but there is a sense that the editor was actually present. In any event, the book presents the trial day to day—seven years' worth!—with extensive quotations from the principals. The editor also comments on how the various speeches and bits of repartee were received. The speeches themselves, some of which went on for days, were recorded by shorthand writers, probably employed by Debrett, but in some cases there exists more than one version. This book, which is in minuscule type, does not have consecutively numbered pages. The editor has divided the material into eight parts, each of which has its own numbering schemes. In the unlikely event that a reader wishes to pursue this reference, I have given the part, or parts, followed by the internal page numbers. Hereafter *Debrett*. Parts 5 through 8 are consecutively numbered. This sampler can be found in Part VII, pp. 150–154.

4. *Gleig*, I, 6.

5. *Gleig*, I, 9.

6. *Machast*, p. 118.

7. *Gleig*, I, 12–13.

8. *Destiny*, p. 12.

9. For a useful, relatively brief Indian history, see Stanley Wolpert, *A New History of India*, 5th edition (Oxford, 1997).

10. This encounter is discussed graphically in *Keay*, Chapter 14.

11. *Gleig*, I, 244.

12. There is, needless to say, a great deal of biographical material on Clive. Most people know, or think they know, more about him than they do about Hastings and often attribute to him the founding of British India. He certainly played a vital role, but without Hastings it would not have happened. Macaulay wrote a celebrated essay on Clive (Macaulay, *Essays*, II, 670–762; hereafter *Macclive*). One of the strangest books is *The Rape of India* by Allen Edwardes (New York, 1966). Edwardes is fixated on the sexual peccadilloes and the detailed accounts of tortures and mutilations he has ferreted out of the contemporary literature. For example, he claims that when Hastings was captured by the Muslims, he was forcibly circumcised. Certainly Muslims did that to their male prisoners,

but no other biography of Hastings mentions that it was done to him. The book nonetheless contains useful source material which I will occasionally quote if it seems corroborated by other sources. Hereafter *Rape*.

13. *Macclive*, p. 676.

14. *Macclive*, pp. 702–703.

15. *Rape*, p. 136.

16. For excerpts from Holwell's account as well as much other useful information about this affair, see *Echoes*, Chapters 1 and 2.

17. *Echoes*, p. 22.

18. There is some difference as to whether it was twenty-one (*India*) or twenty-three (Holwell).

19. For an account, see P. J. Marshall, *Bengal: The British Bridgehead* (Cambridge, England, 1987).

20. *Feiling*, p. 26.

21. See *Destiny*, p. 33, for samples.

22. Claire Tomalin, *Jane Austen: A Life* (New York, 1997), p. 50. Hereafter *Claire*.

23. David Nokes, *Jane Austen: A Life* (London, 1997), p. 419. Hereafter *Nokes*.

24. *Nokes*, p. 31.

25. *Nokes*, p. 31.

26. *Keay*, p. 322.

27. James Boswell, *Life of Johnson* (Oxford, 1980), pp. 1115–1120.

Chapter 4. HASTINGS, 1769–1772: MADRAS

1. *Bogle*, pp. cxli–cxliii.

2. *Echoes*, pp. 133–134. All of this may seem like the makings of a novel. Indeed, while surfing the net under "Carl von Imhoff" I came upon one. It was written by a man named Victor Barnouw. I know nothing about him except that he has clearly done his homework. He has invented another artist, a young man, an apprentice to Joshua Reynolds, who is also on board the *Duke of Grafton* and observes what happens. Ultimately he goes to Bhutan with Bogle and marries the woman that *he* fell in love with on the trip out to India. The full novel, which is 106 pages, can be downloaded from the net. I do not know if it was ever published. Most of the characters we have met are in it.

3. *Echoes*, p. 134.

4. The full list and the amount each one put up—between 100 and 3,000 pounds, for a total of 30,133 pounds—along with their professions, can be found in Marguerite Eyer Wilbur, *The East India Company* (New York, 1945), pp. 445–458. Hereafter *Wilbur*. This book contains a number of factual errors and should be used with caution. A really good treatment of this material can be found in Brian Gardner, *The East India Company* (New York, 1971). Hereafter *Gardner*.

5. *Feiling*, p. 52.

6. See, for example, *Wilbur*, p. 269. This letter and its impact are also discussed in an essay by H. V. Bowen, "India: The Metropolitan Context," in the *Oxford History of the British Empire* (New York, 1998), II, 530–551. Hereafter *Bowen*.

7. *Gardner*, pp. 93–94.

8. *Feiling*, p. 52.

9. In fairness it should be pointed out that not all biographers agree that Clive shot himself or even that he committed suicide at all. See, for example, R. J. Minney, *Clive of India* (London, 1957). Given that everyone is in agreement that he had tried to kill himself in this way in India, I find it plausible that he did shoot himself.

10. Both these quotations are found on p. 535 of *Bowen*.

11. This remarkable outburst can be found in any of the standard biographies of Clive or in the accounts of the British in India. See, for example, S. M. Burke and Salim Al-Din Quraishi, *The British Raj in India* (New York, 1995), p. 10.

Chapter 5. Hastings in Bengal, 1772–1774

1. *Echoes*, p. 65.

2. See *Echoes* for the full details. This quote is found on p. 172.

3. *Echoes*, p. 174.

4. *Echoes*, p. 177.

5. *Echoes*, p. 179.

6. This term is used this way in *Echoes* to describe Calcutta high society.

7. *Echoes*, p. 123.

8. *Echoes*, pp. 123–124.

9. *Echoes*, p. 126.

10. *Feiling*, p. 87.

11. This jingle can be found in Percival Spear, *The Nabobs* (New Delhi, 1998), p. 65. The translation was supplied by my physics colleague Sudip Chakarvaty (who informs that this was the first time he has used his native tongue since he left Bangladesh in 1958) and then corrected and refined by Rosane Rocher, who is expert in these languages.

12. *Echoes*, p. 137.

13. Eliza Fay, *Original Letters from India, 1779–1815*, with an introduction by E. M. Forster (London, 1925), pp. 174–175. Mrs. Fay was a formidable character. She and her husband made the overland trip via Suez. Her account shows why this was not a very attractive alternative to the ocean voyage. They were attacked by bandits in the desert, and once they reached India they were taken prisoner by Hyder Ali. It took them a year and eighteen days to reach Calcutta. After a relatively short time she and her husband were divorced. Eventually she made two more trips to India.

14. For a useful two-volume biography of North, see Alan Valentine, *Lord North* (Norman, Okla., 1967). Hereafter *Valentine*. This quote is found in I, 25. North, incidentally, was during his father's lifetime a "courtesy lord"—a lord in title only, with none of the privileges.

15. *Valentine*, II, 449.

16. *Valentine*, I, 118.

17. *Valentine*, II, 158. This position was at the time usually referred to as "first minister."

Chapter 6. HASTINGS, 1774–1785

1. *Echoes*, p. 113.

2. *Gleig*, I, 452.

3. Junius, *Letters by the Same Writer* (Philadelphia, 1813), II, 232. In his well-known book about Burke, *The Great Melody: A Thematic Biography and Commentated Anthology of Edmund Burke* (Chicago, 1992)—hereafter *Melody*—Conor Cruise O'Brien takes the position that Francis was definitely the author of the Junius letters and that North knew this. Thus O'Brien claims that Francis's appointment was a bribe to get him to stop writing these letters. The reader should study O'Brien's book to see if the evidence cited seems persuasive. I can only say that I do not agree. This is not the place to go into the history of the attempts to identify Junius, but, as far as I know, nowhere does Francis admit to being the author of these letters. One would have thought that after everyone had died, Francis, even posthumously, might have said something. This is only one of many places where I have disagreements with O'Brien's interpretation of this history. I think the reader is much better served by studying Professor Whelan's analysis of the same body of evidence in the book cited in detail below.

4. *Echoes*, p. 55.

5. *Gleig*, I, 453.

6. There *was* capital punishment in India. Muslim law, which was severe, certainly had it, and the British were regularly executing *dacoits* (highwaymen) when they were captured. In principle, all criminal law in Calcutta was Muslim law while Hindus practiced Hindu civil law, which Hastings had made sure of.

7. *Echoes*, p. 61.

8. Some authors spell this "Mackrabie," but Macrabie seems to be the consensus spelling.

9. *Echoes*, p. 62.

10. *Echoes*, p. 62.

11. The full text of the letter from which I quote can be found in *Echoes*, pp. 62–64.

12. *Feiling*, p. 103. A reader who wants more detail about this period should consult Feiling, with the caveat that he or she will have to digest a pretty hefty diet of probably unfamiliar fare.

13. The introduction that Halhed wrote for this translation, along with the letters that Hastings and Halhed wrote to the directors, can be found in P. J. Marshall, ed., *The British Discovery of Hinduism in the Eighteenth Century* (Cambridge, England, 1970). Hereafter *Discovery*. A very interesting biography of Halhed is Rosane Rocher's *Orientalism, Poetry, and the Millennium: The Checkered Life of Nathaniel Brassey Halhed, 1751–1830* (Columbia, Mo., 1983).

14. *Gleig*, I, 403.

15. *Feiling*, p. 103.

16. Two highly useful discussions of these matters, besides the biographies already cited, are Frederick G. Whelan, *Edmund Burke and India* (Pittsburgh, 1996) (hereafter *Whelan*), and P. J. Marshall, *The Impeachment of Warren Hastings* (Oxford, 1965), hereafter *Marshall*.

17. *Whelan*, p. 141.

18. *Echoes*, p. 209.

19. *Echoes*, p. 212.

20. *Echoes*, p. 238.

21. *Echoes*, p. 222. This wonderful book is long out of print, but if you can find a copy it is worth reading for these transcripts alone. There is a relatively inexpensive facsimile edition.

22. *Bogle*, p. cxlviii.

23. The full text of this letter can be found in *Gleig*, I, 471–476.

24. From Sir Nathaniel Wraxall, *Historical Memoirs of My Own Time* (London, 1904), pp. 301–302. Hereafter *Wraxall*.

25. Should anyone care to read it, it can be found in a small collection entitled *Two Anglo-Saxon Plays* (New York, 1928).

26. *Machast*, pp. 129–131.

27. *Gleig*, I, 517–518.

28. In many books this name is spelled Macleane. But in Hastings's letters, quoted in Gleig, this is the spelling, so I have adopted it.

29. The reader who is interested can find part of it, along with a fuller description of the trial, in *Echoes*, pp. 66–108.

30. *Machast*, p. 154.

31. For the full text, see the reference in *Echoes* above.

32. *Echoes*, pp. 113–114.

33. *Echoes*, p. 117.

34. *Bogle*, p. cxlix.

35. *Gleig*, II, 108–109.

36. *Gleig*, II, 111–112.

37. *Feiling*, p. 182.

38. The full letter can be found in *Gleig*, II, 157–161.

39. *Gleig*, III, 138–139.

40. *Echoes*, pp. 302–303.

41. *Gleig*, III, 215.

42. *Feiling*, p. 191.

43. For more details, see the delightful *The Nabobs* by Spear.

44. *Debrett*, Part IV, pp. 94–95.

45. *Feiling*, p. 214.

46. Sophia Weitzman, *Warren Hastings and Philip Francis* (Manchester, England, 1929), p. 351. Hereafter *Weitzman*.

47. This quotation is taken from G. W. Forrest, ed., *Selections from the letters, despatches, and other State papers preserved in the Foreign Department of the Government of India, 1772–1785* (1890), II, 711. In short, it was an official document.

48. *Feiling*, p. 228.

49. *Weitzman*, p. 355.

50. *Gleig*, II, 255–256.

51. This is quoted in *Marshall*, p. 106. Both *Marshall* and *Destiny* have good accounts of the Benares incident. The one in *Feiling* is somewhat harder to follow.

52. For a useful brief summary, see the article by J. L. Brockington, "Warren Hastings and Orientalism," in *Impeachment*, pp. 91–108.

53. For a brief description of the expedition and its personnel, see *Bogle*, pp. lxxi–lxxv.

54. See Collister, *Bhutan and the British*, for several examples.

55. This letter is quoted in full in *Discovery*, pp. 184–191.

56. The speech may be found in many sources on Burke. I have used Peter J. Stanlis, *Edmund Burke: Selected Writings and Speeches* (Garden City, N.Y., 1963), pp. 367–389. Hereafter *Speeches*. Mr. Stanlis seems to belong to the large school of commentators who assume that everything Burke claimed about the abuses of the Company and about Hastings was literally true. As I will make clear, I strongly disagree.

57. *Speeches*, pp. 376–377.

58. *Machast*, p. 211.

59. Professor Rocher has pointed out to me that the Asiatick Society had a manuscript and book collection that are still in the possession of its modern counterpart. She also notes that the Writers Building was built not by the Company but by private speculators who seemed to have had a connection to Barwell. The Company eventually bought it.

60. See especially *Melody*, Chapter 1.

61. Macaulay, *Historical and Critical Essays*, III, 654. Hereafter *Rock*.

62. This quotation may be found in *Melody*, p. 114. It is taken from a draft of Burke's speech. Verbatim accounts of speeches in Parliament were not available until after 1783, when journalists were first allowed to report them. This preceded the Hastings impeachment trial, which is why we have such full documentation of the speeches delivered at the trial.

63. I take some of my information from Isaac Kramnick, *The Rage of Edmund Burke* (New York, 1977). Hereafter *Rage*. I am well aware that Professor Kramnick's book, with its psycho-sexual interpretation of Burke's behavior, is anath-

ema to many Burke scholars. Nonetheless I found in Kramnick's book documentary material that I did not find elsewhere. What I discuss is based on that material and not on an interpretation of it.

64. In *Rage* the case is made that it had a homosexual component and that Burke's sexual "ambiguity" fed the rage that he expressed in his most polemic speeches, which sometimes did have sexual references. This is a discussion we can safely leave to the experts.

65. Quoted in *Rage*, p. 72.

66. *Weitzman*, p. 335.

67. This appeared in the *General Evening Post*, April 8, 1773. I have taken it from the discussion in *Melody*, p. 264.

68. Quoted in *Feiling*, p. 128.

69. *Weitzman*, p. 223.

70. *Weitzman*, p. 224.

71. *Feiling*, p. 283.

72. *Feiling*, p. 283.

73. *Weitzman*, p. 142, n. 2.

74. *Valentine*, II, 274.

75. *Wraxall*, p. 324.

76. *Gleig*, II, 486–487.

77. *Wraxall*, pp. 343–344.

78. *Speeches*, pp. 377–378.

79. See *Marshall*, pp. 24–25, for more details.

80. Oddly, he gives 208 to 106 as the count in favor, which differs from the one in *Valentine*, II, 383. I have used Valentine's number. Both numbers reveal the same thing—that the House voted two to one in favor of the bill. The entire letter can be found in *Gleig*, III, 99–104.

81. *Valentine*, II, 388. Valentine's account of this affair is savorous. He does not focus much on Hastings since he is writing a biography of North. An equally savorous account can be found in *Wraxall*, p. 597 *et seq.* Wraxall was there and was a participant. He voted against the bill in the House of Commons.

82. *Echoes*, p. 325.

83. Alfred Spencer, ed., *Memoirs of William Hickey*, 4 vols. (reprinted Watford, England, 1950). Hereafter *Hickey*.

84. *Hickey*, III, 245.

85. *Gleig*, III, 108.

86. The entire letter may be found in *Gleig*, III, 173–175.

87. *Feiling*, p. 310.

88. *Gleig*, III, 160.

89. Some commentators say that Hastings brought yaks back with him. Having had some experience with yaks, I find this highly unlikely. Feiling says "cows," and perhaps they were the breed of cow and yak that one usually sees at moderate altitudes in Nepal. A true yak is really a high-altitude animal.

Chapter 7. THE DIARIES OF FANNY BURNEY

1. At this time there is, alas, no definitive edition of the diaries of Fanny Burney. I have used the beautiful six-volume edition edited by her niece Charlotte Barrett, published in 1842–1846. The version I have was published by Macmillan (New York, 1904). Hereafter *Burney.* This entry will be found in II, 297. Charlotte Barrett did not try to investigate what lay underneath the blacked-out portions of Fanny Burney's diaries, something that modern scholars are trying to do.

These six volumes cover the period from 1778 to 1840, which is the time frame of Burney's acquaintance with Hastings and the trial and its aftermath. In addition there are two volumes of journals, edited by Annie Raine Ellis, that cover the period from 1768 to 1778. These were published in 1889 and then reprinted in 1971 (Freeport, N.Y.), hereafter *Early Burney.* A recent biography of Burney is Kate Chisholm, *Fanny Burney: Her Life, 1752–1840* (London, 1998). Hereafter *Chisholm.* I find Ms. Chisholm's offhand references to Hastings, however, to be totally misguided. If her list of references is complete, she seems never to have read anything about Hastings or eighteenth-century India.

2. *Chisholm,* p. 1.

3. I follow the general usage and call them journals rather than diaries. They do not really record daily events and, as I will explain, contain a great deal of material not written by Burney at all.

4. This essay can be found in Macaulay, *Critical and Historical Essays,* Vol. III. The quotation is on p. 335. Hereafter *Macburney.* This is actually close to the Burney family's original name.

5. *Early Burney,* II, 47–48.

6. *Early Burney,* II, 55.

7. *Macburney,* pp. 347–348.

8. This quotation is, of course, part of the Burney lore. I have taken it from the introduction to the 1982 edition of Burney, *Evelina,* published by Oxford University Press, New York, and written by Edward and Lilian Bloom. Hereafter *Evelina.* One can find it on p. ix of their introduction.

9. *Chisholm,* p. 43.

10. *Evelina,* p. 1.

11. *Early Burney,* II, 153–154.

12. *Early Burney,* II, 154.

13. *Burney,* I, 90. This is from the entry of August 28, 1778.

14. *Macburney,* p. 388.

15. *Burney,* II, 88.

16. *Burney,* II, 91.

17. *Burney,* II, 361.

18. Quoted in *Chisholm,* p. 69.

19. An enjoyable recent book on George III and his family is Christopher

Hibbert, *George III, A Personal History* (New York, 1998). The reader will find a good deal of material taken from Burney's journals. I was disappointed to find very little about India and nothing at all about Hastings.

20. *Macburney*, p. 358.
21. *Macburney*, p. 362.
22. *Burney*, II, 272.
23. *Burney*, II, 280.
24. *Burney*, II, 320.
25. *Burney*, II, 319–320.
26. *Burney*, II, 321.
27. *Burney*, II, 363–364.
28. *Burney*, II, 365.
29. *Macburney*, pp. 358–359.
30. For whatever reason, in Burney's journal he is given the fictitious name of Colonel Fairly. This, it seems to me, argues clearly for her intention that these journals should be read by others.
31. This entire episode may be found in *Burney*, II, 441–443.

Chapter 8. THE TRIAL OF WARREN HASTINGS

1. This spelling for this office is still in use.
2. *Burney*, III, 412–413.
3. The full letter may be found in *Gleig*, III, 238–244.
4. See, for example, *Weitzman*, p. 172 *et seq* for this quote and an account of these early maneuvers.
5. Both men, incidentally, had controversial wives. Oppenheimer's wife had been married to a Communist, which was well known to the authorities who cleared him to build the atomic bomb, but which resurfaced in these hearings.
6. *Weitzman*, pp. 187–188.
7. *Weitzman*, p. 175n.
8. *Weitzman*, p. 175.
9. *Weitzman*, p. 175.
10. See *Marshall*, p. 39 *et seq* for this quotation and a discussion of this phase of the impeachment process.
11. *Debrett*, preface, p. x. This rendering, and those that follow, were made by whatever means the anonymous editor of this compilation employed. I will spare the reader the original rendering where "salaries" are printed as "falaries." I have also corrected an obvious mistake in the numbering.
12. *Debrett*, preface, p. xi.
13. *Destiny*, p. 380.
14. *Burney*, II, 360.
15. The full letter may be found in *Gleig*, III, 286–291.

16. *Debrett,* preface, p. xi.

17. *Debrett,* preface, pp. xi–xii.

18. "Machast," p. 217.

19. I am grateful to Professor Whelan for this suggestion. Precisely this scenario is spelled out in a contemporary account. See Nathaniel Wraxall, *Posthumous Memoirs of His Own Time* (Philadelphia, 1836), p. 219 *et seq.* Wraxall was a shrewd observer of his parliamentary colleagues and provides a balanced view of the trial, which he witnessed.

20. For a description of this and a recent account of Sheridan's life, see Fintan O'Toole, *A Traitor's Kiss: The Life of Richard Brinsley Sheridan* (New York, 1998). Hereafter *Kiss.* While I do not agree with O'Toole's evaluation of Hastings, I found much in this book useful.

21. Quoted in *Kiss,* p. 218.

22. *Kiss,* p. 220.

23. *Debrett,* Part 1, p. 2.

24. *Debrett,* Part 1, p. 2.

25. See *The Works of the Right Honourable Edmund Burke* (London, 1813), xi, 370 *et seq.*

26. *Burney,* III, p. 415.

27. *Burney,* III, p. 416.

28. *In the Matter of J. Robert Oppenheimer,* Transcript of Hearing Before Personnel Security Board, U.S. Atomic Energy Commission (Washington, D.C., 1954).

29. In *Macburney* Macaulay complains about Burney's lack of knowledge of India. But I think he misses the point I have been trying to make about her novelist's intuition.

30. This remarkable colloquy can be found in its entirety in *Burney,* III, 414–435.

31. Quoted in *Marshall,* p. 27.

32. *Burney,* III, 446.

33. This quotation may be found in *Melody,* p. 366, where this part of the trial is discussed in some detail.

34. *Melody,* p. 370. Much of the speech can be found in *Speeches,* p. 394 *et seq.*

35. *Melody,* p. 371.

36. This may be found in full in *Debrett,* Part I, p. 7.

37. Burney's reaction to Burke's speech and her encounter with him may be found in *Burney,* III, 448 *et seq.* The quotations that follow are taken from this source.

38. This debate may be found in *Debrett,* Part I, p. 9.

39. *Debrett,* Part I, p. 10.

40. *Burney,* III, 465–467.

41. *Debrett,* Part I, p. 52.

42. *Debrett,* Part I, p. 74.

43. *Debrett*, Part I, pp. 99–100.

44. Quoted in *Feiling*, p. 357.

45. *Burney*, IV, 117.

46. *Burney*, IV, 120.

47. This remarkable episode may be found in full in *Burney*, IV, 242–251.

48. Quoted in *Gleig*, III, 347, along with other specimens such as "He gorged his ravenous maw with an allowance of two hundred pounds a day" and "He never dines without creating a famine."

49. *Debrett*, Part II, p. 17.

50. *Debrett*, Part II, p. 18.

51. *Debrett*, Part II, p. 33.

52. *Debrett*, Part II, p. 35.

53. *Debrett*, Part II, p. 39.

54. Quoted in *Melody*, p. 397.

55. It is puzzling what Hastings meant. Could he really not have remembered that he was nearly sixty?

56. *Debrett*, Part IV, pp. 66–67.

57. The entire speech may be found in *Debrett*, Part IV, p. 81 *et seq.* The figures on the numbers of sitting Lords may be found in *Marshall*, p. 85, as well as in *Debrett*.

58. *Burney*, IV, 462.

59. *Debrett*, Part IV, p. 97.

60. *Debrett*, Part IV, p. 103.

61. *Burney*, V, 58.

62. *Debrett*, Part VI, p. 63.

63. This entire account may be found in *Debrett*, Part VI, p. 94 *et seq.*

64. *Debrett*, Part VII, p. 122.

65. *Debrett*, Part VII, p. 154.

66. *Debrett*, Part VII, p. 154.

67. *Debrett*, Part VII, p. 144. This page number may seem odd compared to the previous ones, but the Debrett editor has not given the entire verbatim transcript of Burke's nine-day speech. He has collected the invective in one place, hence the previous references.

68. *Debrett*, Part VIII, p. 158.

69. *Debrett*, Part VIII, p. 159.

70. *Debrett*, Part VIII, p. 160.

71. *Debrett*, Part VIII, p. 184.

72. *Debrett*, Part VIII, p. 193.

73. *Debrett*, Part VIII, p. 203.

74. The full set of charges and the details of the vote may be found in *Debrett*, Part VIII, p. 267 *et seq.*

75. *Debrett*, Part VIII, p. 271.

Chapter 9. EPILOGUE: FINAL YEARS

1. *Burney,* V, 253.
2. *Chisholm,* p. 159.
3. Alas, I found no reference to Mrs. Grand in Burney's journals.
4. *Burney,* V, 171.
5. *Debrett,* Part VIII, pp. 290–291.
6. *Gleig,* Vol. III, p. 355.
7. *Debrett,* Part VIII, pp. 302–303.
8. *Debrett,* Part VIII, p. 306.
9. *Debrett,* Part VIII, p. 306.
10. For a more detailed account, see P. J. Marshall, *East Indian Fortunes: The British in Bengal in the Eighteenth Century* (Oxford, 1976). For details on Nobkissen, see *Marshall.*
11. *Weitzman,* p. 195.
12. *Melody,* pp. 579–580.
13. *Melody,* pp. 582–583.
14. *Burney,* V, 332–333.
15. See *Weitzman,* for example.
16. See *Melody,* for example.
17. For a nice discussion of this aspect of Cornwallis's career, see Franklin and Mary Wickwire, *Cornwallis: The Imperial Years* (Chapel Hill, 1980).
18. *Hickey,* III, 306.
19. *Feiling,* Chapter 27, has a good description of Daylesford as it was then.
20. See, for example, *Wraxall.*
21. *Gleig,* III, 428–429.
22. *Gleig,* III, 445.
23. Professor Rosane Rocher has pointed out that colonial servants' education also changed. Civil servants were educated at Haileybury College and military personnel at Addiscombe Academy. Thus they were not only indoctrinated against the "lures of the east" but they arrived in India in their twenties, not their late teens, so that their social attitudes were more firmly fixed.
24. *Gleig,* III, 460–461.
25. John Gore, ed., *The Creevey Papers* (London, 1963), pp. 49–50.
26. I am grateful to Professor Rocher for calling it to my attention.
27. *Burney,* VI, 416.
28. I am grateful to Sir Anthony Bamford for correspondence about Daylesford and for sharing some beautiful photographs of the estate.

BIBLIOGRAPHY

Jeremy Bernstein. *In the Himalayas.* New York: Lyons Press, 1996.

James Boswell. *Life of Johnson.* Oxford: Oxford University Press, 1980.

Edmund Burke. *Selected Letters of Edmund Burke.* Ed. Harvey C. Mansfield, Jr. Chicago: University of Chicago Press, 1984.

————. *Selected Writings and Speeches.* Ed. Peter J. Stanlis. New York: Doubleday, 1963.

————. *The Works of The Right Honourable Edmund Burke.* Vol. XI. London: F. C. and J. Rivington, 1813.

Frances Burney. *Cecilia; or Memoirs of an Heiress.* New York: Oxford University Press, 1988.

————. *Diary and Letters of Madame D'Arblay.* 6 vols. Ed. Charlotte Barrett. London: Macmillan, 1904.

————. *The Early Diary of Frances Burney, 1768–1778.* Vol. II. Ed. Annie Raine Ellis. Freeport, N.Y.: Books for Libraries Press, 1971.

————. *The Early Journals and Letters of Fanny Burney.* Vol. I. Ed. Lars E. Troide, Montreal: McGill-Queen's University Press, 1988.

————. *Evelina; or the History of a Young Lady's Entrance into the World.* New York: Oxford University Press, 1998.

————. *The Wanderer; or Female Difficulties.* New York: Oxford University Press, 1991.

H. E. Busteed. *Echoes from Old Calcutta.* New Delhi: Asian Educational Services, 1999.

Geoffrey Carnall and Colin Nicholson, eds. *The Impeachment of Warren Hastings.* Edinburgh: Edinburgh University Press, 1989.

Kate Chisholm. *Fanny Burney: Her Life, 1752–1840.* London: Chatto & Windus, 1998.

Peter Collister. *Bhutan and the British.* London: Serindia, 1987.

Thomas Creevey. *The Creevey Papers.* Ed. John Gore. London: B. T. Batsford, 1963.

A. Mervyn Davies. *Strange Destiny.* New York: G. P. Putnam, 1935.

Debrett. *The History of the Trial of Warren Hastings.* London: Debrett, 1796.

Henry Dodwell. *Dupleix and Clive, The Beginning of an Empire.* London: Frank Cass, 1967.

Allen Edwardes. *The Rape of India.* New York: Julian Press, 1966.

Michael Edwardes. *Warren Hastings: King of the Nabobs.* London: Hart-Davis, MacGibbon, 1976.

Eliza Fay. *Original Letters from India, 1779–1815.* London: Hogarth Press, 1925.

Keith Feiling. *Warren Hastings.* London: Macmillan, 1954.

Lion Feuchtwanger. *Two Anglo-Saxon Plays.* New York: Viking Press, 1928.

Peter Fleming. *Bayonets to Lhasa.* Oxford: Oxford University Press, 1985.

Brian Gardner. *The East India Company.* New York: McCall, 1971.

G. R. Gleig. *Memoirs of the Life of the Right Hon. Warren Hastings, First Governor-General of Bengal.* 3 vols. London: Richard Bentley, 1841.

Christopher Hibbert. *George III: A Personal History.* New York: Basic Books, 1998.

William Hickey. *Memoirs of William Hickey.* 4 vols. Ed. Alfred Spencer. London: Hurst & Blackett, 1950.

Lawrence James. *Raj: The Making and Unmaking of British India.* New York: St. Martin's Press, 1998.

Junius. *Letters by the Same Writer.* Philadelphia: Bradford and Inskeep, 1813.

John Keay. *The Honourable Company.* New York: Macmillan, 1994.

Russell Kir. *Edmund Burke.* New Rochelle, N.Y.: Arlington House, 1967.

Isaac Kramnick. *The Rage of Edmund Burke.* New York: Basic Books, 1977.

Alfred Lyall. *Warren Hastings.* Freeport, N.Y.: Books for Libraries Press, 1970.

Thomas Babington Macaulay. *Critical and Historical Essays.* 3 vols. Boston: Houghton, Mifflin, 1900.

Clements R. Markham, ed. *The Mission of George Bogle to Tibet and the Journey of Thomas Manning to Lhasa.* New Delhi: Manjusri, 1971.

P. J. Marshall. *East Indian Fortunes: The British in Bengal in the Eighteenth Century.* Oxford: Clarendon Press, 1976.

———. *The Impeachment of Warren Hastings.* Oxford: Oxford University Press, 1965.

———. *The New Cambridge History of India.* Vol. 2, *Bengal: The British*

Bridgehead. Eastern India, 1740–1828. Cambridge, England, Cambridge University Press, 1987.

P. J. Marshall, ed. *The British Discovery of Hinduism in the Eighteenth Century.* Cambridge, England, Cambridge University Press, 1970.

R. J. Minney. *Clive of India.* London: Jarrolds, 1957.

Pendrel Moon. *Warren Hastings and British India.* New York: Collier, 1962.

Lewis Namier. *Crossroads of Power.* Freeport, N.Y.: Books for Libraries Press, 1970.

David Nokes. *Jane Austen: A Life.* London: Fourth Estate, 1997.

Conor Cruise O'Brien. *The Great Melody: A Thematic Biography and Commented Anthology of Edmund Burke.* Chicago: University of Chicago Press, 1992.

Fintan O'Toole. *A Traitor's Kiss: The Life of Richard Brinsley Sheridan.* New York: Farrar Straus and Giroux, 1998.

Rosane Rocher. *Orientalism, Poetry, and the Millennium: The Checkered Life of Nathaniel Brassey Halhed, 1751–1830.* Columbia, Mo.: South Asia Books, 1983.

Percival Spear. *The Nabobs.* New Delhi: Oxford University Press, 1998.

Lucy S. Sutherland. *The East India Company in Eighteenth-Century Politics.* Oxford: Oxford University Press, 1952.

Bryn Thomas, et al. *India.* Hawthorn, Australia: Lonely Planet, 1997.

Claire Tomalin. *Jane Austen: A Life.* New York: Alfred A. Knopf, 1997.

L. J. Trotter. *Warren Hastings.* Freeport, N.Y.: Books for Libraries Press, 1972.

Alan Valentine. *Lord North.* 2 vols. Norman: University of Oklahoma Press, 1967.

Sophia Weitzman. *Warren Hastings and Philip Francis.* Manchester: Manchester University Press, 1929.

Frederick G. Whelan. *Edmund Burke and India.* Pittsburgh: University of Pittsburgh Press, 1996.

Franklin and Mary Wickwire. *Cornwallis: The Imperial Years.* Chapel Hill: University of North Carolina Press, 1980.

Stanley Wolpert. *A New History of India.* Oxford: Oxford University Press, 1997.

Nathaniel William Wraxall. *Historical Memoirs of My Own Time.* London: Kegan Paul, et al., 1904.

———. *Posthumous Memoirs of His Own Time.* Philadelphia: Lea and Blanchard, 1836.

INDEX

NOTE: Noncontinuous references are sometimes abbreviated using *f* and *ff*. *f* abbreviates "and on the next page" whereas *ff* abbreviates "and on each of the next two pages." Page numbers in italics indicate illustrations.

A NOTE ON THE AUTHOR

Jeremy Bernstein was born in Rochester, New York, and educated at Harvard University. He is a theoretical physicist who is now professor emeritus of physics at the Stevens Institute of Technology. He has held appointments at the Institute for Advanced Study, the Brookhaven National Laboratory, CERN (the European Organization for Nuclear Research), Oxford University, the University of Islamabad, and the École Polytechnique. He has written some fifty technical papers and three technical monographs, most recently *Kinetic Theory in the Expanding Universe* and *An Introduction to Cosmology*.

Mr. Bernstein is perhaps best known for his writings for non-scientists, including *Albert Einstein* (nominated for a National Book Award); *Three Degrees Above Zero*; *Mountain Passages*; *Science Observed*; *The Tenth Dimension*; *Cosmological Constants*; *Quantum Profiles*; *Cranks, Quarks, and the Cosmos*; and *Hitler's Uranium Club*. He has traveled extensively in the Indian subcontinent; his most recent book on these travels is *In the Himalayas*. From 1961 to 1993 he was a staff writer for the *New Yorker*. Among a great many honors and awards, he has won writing prizes from the American Association for the Advancement of Science, the American Institute of Physics, and the American Alpine Club. He lives in New York City and Aspen, Colorado.